Michael Kuhn, Hebe Vessuri (eds.)

Contributions to Alternative Concepts of Knowledge

BEYOND THE SOCIAL SCIENCES

Edited by Michael Kuhn, Hebe Vessuri, Shujiro Yazawa

ISSN 2364-8775

1   *Michael Kuhn, Shujiro Yazawa (eds.)*
    Theories about and Strategies against Hegemonic Social Sciences
    ISBN 978-3-8382-0586-1

2   *Michael Kuhn*
    How the Social Sciences Think about the World's Social
    Outline of a Critique
    ISBN 978-3-8382-0892-3

3   *Michael Kuhn, Hebe Vessuri (eds.)*
    The Global Social Sciences
    —Under and Beyond European Universalism
    ISBN 978-3-8382-0893-0

4   *Michael Kuhn, Hebe Vessuri (eds.)*
    Contributions to Alternative Concepts of Knowledge
    ISBN 978-3-8382-0894-7

Michael Kuhn, Hebe Vessuri (eds.)

CONTRIBUTIONS TO ALTERNATIVE CONCEPTS OF KNOWLEDGE

ibidem-Verlag
Stuttgart

Bibliografische Information der Deutschen Nationalbibliothek
Die Deutsche Nationalbibliothek verzeichnet diese Publikation in der Deutschen Nationalbibliografie; detaillierte bibliografische Daten sind im Internet über http://dnb.d-nb.de abrufbar.

Bibliographic information published by the Deutsche Nationalbibliothek
Die Deutsche Nationalbibliothek lists this publication in the Deutsche Nationalbibliografie; detailed bibliographic data are available in the Internet at http://dnb.d-nb.de.

∞

Gedruckt auf alterungsbeständigem, säurefreien Papier
Printed on acid-free paper

ISSN 2364-8775

ISBN-13: 978-3-8382-0894-7

© *ibidem*-Verlag
Stuttgart 2016

Alle Rechte vorbehalten

Das Werk einschließlich aller seiner Teile ist urheberrechtlich geschützt. Jede Verwertung außerhalb der engen Grenzen des Urheberrechtsgesetzes ist ohne Zustimmung des Verlages unzulässig und strafbar. Dies gilt insbesondere für Vervielfältigungen, Übersetzungen, Mikroverfilmungen und elektronische Speicherformen sowie die Einspeicherung und Verarbeitung in elektronischen Systemen.

All rights reserved. No part of this publication may be reproduced, stored in or introduced into a retrieval system, or transmitted, in any form, or by any means (electronic, mechanical, photocopying, recording or otherwise) without the prior written permission of the publisher. Any person who does any unauthorized act in relation to this publication may be liable to criminal prosecution and civil claims for damages.

Printed in the EU

Table of Contents

Acknowledgements 7

Chapter 1:
The misery of defining what scientific knowledge is—and what not 9
Michael Kuhn and Hebe Vessuri

Section I: Alternative concepts of knowledge

Chapter 2:
Towards a dialogue between knowledge systems. Learning experiences in indigenous contexts in Mexico 21
Juan Pablo Vázquez Gutiérrez and Pablo Reyna Esteves

Chapter 3:
Alternatives to Nostalgia for Colonial Ethnology in the African Postcolonial Theory 41
Léon-Marie Nkolo Ndjodo

Chapter 4:
The Interlinkages between Western and Indigenous Psychology in 20th- and early 21st-century India 73
Christiane Hartnack

Chapter 5:
Knowledge as Interaction: An Alternative Epistemology from Rural Mexico 85
Roger Magazine

Chapter 6:
Indigenous knowledge in the social sciences: *comunalidad* and the challenge to Western categories 101
Claudia Magallanes-Blanco and Leandro Rodriguez-Medina

Chapter 7:
What can Science and Technology Studies do with and for Latin America? 123
Ivan da Costa Marques

Chapter 8:
Decolonising social sciences in remote Australia 143
Michael Christie

Chapter 9:
Culturalising Social Knowledges as a Critique of Euro-American Social Sciences: Learning from Deconstructing Poverty in the Shadow of Gandhian Social Theory 151
Kumaran Rajagopal

Chapter 10:
Rereading of Metaphysical Foundations of Humanities in the Light of the Qur'an's Teachings 163
Qodratullah Qorbani

Section II: Contributions to the discourse about alternative concepts of knowledge

Chapter 11:
What is foreign knowledge? 187
Leandro Rodriguez Medina

Chapter 12:
Alternatives to the Globalising Humanities and Social Sciences: Comments to the ideas presented at the Mexico WSSHNetwork workshop 231
Michael Christie

Chapter 13:
Some comments about spatiological thinking—the final universalisation of the "European" social sciences 243
Michael Kuhn

Biographical Notes 269

Acknowledgements

This book presents social thought about **"Contributions to Alternative Concepts of Knowledge"** with contributions from social scientists across the world reflecting on the contemporary social sciences, in particular on alternative concepts of knowledge, social thought initiated by discourses on three WorldSSHNet events:

- The thinkshop about *"Multiple Epistemologies - Science and Time - Science and Space - Science and Culture - Science and Society"*, held at Universidad Iberoamericana, Mexico City, Mexico, 22–23 February 2013, funded by the Wenner Gren Foundation,

- The thinkshop about *"The global social science world - beyond the 'Western' universalism"*, held at and funded by the University for Applied Sciences, Zwickau, Germany, 27–29 September 2013,

- The WorldSSHNet panel on the *"Eighth Congress of the International Asian Philosophical Association"*, held at the Süleyman Demirel University in Isparta, April 30th to May 3rd 2016.

This book publishes the papers resulting from the discourses on these events and disseminates them to invite last but not least those academics who could not participate in our events but who can thus join these controversial debates.

The editors of this book want to take the opportunity to thank all participants of the WorldSSHNet activities, those who contributed papers to the events, those who contributed chapters to this book and all others who contributed in several other ways to our thinkshops and thus also supported the publication of this book.

We gratefully acknowledge the editorial and financial contributions of Professor Michael Christie, of the Northern Institute, Charles Darwin University, Northern Territory, Australia.

As a funding organisation that goes beyond paying lip service to the issues of inter-disciplinary and inter-national social science activities, but really supports them, we wish to express our gratitude to the Wenner-Gren Foundation for funding our thinkshop in Mexico City.

We, the editors, consider this book not as the end, but as another point of departure for further controversial debates and would like to take this opportunity and invite readers to contribute to the continuation of these conversations with their critical comments.

Those who are interested in the WorldSSHNet may visit our www: http://www.worldsshnet.org/

Michael Kuhn and Hebe Vessuri

Chapter 1:
The misery of defining what scientific knowledge is—and what not

Michael Kuhn and Hebe Vessuri

This book publishes contributions to the debate about alternative concepts of knowledge and it does this with an implicit question mark, in the sense that they are contributions to a controversial debate, both with regard to what alternative concepts of knowledge are, and to the question compared to which knowledge alternative concepts of knowledge are alternatives.

The European social sciences answer this question with their typical way to discuss any controversial issue as the answer to the question of what one defines what scientific knowledge is and what not—and by translating the question what the cognitive nature of alternative knowledge is into the methodological question of what one defines as scientific knowledge; alternative concepts of knowledge are seen as deviating from what the European social sciences define as what scientific knowledge is. What else could a science approach do, that insists that what knowledge is and what it is not, depends on ex ante definitions of its topic, its approach and its methods, and therefore answers the question of what alternative knowledge is, also depending on what one defines ex ante as scientific knowledge and, thus, on what the alternatives to this knowledge are. Just as judging about any social sciences theory must be a matter depending on such ex-ante definitions, choices of both how any object of thinking is approached through meta theories and what the chosen methods for thinking are, the question what is alternative knowledge, is also made a matter of definition.[1]

Though the social sciences approach to theorizing via such ex ante definitions, which allow any contradictory and exclusionary

---

[1] Needless to say, that unlike defining what scientific thinking is, what the cognitive operations from describing to concluding etc. are, can be a topic of theorizing about scientific thinking. A commendable reading in this regard might be an old book from Hegel, the "*Phenomenology of Spirit*."

thought as scientific knowledge, would also allow to define any other than the European concept of knowledge as arbitrarily as scientific knowledge, the European approach to sciences has defined that the attributes of what this European approach to science considers as scientific knowledge must be exclusively defined as scientific knowledge. It has thus established this approach to social thought as the scientific reference system against which any other knowledge that does not coincide with the European definitions of what science is, is non-scientific knowledge, as in this sense alternative knowledge.

Such knowledge, deviating from the European definitions, has been earlier labelled and discredited as indigenous knowledge and excluded from the privilege of belonging to those sciences that claim to decide about what scientific knowledge is, no matter what this knowledge is saying. Thanks to a more recent redefinition of what the very European sciences consider as science, the same knowledge has become via the post-colonial discourses by social scientists such as Wallerstein, Gadamer or Foucault a now welcomed approach to knowledge and is since then a contribution to what the European approach to social sciences consider as scientific knowledge. Without ever arguing about what any knowledge tells us about the world, simply because it does now fulfil the new definitions of what the European sciences defined as scientific knowledge. No matter what this knowledge is telling us about the world it now contributes to knowledge. Knowledge is considered as scientific thought or not according to what the European metatheorists define as knowledge, either excluded or generously invited by thinkers of the European science tradition—thinkers from Merton to Foucault—to contribute to what the European post war II social sciences define as belonging to the scientific universalism or to what Wallerstein, in his contribution to the post-colonial discourses, defines as the universal universalism, both knowing what knowledge is and what it is not without making any attempt to understand what this knowledge is about.

And this, judging about knowledge without judging about what knowledge says, is only consequent. Since the European social science approach also decided per definition that social sciences cannot create any objective knowledge, they can neither decide about what scientific knowledge is via what the knowledge says, but again via definitions, they may be more exclusive or inclusive definitions.

Chapter 1: The misery of defining what scientific knowledge is

How else but by definition, of what knowledge is and what it is not, could an approach to social science decide about what alternative knowledge is, an approach which per definitions of social sciences thinking—definitions created from Kant via Popper to Foucault—also defines *the* dogma that social sciences can only create relative objective knowledge, relative to the ex ante choices of theories through which social sciences theorize. Hence, any knowledge, no matter what it says, no matter whether it contradicts other knowledge, any knowledge must be accepted as knowledge, as long as it follows the rules the dogmas the European social sciences established via definitions about what counts as scientific knowledge.

Rather than the indigenous forms of knowledge, that the European social sciences once discredited and excluded and then later invited as contributing to what they consider as knowledge, it is this dogmatism of the European approach to social science that discredits them, an approach to science that only knows to decide about knowledge via definitions, definitions not only of what this approach considers as knowledge but also of what it considers as science.

The congenial partner of this tautological concept of social thought, defining what knowledge is in accordance to what it defines as being knowledge or not, is inevitably the arrogance with which this European approach to social thought glosses over the fact, that these very debates, deciding about what scientific knowledge is and what not via definitions, at the same time frankly admit that they have not any secure knowledge. As T. Kuhn, otherwise admired as a witness for the dogma that there is no objective knowledge, phrases it: There is no knowledge the social sciences created in a 200 years history, which until today could be considered as a paradigm, such as any secure knowledge in the natural sciences.

And this is truly frivolous: Insisting on the one hand on their definition that social sciences by their nature cannot create any objective knowledge, insisting that social sciences are not able to create any objective theories, and at the same time defining what this approach to social thought considers as scientific knowledge and what not, is a truly unique combination of non-knowing and arrogance claiming to decide about what knowledge is and what it is not.

It is this uniqueness of a concept of scientific knowledge that only securely knows that it does not have any secure knowledge and at the same time is arrogant enough to decide what scientific knowledge is and what it is not. It is this very combination of not-knowing anything, but deciding about what knowledge is that this book does not want to share nor contribute to and to discuss alternative concepts of knowledge again by alternative ways of defining what science is and what it is not.

Needless to say, one could indeed trace the cognitive procedures of how the concepts of knowledge presented in this book construct social thought and from there to see if and how they do this in any other way, different from the ways the European social sciences ways of theorizing do. This ambitious project is not what this book can offer, though it would indeed be worthwhile doing it.

However, without doing this ambitious project, tracing how the alternative concepts of knowledge in this book construct social thought and in which respects these modes of creating knowledge deviate from what it claims being an alternative to—the European social sciences -, this much can be said: All the concepts of knowledge in this book discuss these alternative concepts of knowledge in a tension between presenting them as forms of knowledge which create insights that can be shared with other forms of knowledge creation, and at the same time as knowledge that aims at forms of knowledge, which represent a unique and authentic view on what they think about.

Though a few chapters reflect on the issue of the ambiguity of the debates about alternative concepts of knowledge, in general this book is less ambitious and does not intend to elaborate on such epistemological issues incorporated in the alternative concepts of knowledge it presents. It rather modestly presents a few examples of social thought which consider themselves as alternative concepts of sciences and, by presenting them, this book tries to make a contribution, not the those definitional discourses, but to the question of what the knowledge is saying these alternative concepts of knowledge create and what kind of knowledge they add to the knowledge social sciences have and work with. Therefore, this is already very worthwhile doing, considering the fact that the definitional social sciences throughout their 200 years history boasted not having created any secure knowledge. May be, other alternative approaches to knowledge do.

Chapter 1: The misery of defining what scientific knowledge is

To do this, contributing to this discourse and not to its definitions, this book consists of two sections: Section I, from chapter 2 to 9 presents and discusses alternative concepts of knowledge. Section 2 contributes three chapters 10, 11 and 12, to the contemporary discourses about alternative concepts of knowledge, alternatives to the "European" social sciences.

In chapter 2 Vazquez Gutierrez and Reyna Esteves discuss the results of an educational and academic experience in Mexico, doubly interested in the dialogue between knowledge systems and the university tasks. They begin by looking into the indigenous world and its challenges in the construction of a dialogue between knowledge systems. In particular, they consider the situation of indigenous peoples in Mexico, the persistence of institutionalized racism and discrimination, and a critique of monocultural thinking. Next they describe the challenges faced by the University system in its attempts to generate dialogue with indigenous peoples, and consider questions around constructing an intercultural dialogue. The authors go deeper into their own experience in the Iberoamerican University, offering a glance from Jesuit Universities, and they briefly revise their projects and initiatives and offer some questions and dilemmas around their practices.

Chapter 3 is certainly a most exciting example of how thinking about alternative concepts of knowledge is caught in the above tension between the underlying aim to create authentic concepts of knowledge deviating from what is mostly coined as "Western" knowledge or rationality and the other intention to present such alternative, authentic concepts of knowledge, representing a unique view on the world of the social, as a concept of thinking that can be shared by what it opposes, the very Western way of thinking and their theories. Njodo argues passionately against the construction of authentic concepts of knowledge in discourses among scholars in Africa advocating that it was the nature of African minds to refuse the concept of rationality the thus rejected concept of the European social sciences imposed on the knowledge scene in Africa, accusing them of ultimately racist ideas, the very racist views colonial thinking created about the "natives", racist ideas these discourses not only accept but now propagate themselves as the real nature of African minds. He then suggests other alternative concepts of knowledge against the European social sciences' concept of knowledge; he discusses theorizing in Africa along historical roots, and he strikingly presents concepts of thinking which coincide with the very roots of thinking that emerged in parallel to the European concept of nation state in the social sciences generated in Europe and that accordingly constructed the concept of rationality, founding the ways social sciences were since then practising thinking.

The project seeking alternative concepts of knowledge to the European social sciences is certainly motivated by some scientific discontent with the knowledge they create and seeks for other ways of theorizing about the social, and is thus mainly a scientifically inspired project. However, in the context of the emergence of a decolonized world it is also obvious that many projects aiming at alternative concepts of knowledge, mainly those discussed under the notion of indigenous knowledge aiming at authentic knowledge are motivated by political considerations. Chapter 4, by Christine Hartnack, reflecting on the nexus between the political developments in India is therefore most worthwhile reading. Unlike in the realm of political science, of economics or of sociology, politically inspired motivations seeking for alternative concepts of knowledge might sound less surprising. Hartnack however discusses the case of Psychology and how the discourse about indigenous concepts of knowledge in psychology are massively affected by very political, to avoid saying nationalistic, motivations. She traces the historical interconnections between indigenous psychology and the psychological theories in the European science world and how they are developing with the changing political rationales and agendas of new nation-state India and its integration into the world of nation states and their "modern" rationales of the project adjusting India to the project of global "neo-liberalism." In this sense, this chapter lectures us about the extent to which a social science discipline, which at first glance might seem to be less infected by political influences and its discourses about indigenous knowledge is a very politically inspired project, ranging from considerations about academic career perspectives towards simply nationalistic motivations, creating alternatives concepts of knowledge as a matter of sheer nationalism.

On the lookout for ethnocentric, false universalisms, Roger Magazine in Chapter 5 is concerned with the possibility that anthropological "theory" reveals the "local-ness", the ethnocentrism and thus the limits of established theory, and in his paper he aims

Chapter 1: The misery of defining what scientific knowledge is

to show how ideas or theories of the people studied can be incorporated into scientific theory in an attempt to move beyond our own conceptualization of the world. Based on his own ethnographic research he proposes that people in Tepetloaxtoc are linked together by their activities, they need each other to be able to act. This is because actions involve two subjects rather than one: the first who motivates and the second who performs the action. This contrasts with the form that this relationship usually takes in the modern world in which individuals are naturally endowed with the ability to act. In Tepetloaxtoc what people create or produce is not a thing, inert, de-subjectified and ready to have its singular objective reality revealed once produced, but rather subjectivity and action, which continue to transform themselves and others after their creation.

Magallanes Blanco and Rodriguez Medina deal in chapter 6 with recent developments around the notion of Indigenous Knowledge and try to illustrate the richness of a local contribution to our understanding of community media as well as the need to in-breed some western(ized) knowledge about societal relations with theoretically sound and empirically relevant ideas coming from the "South". They explore the concept of *comunalidad* as the result of a series of personal and community processes of struggle in the southern state of Oaxaca, Mexico, during the 1970s and 1980s. They argue that Indigenous Knowledge is valuable, not only because of its cultural and geographic roots, its embeddedness in ancient traditions, but also because of its explanatory power and potential usefulness beyond its context of production.

Chapter 7 from Ivan Marques might serve as an example of the above mentioned tensions between the desire to create authentic forms of knowledge and the desire to get these alternative concepts of knowledge after all and in particular acknowledged by those European concepts of knowledge they intend to oppose. In fact, strictly speaking, this chapter does not present any alternative concept of knowledge, but presents thought, somehow representing the struggle between the aim to create an authentic concept of knowledge that must thus deviate from the European concept of science and that, at the same time, is so keen to become a part of the global knowledge scenery the very European social sciences orchestrate, by setting up the scientific standards of this global social science orchestra.

Christie's chapter 8 on Australian Yolnu thinking is about revisiting what he takes, following Viveiros de Castro, as the colonial urge 'to explain, interpret, contextualise and rationalise', while proposing 'to use indigenous thought, draw out its consequences, and ascertain the effects it may produce on our own way of thinking'. Although he does not engage in either criticizing the former discourse nor in developing the latter alternative, he comments on an initiative to which he was related. In an experience about housing for Aborigines, he was faced with the need of representing the needs of Aboriginal housing that led him to engage in Australian Aboriginal metaphysics, being forced to un-think both time and monologue.

Kumaran Rajagopal resumes in chapter 9 the criticism of the idea of poverty he made in a former contribution (forthcoming). He argues that poverty has come to acquire such naturalness that we no longer treat it as a concept whose constructedness needs to be critically inquired into. Having come to regard poverty as 'material resourcelessness' arising out of the alleged lack of imitativeness or development ambition of the so called 'poor' nations or 'poor' individuals, the resource-rich people have successfully reduced poverty to personal failure of the material-poor. This manner of absolutisation of poverty along simple economistic lines has resulted in emptying the concept of its moral, cultural and collective connotations. The moral universe of the resource-rich has come to encompass all the inhabitants of the planet so much so that evolving a critical analysis has become nearly impossible. He finds the Gandhian framework offers such an alternative moral universe making a critique likely. His article aspires to learn from Gandhian social theory and lists the benefits of deploying it for a liberating understanding of poverty as well as for imagining the possibility of an alternative social knowledge making.

In chapter 10 Qorbani discusses an alternative way of seeing humanities through the view of the Quran. He argues that humanities, in their extensive meaning, concern some significant facts like society, human being, his/her thought and social behaviours. Humanities try to get global laws of society and humans based on the ways of their approaches to humankind, society and their relations, while human restrictions prevent their comprehension by empirical investigation. On the contrary, getting universal laws and rules concerning humans and society is achievable through application

Chapter 1: The misery of defining what scientific knowledge is 17

of religious and metaphysical foundations. Qorbani argues that the Qur'an, as a divine, revealed and infallible book, has some prominent teachings regarding God, human being, society, global humankind and social traditions and laws, which makes it possible to form a kind of efficacy worldview and functional metaphysical thought for "human being" that can be considered as foundations of humanities and social sciences. In his view, by using the Qur'anic teachings, it is possible to build a new anthropology and cosmology in which to reform our philosophical thoughts of the world, societies and the place of human beings towards God.

The book's second section discusses under the headline "Contributions to the discourse about alternative concepts of knowledge" the notion of alternative concepts of knowledge with three contributions.

Leandro Rodriguez Medina engages in chapter 11 in an exploration of new modes of knowledge production in the context of globalization, the so-called knowledge (or information) society and information technologies as mediations that have transformed communication. His main concern is to elaborate the distinction beween foreign and local knowledge and explore its potential usefulness. The category becomes handy for understanding and analysing practices of knowledge production. Management and business are the two areas that have produced the most knowledge on this topic. Rodriguez Medina contends that this literature can provide important insights not only into the nature of foreigness but also into social and organisational aspects of knowledge use and circulation. He then discusses implications of his general argument. First, although foreign knowledge—and perhaps any knowledge—calls for interpretation, one role of peripheral scholars has been to profusely introduce premises to foreign ideas in order to adapt them to local realities. Second, their labels should be problematized, in particular those used to organize knowledge. Due to their peripheral position in the international division of academic labor, those scholars need to create new classificatory systems that connect foreign knowledge to local production.

In his second contribution to this book in chapter 12 Christie attempts to look at the alternatives to the globalising humanities and social sciences, "GHSS". Among his basic assumptions are the following: all knowledge is local, alternatives to the "GHSS" are manifold, knowledge is a cultural, social and political process; the new globalising knowledge practices exist in dynamic tension with their alternative. He then touches on the politics of alternatives to the Globalising HSS, deliberate marginalisation by the governmentalities of globalisation, deliberate dissociation from institutional forms, persistent pre-globalised (including indigenous) practices, alternative practices and sources created by globalised capital. Finally, he briefly touches on some epistemological features of alternatives to "globalising HSS".

The final chapter 13 by M. Kuhn does not present any alternative concept of knowledge either, but reflects on these discourses, which discuss the various forms and notions under which alternative concepts of knowledge, such as local or indigenous knowledge, or in the case of chapter 10 in this book "foreign" knowledge, are presented as alternative approaches to the European concepts of social thought, the European social sciences. In his chapter he argues that such alternative forms of knowledge are, firstly, no alternatives to the ways the European social science practice thinking about the social, since it is the very European social sciences, which found their way of thinking on thinking with and through constructs of nation-states, that is nationally confined social entities. Secondly, he argues, motivated to create alternative social thought from the views of the new independent states on the world's social, it is the merit of mainly those social sciences from the former colonized world and their contributions to the post-colonial discourses, to question the historical anachronism of social sciences which present nationally confined knowledge as knowledge that applies to all social constructs across the world's social, disregarding whether they are nationally or non-nationally constructed socials. However, as it stands, this critique advocating authentic social thought ends up obliterating the oddity of a global monopole on nationally confined thinking and spreads this very way of European way of thinking under the labels of local or indigenous knowledge as the only thereby finally universalised European way of theorizing about the social. It is the ironic achievement of the critics labelling their opponents as the "Western" social sciences and their "Eurocentrism", to make this very European way of thinking on nationally confined socials the universalized concept of knowledge ruling social science thinking across the world as a multiplicity of globally "provincialized" thought.

Section I:
Alternative concepts of knowledge

Chapter 2:
Towards a dialogue between knowledge systems. Learning experiences in indigenous contexts in Mexico

Juan Pablo Vázquez Gutiérrez and Pablo Reyna Esteves

Introduction

This paper objective is to submit for discussion the results of an educational and academic experience that takes place in indigenous contexts in the North and Southeast of Mexico. We believe that presenting it may help in the thinking of the dialogue between knowledge systems, as well as about the university's tasks.

Despite the self-critical tone of this paper, the experience to which we refer below is very valuable. It is the resulting effort of many colleagues working with the Interculturality and Indigenous Affairs Program (PIAI, for its acronym in Spanish) of the Iberoamerican University during the past six years.

The paper is divided in four parts. In the first section we describe the difficulties of Mexican indigenous peoples and in the second section we discuss the challenges towards an education open to the dialogue between knowledges. In the third section we present our work experience highlighting its major accomplishments. Finally, we consider the limits of this experience and raise some relevant questions to reflect upon.

I. The indigenous world and the challenges in the construction of a dialogue between knowledge systems

I.1. The situation of indigenous peoples in Mexico

Mexico is one of the most culturally diverse countries in Latin America. According to the Catalogue of National Indigenous Languages produced by the National Institute of Indigenous Languages (INALI for its acronym in Spanish) there are 68 native linguistic groups in our country. These 68 groups belong to eleven linguistic families, in which 364 dialects (INALI, 2008:38) are spoken. Each of these languages reflects a unique worldview, with elements that allow it to establish specific relationships with its surroundings. This linguistic diversity brings about enormous cultural wealth, as much for the combination of knowledge practices it contains, as for the different approaches to reality that become possible.

Indigenous cultural diversity in Mexico is legally acknowledged in the Constitution, in its 2nd Article. There, the multicultural composition of our country is recognized.[1] However, this recognition is denied in practice due to the policies developed by the Mexican government.

Currently Mexico is still a deeply unequal country. Here the faces of poverty have a clear geographic location, and a precise allocation of gender and ethnicity. In terms of income, access to goods and quality of life rates, indigenous peoples invariably occupy the lowest positions on the scale.[2]

This situation has become critical in recent years. Asymmetric effects of globalization have weakened the economy of indigenous

---

[1] Mexico is one of the countries with the largest indigenous population in Latin America (Zolla and Zolla, 2004:39). According to the Population and Housing Census 2010 (INEGI, 2011), about 15.7 million people (13.9% of the national total) are recognized as indigenous. Cf CONAPO, 2011:1.

[2] According to government studies, in 2012 44.2% of the total population of Mexico was in some degree of poverty. 11.2% is in extreme multidimensional poverty. Of these areas, 75% is indigenous population (CONEVAL, 2013:3). That same year the 50 municipalities with the lowest human development had the largest indigenous population. Cf CONAPO, 2011:52; Schmelkes, 2013:7.

peoples. Given this situation, the choices of these groups are reduced to resisting in precarious subsistence, if not to accept forced migration. The rise in violence and insecurity has become an additional factor that threatens possibilities of development of these peoples. Territorial dispossession to exploit the natural resources of the lands historically inhabited by indigenous peoples has intensified in the last 30 years.[3] The presence of all these issues challenge social cohesion. The indigenous armed uprising of 1994, which originated in Chiapas, is an example that highlights the relevance of conflicts in the Mexican context. This movement embodies a reaction, among others, from the effects of an economic and social model that reproduces conditions of dispossession, inequality and exclusion.

I.2. Institutionalized racism and discrimination

Despite the efforts to promote more tolerant and inclusive customs, Mexico is still a profoundly discriminatory country. Compared with the overall national population, indigenous groups suffer the effects of exclusion in two ways. They are the poorest as well as the most discriminated against (Vázquez, 2012a: 217).[4]

Mexican society gives indigenous status a very poor consideration. Negative connotations associated with the word "Indian" are part of an ideology born in our colonial past, that has been strengthened throughout history.

The role of schooling has been key in this story. Education has helped shape a national identity that exalts Mexico's indigenous heritage. However, this acknowledgement is only formal and has not achieved much for the Indigenous people. Rarely are our indigenous roots considered as an active factor of our present

---

[3] The mining concessions given since 2000 are equivalent to 26% of the country. In the last ten years, Canadian mining companies have extracted more gold than during the colonial period (La Jornada, 2011).

[4] In this regard, the National Survey on Discrimination in Mexico findings are illustrative (CONAPRED, 2010). 4 out of 10 Mexicans believe that the rights of homosexuals, indigenous and migrants are not respected in the country.;4 in 10 surveyed say they are not willing to cohabit with people of different race or culture. Moreover, on surveys to members of various ethnic groups, respondents identified as main problems in their ethnic group discrimination, poverty and lack of government actions that give them effective support (CONAPRED, 2010:22, 36, 52–54).

condition. So we are taught to admire the ancestral indigenous peoples, while the present indigenous people are ignored and discriminated against, thus denying them a chance for a viable future.(Vázquez, 2012b: 49).

Behind this concealed rejection of the indigenous condition is a profound ignorance and a tendency to simplify things. The indigenous world is usually seen as a *uniform* reality—veiling its enormous diversity—whilst situating it as a reality *separate* from the rest of Mexican society.

This division would seem to lead to a confrontation between two visions of our country. On the one hand, the *urban-mestizo Mexico* is pictured as the "present ideal" of a nation integrated into the global order. On the other is the "*deep Mexico*", with its indigenous influence that has shaped us and is part of us, but whose presence we strive to erase. In this way a culture of discrimination prevails in our country, which is not, however, viewed as racist and ethnocentric.[5]

I.3 Critique of the monocultural thinking

In Mexico there are many expressions of ethnocentrism and discrimination based on ethnic origin. Recognition and discussion of these issues become increasingly necessary, as this type of violence is exerted systematically in different spaces of everyday life. In this situation, how should we think about the possibilities of development of indigenous peoples and their participation in the national context?

The following frameworks show the main ways in which this question has been answered.

> a) *A model of an assimilationist cultural relation, or one based on the integration of an alleged minority, subordinated to a supposed national majority* (Etxeberria, 2004:23–24).

According to this model, the recognition of multiculturalism has been generally understood in Mexico from parameters where the differences are recognized, regulated and apparently tolerated.

---

[5] An interesting anthropological reflection on this problem is made by Bonfil, 1987.

However, this apparent acceptance is always performed within the boundaries of a limited liberal scheme. Under this scheme, indigenous communities are forced to comply with participation models beyond their cosmovision[6] and traditions. In this way their supposed inclusion in the nation's development and the recognition of their rights are always conditional upon the acceptance of regulations that deny the cultural specificities of their indigenous worlds (Vázquez, 2012a: 220).

> b) *A model of colonial relations and welfare assistance, based on the original plunder and destruction of the indigenous world.* In this model, native groups are offered a conditional incorporation into a clientelistic—quid pro quo—participation in social assistance schemes provided by the State (Etxeberria, 2004:23–24).

According to this perspective, indigenous people are considered marginalized individuals. This situation places them as *objects of attention* of the state's social programs. The contribution of indigenous peoples to the country is considered void, and they are seen as a "problem". In that sense, the transformation of their worldviews, forms of organization and lifestyles is considered a priority in order to make them compatible with the guidelines required by "development".

Although the two models described are significantly different, they share relevant components. In both visions, the indigenous peoples are denied their identity and their potential as *subjects of law*. Such denial is transferred to other basic dimensions that refer to their exclusion, as individuals *capable of dialogue* and *political*

---

[6] For the purpose of this text we use the concept cosmovision as the set of meanings, values and representations that an specific social group uses for defining its own world, the way the group relates to it, and its collective identity. Even though a group's cosmovision is not completely present and totally coherent in daily life, it is constant and significant. Cosmovision functions as framework that guides and signifies our actions. As this framework is socially shared, cosmovision becomes a distinctive haracteristic of an individual's membership to the cultural groups that shares this forms of being and of understanding the world.

skills to effectively participate in the construction of a pluricultural nation.[7]

These models are also based on a shared support that originates from a monocultural thinking[8] practice (Santos, 2009:110).

Monocultural thinking functions, according to Santos, is a dominant form of interpretation of reality. A central feature of these ways of thinking or "monocultures" of knowledge is that they set themselves up to be the only form of understanding, denying other possibilities of knowledge. This imposition leads to the construction of a one-dimensional worldview and to the imposition of knowledge systems assumed and presented as universal (Santos, 2009:111–112). Also, the empire of monocultural knowledge leads to a fiction that becomes fact, of the existence of *only one reality and present time*. Faced with this one-dimensional world image, other forms of knowledge or rationality are seen as different, strange, inefficient and unproductive (Santos, 2009:113).

In the monocultural discourse, the conflicts that arise from the relationships between different groups and different rationalities are silenced, or incorporated in a subordinate way to the dominant logic of the global system. The monocultural understanding showcases a world aimed towards "progress". In this imagined world, the most diverse worldviews merge and articulate amongst themselves without complication. The result of this idealized image is one of a technological world, with articulated uniform meanings, which in its apparent integration produces universal and undifferentiated meanings and references.

Based on this monocultural thinking, most of the dominant interpretations of multicultural coexistence are established. Under

---

[7] This pattern of thinking and relationship includes not only government programs, but sometimes even to international organizations, funding agencies, NGOs and universities (Vázquez, 2012:220).

[8] The idea of monoculture is used by Santos to highlight that some practices and knowledges are presented as if they were universally valid and are imposed over other forms of knowledge. This idea of monoculture goes against the idea of cultural diversity. The imposition of monocultural knowledges is done by marginalizing and making invisible other forms of knowledge. In this sense, what is not seen is invisibilized by a social act in which it is produced as inexistent. This reduces the world's diversity into one and only, auto-assumed as universally valid, form of knowledge. Any monocultural idea of the world possesses a limited understanding of the world and of itself. Cfr. Santos, 2009: 110–113

this way of thinking, multicultural coexistence is understood as a peaceful and distant relationship between different cultures. Therefore, a dominant version of multiculturality and multiculturalism is strengthened, where the world is seen as a diverse place without conflict; a world united in a single voice through globalized messages and icons. Beyond their outreach and consumption with ideological goals, this homogenized image of cultural diversity does not require nor encourage genuine communication and mutual understanding between the "culturally distinct"[9].

II. Challenges faced by the University system in its attempts to generate dialogue with Indigenous peoples

I.4. Questions and challenges around constructing an intercultural dialogue

Having considered the previous arguments, several questions arise:

In a world with undeniable cultural differences, is mutual understanding possible? How can it be achieved? Which elements can foster intercultural dialogue? Moreover, how can horizontal dialogue between cultures in a global framework emerge?

From our own experience, we consider it necessary to establish our approach to the concept of "intercultural dialogue".

First, it should be noted that the claim for intercultural communication is, as of today, only a *future project* and not a reality. Nonetheless, this should not be a disincentive from the work to attain it. Interculturality is an aspiration visible on the horizon, even in the context of a globalized society, precisely because reality poses it as a challenge, a question, and a necessity.

---

[9] We use the concept of culturally distinct to highlight that human acts and relationships are always local and cultural. Even in the areas most influenced by globalization and communications technology, individuals always act with a specific language, culture, and knowledge. The predominance of monocultural forms of knowledge tend to hide these differences.

As an aspiration, intercultural dialogue assumes as its first requisite the establishment of horizontal relationships open to the possibility of another "culturally distinct".

In this sense, it is impossible to establish an intercultural dialogue that is based only on a certain type of content, assumed as universal and necessary.

Behind this consideration are the power relations that emerge when trying to build agreements between different parties, each one having their own idea of reality.

Faced with the challenges arising from the huge social and cultural diversity of Mexico, finding less violent, unjust and homogenizing ways to relate becomes an imperative.

In this sense, the intercultural approach seeks to open dialogue, encounter and mutual learning processes among different cultures. Interculturality is an ethical and political approach, since it demands working to put an end to the lacerating conditions of economic and social inequality predominant in our country.

At the same time the development of interculturality entails a self-critical reflection of us as individuals, of our institutions, as well as of our societies as a whole.

Finally, an effective intercultural dialogue demands more from civil society and State institutions than mere consciousness about the value of diversity. Concrete actions that modify the logic of dominant relations are needed, in order to produce more horizontal and inclusive policies, customs and coexistence models. Moving forward to acknowledge cultural differences and strengthen historically marginalized groups is also needed, as well as constructing spaces that favor communication and agreements between "cultural distincts".

In short, new forms of institutionalism are needed, to exercise differentiated rights and pluricultural forms of political participation. In universities' particular contexts all this leads to a radical questioning of the social responsibility of our institutions, in face of the difficulties of indigenous peoples in the country. All this leads to a reassessment of our most important tasks, in order to offer strategic support to the development proposals that these actors define.

- Educational projects within indigenous contexts, undertaking an intercultural approach, are difficult, and complex, especially when you are working inside a traditional university with its own institutional conditions. Among other things, you take the risk of reproducing work schemes and knowledge that deny horizontality and dialogue, imposing ethnocentric or hierarchical ways of thinking.

- Building an intercultural relationship between the university and indigenous communities and processes requires constant revision of silenced assumptions and everyday teaching practices.

- The processes accompanied throughout the years of the PIAI's work, have many times gone beyond the boundaries of its own program rules, opening new possibilities of construction.

- The university's institutional conditions are a constant challenge for building processes with potential for interculturality. The University's order of action and knowledge is inherently disciplinary. The disciplinary approaches to reality frequently operate as monocultural ways of thinking.

- The university's disciplinary discourses are sometimes contrary to a horizontal dialogue with other kinds of knowledge. Their structure and modes of operation (as heirs of modern Western thought), generate a closed discourse, with undisputed assumptions, which are often assumed as valid in a universal sense. When confronted by indigenous knowledges, the university's disciplinary discourse is not able to question its own presuppositions. The University's monodisciplinarity is limited, and it should gradually transform itself, starting from the relationship with other practices and knowledge.

More than once, we have been mistaken in taking the word of one indigenous person (as well as his political views and cultural perspectives) as representative of a whole cultural group. This faulty generalization is caused by the widespread ignorance that universities have in relation to the reality of indigenous societies and by the urgency in which we work, in order to generate the results that our institutions require. A constant dialogue, limited to our counterparts and key informants, is often the only possible way we can carry out our work. If we do not explore and make explicit these limitations over time, we could be led to confuse our relationship with a limited group of individuals as if it was a relationship with a community as a whole. Without minimizing the perspective of these members, an unintended consequence of this style of communication could be producing a "relationship of elites" not very representative of the communitarian processes that we try to develop.

Due to the long process of conquest, pillage and discrimination they have suffered, indigenous communities and organizations are suspicious of the processes promoted by external actors. As a result, the first goal in the building of relationships with the communities is the creation of a bond of trust. This point might seem trivial, but it is very important. This trust can only be constructed when all the participants are related in an open way and assume their respective limitations and ignorance. Working from the recognition of mutual ignorance, allows the university to question its own learning capabilities.

III. Our own experience from the Iberoamerican University

II.1 Higher Education, multiculturalism and indigenous peoples.
A glance from Jesuit Universities

For years in Mexico, universities and colleges have assumed the task of bringing education to students from historically excluded populations. Such is the case of indigenous people, which have become present in diverse scholarly and academic spaces.

As the inclusion of indigenous children and youth to the national educational system—from kindergarten to college—has become a rising trend, the intercultural approach has become widespread in the system's curricula, including that of the Jesuit Colleges and

Universities associated in the Jesuit University System (henceforth SUJ). The SUJ is formed by eight higher education institutions trusted or associated with the Mexican Province of the Society of Jesus. The SUJ's main purpose is to transform society into a fair one, where solidarity for the poor and excluded is privileged. (SUJ, 2013).[10]

In this institutional framework, the Interculturality and Indigenous Affairs Program (PIAI), created in 2006 within the Iberoamerican University, tries to articulate the University's social and educational projects with indigenous peoples' needs and conflicts.

II.2 Our Projects and initiatives

The PIAI's mission is "create the spaces where the University members can contribute, based on their own knowledge fields, to the understanding of multicultural Mexico and to the transformation of the nation's social and cultural inequalities" (PIAI-UIA, 2011:1).[11] PIAI promotes the integration of working groups with academics, social organizations and institutions concerned with promoting the intercultural debate and the development of indigenous peoples in Mexico. This work has mainly focused on learning and research processes in three indigenous regions:

a) <u>Northern region. State of Chihuahua</u>. Developing projects with *Raramuri* indigenous peoples. Project coordinated with the Jesuit Mission based on the *Sierra Tarahumara,* the Instituto Tecnológico de Estudios Superiores de Occidente (a university that belongs to SUJ) and *Émuri Integrated Services,* a civil society group (SINE).

b) <u>South-East. State of Chiapas</u>. *Tseltal* indigenous area. Collaborative work with the Jesuit Mission based in Bachajón, Chiapas.

---

[10] For a review of SUJ's structure, objectives and projects, cf. http://www.suj.org.mx/ideario.htm

[11] See also http://www.uia.mx/web/site/tpl-Nivel2.php?menu=mgPerfil&seccion=cdIndigenas

> c) South-East. State of Oaxaca. Ayuuk indigenous area. Collaborative projects with the Intercultural Ayuuk Institute (ISIA), an indigenous intercultural higher education institute associated to the SUJ.

The PIAI conceives its role as team work collaborator, not as a lead, in the processes developed and manifested by indigenous groups and communities. In this regard, PIAI considers that the knowledge produced by the university should be re-thought within a non-hierarchichal framework with other kinds of knowledge. PIAI promotes the formation of interdisciplinary, interinstitutional and intercultural working groups that focus on the generation and application of socially relevant knowledge. The intercultural approach respects diversity and is committed to dialogues between knowledges.

We briefly describe the main projects developed in the regions named above.

II.3.1 Collaborations in the Sierra Tarahumara [12]

> a) "Raramuri culture and the curricula of elementary education. Analysis and integration proposals." The project collaboration group was formed of elementary education teachers from Raramuri schools, academics and students from the Education Department of the Iberoamerican University, academics from ITESO, the Jesuit Mission in Sierra Tarahumara, and the civil organization Émuri Integrated Services (SINE). Elementary school teachers from two schools in the Sierra Tarahumara have accompanied the process through participatory research and self-reflection. Along with the participating teachers, a methodology was designed, to develop the curricula, which considered the social and cultural environment thereby helping to improve the cultural relevance of education in the region.

---

[12] 1) http://jesuitasentarahumara.wordpress.com 2) http://jesuitasentarahumara.wordpress.com/galeria-fotografica/del-baul-de-los-recuerdo-del-p-diaz-infante/attachment/31/

b) As a result of these collective experiences, we have started to work on the creation of a Tarahumara Intercultural Studies Center. Its main tasks will include the gathering and systematization of the region's relevant data, such as a natural resources observatory. The aim of this process is to articulate a long-term strategic partnership with the social and educational works of the Jesuit Mission in the Tarahumara region.

c) The Jesuit Mission in Sierra Tarahumara, SINE, ITESO, and UIA have launched a Masters in Knowledge Management and Education designed for teachers who work in indigenous communities. As part of the academic programme, SINE guides the students on their field work and in their research projects.

II.3.2 Collaborations with the Jesuit Mission in Bachajón, Chiapas [13]

Main projects:

a) The recovery of traditional knowledge in Tseltal communities of Chiapas was promoted, as a result of the research project entitled "Concerning *cosmovisional* and sociopolitical organization in Latin American indigenous communities" (2008–2011). Such recovery entailed the development of systematization workshops.

b) As a result of the systematization of traditional Tseltal knowledge, three certified courses, desgined for community members and young Tseltal people were developed and delivered, within these themes:

- Tseltal indigenous law and legal system.
- *Jcanan qu'inal lum* (Caretakers of Mother Earth).
- *Jpoxtaywanej* (Health Promotion).

---

[13] See http://misiondebachajon.sjsocial.org/

These diploma courses were carried out during two years and were attended by more than 150 students in the three programs. The results were published in the book "Indigenous Peoples, State and Human Rights. Nasa at Colombia and the Tseltal at Mexico" published by the UIA and the University of Deusto in 2012 (cf.. Etxeberria, Muñoz and Vázquez, 2012).

II.3.3 Collaborations with the Intercultural Ayuuk Institute (ISIA) [14]

Main processes:

a) In this section, a research project linked to the ISIA is discussed: "Analysis of the working environment in the Ayuuk region of Oaxaca. Identification of the capacities and limitations for work integration of graduates from ISIA". The main results of these projects are: i) The creation of an updated graduate's data base. ii) Identification of the main problems faced in employment in the region. iii) The construction of linking strategies and social entrepreneurship facing the challenges of employment.

b) Teaching practices at the ISIA: interinstitutional collaboration as an intercultural space and the role of entities that support teaching. Throughout the development of this project different gatherings between students and professors have been generated to recollect and systematize successful teaching practices from an intercultural perspective that contribute to improve the students' academic training.

Both projects aim to advance interinstitutional strengthening and knowledge exchange, as well as to strengthen the ISIA as a relevant educational offering, consistent, and of quality to the indigenous youth of the region.

It is essential for the PIAI to link knowledge and university practices with knowledge and practices of indigenous communities.

---

[14] http://www.isia.edu.mx/

The goal behind this is to build intercultural alternatives in education and development, which are linked to the needs of communities and indigenous organizations in the country. That is why one of its main tasks is to promote collaboration between the departments and service areas of the UIA with the aforementioned projects. The forms of collaboration are very diverse. Here we will mention only the chore teaching collaboration and support to the management at the ISIA, where the scope of our participation as a university is greatest.

- PIAI participated in the design and development of ISIA, as well as the educational principles and curriculm design.

- UIA has been responsible of more than 120 courses in the three undergraduate programs offered in ISIA (Communication and Social Development; Administration and Sustainable Development; Intercultural Education). More than 80 UIA teachers have taught at ISIA. On average, 10 courses are delivered each semester.

IV. Some questions and dilemmas around our own practice

We have described the main iniciatives carried out in this work. As a conclusion, we consider it necessary to present some of the limits and some self-critical considerations emerging from our experience. These reflections are presented in short statements, with the intention to reveal topics and questions for further analysis.

- On the way we have faced different kinds of obstacle. One of them regards to the operating conditions of our projects. Despite the interest of the university to stay close to the processes that it supports, the geographical remoteness and the existence of different work conditions and practices from our counterparts in each region, has occasionally led to communication problems and undesired results. Some of these have resulted, for example, in the adoption of arbitrary, bureaucratic actions, which have been outside the interests and worldview of the participants. When this happens we have distanced ourselves from the goal of promoting culturally relevant learning processes.

- Originally the PIAI was not designed to be a program aimed for the education of students or the creation of research projects. Initially, its mission was to participate as a space of connection and support in the development of intervention projects. Over the years and due to its own practice, the PIAI has had to expand its profile and fields of action. In the everyday work we have learned to develop new tools and concepts of work.

- The PIAI has assumed as a working principle, the ongoing modification of its own work, adapting itself to the times, logic and demands of practice itself, accepting the inevitable existence of gaps and blind spots. Therefore, the PIAI has no choice but to reconsider, on the basis of its real world experience, its own assumptions, limited by the conditions of a university that belongs to the Jesuit University System.

- One of our key lessons involves the certainty that the university cannot deal alone with the problems of the Mexican indigenous context. In this regard, it has been necessary that the PIAI learns to promote interdisciplinary and interinstitutional collaborations in each project that it supports. Those who work at the university do not have employment conditions which would allow them to remain for extended periods in the remote indigenous regions in which we work; so because of this restriction, collaboration with our local partners (civil society and community representatives) is fundamental to the development of each project.

- Being compelled to work in collaborative and co-responsible ways, universities must recognize and

Chapter 2: Towards a dialogue between knowledge systems 37

accept their limitations, their ignorance and their arrogance in pretending to be the only of the most significant holder of knowledge. Humility and openness, essential features for the construction of an intercultural dialogue, are not intrinsic features of the university, used to consider itself as the institutional carrier of truth. According to what we have said here, we explicitly abandon the idea of the university's knowledge as an expert and infallible one. However, this does not mean we give up the rigor and supervision required by our own epistemological traditions.

- Relationships with other actors and institutions are, also, subject to constant revision. The characteristics of our labor require us to establish a dialogue with indigenous colleagues in the regions in which we participate.

- Universities, even with all their limitations, can and should be a privileged space to promote the social and political processes that lead to interculturality. In this sense, PIAI assume its ethical and political responsibility to build a university from the margins, from the frontiers with indigenous communities. Our labor is not that of an intellectual avant-garde, but the one of a reflexive rearguard. One that, placed always behind the processes and communities, contributes to the process with analysis and feedbacks.

To assume an ethical and political commitment to the promotion of interculturality implies the need to change the timing of a university's practice. The university should adapt its structures and processes in order to effectively respond to emerging and urgent needs that indigenous communities face every day.

- The university can and should become a space for the widespread acknowledgement of the status of indigenous peoples and communities. Due to its nature and condition, the university can serve as a resonance chamber around relevant social issues. For this, it can use its social, political and economic capital. The university may become also an important interlocutor that allows the communities to rethink themselves and face their own contradictions and oppressions. Primarily, those issues associated with gender relations, identity changes and cultural changes in the emerging forms of family and community violence. All of these complexities and contradictions are involved in the huge challenge of thinking and seriously addressing the construction of more just social relations, in a context of respect for diversity, be it of any kind.

- Intercultural dialogue demands that dialogue partners acknowledge the blind spots of their own culture (and its different forms of ethnocentrism) and demonstrate the will to "open" to the understanding of other ways of interpreting reality. The possibility of horizontal communication between "cultural distincts" implies mutual recognition of differences, as the starting point for progress towards strategies and meeting points that promote understanding. In this sense, the adoption of an open mind towards intercultural dialogue means not merely formal learning content, but the development of practices that involves a personal change not only of the rational order, but also in terms of values and orientations towards the world. The intention is to produce a deep, structural change in our own cultural devices and our most natural orientations. The acquisition of skills for intercultural dialogue is, therefore, not a result of a traditional teaching practice, but rather the outcome of participation in significant and crucial experiences that move us, as they pose significant practical challenges arising from the specific relationship with the other "cultural distinct". Developing an intercultural communication actually means something more than mere awareness of diversity; it assumes a "movement of place" beyond our own spaces of comfort, supported by what our culture appears to us as the most obvious and natural. In this sense the encounter with different cultures promotes changes in our own preconceptions of the world.

- Intercultural dialogue demands respect for other cultures. However, this respect is not equivalent to lack of critique. Intercultural relationship is not conflict free. Intercultural dialogue is not about denying our own cultural affiliation (pretending to be some other), it is about understanding ourselves and understanding the other. As it happens in the attempt at communication between different languages, it requires a cultural translation that will inevitably produce misinterpretations and misunderstandings. Ultimately the claim of intercultural dialogue recognizes the enormous complexity involved in the everyday coexistence and understanding between the cultural others. Basically, its approach refers to a fundamental challenge to democratic life and the effective exercise of individual and group rights: how to build, under equal conditions, ways of understanding and consensus around the fundamental issues of the collective life, from the recognition of our differences and our diverse cultural situation.

References

Bonfil Batalla, G. (1987). *México profundo: una civilización negada*. México: Grijalbo.

Consejo Nacional de Evaluación de la Política de Desarrollo Social (CONEVAL). (2013). "Indicadores de medición de pobreza. Origen étnico y nacional, 2008–2010." Available in internet http://web.coneval.gob.mx/Informes/Interactivo/Medicion_pobreza_2010.pdf

Consejo Nacional de Población (CONAPO). (2011). Índice de marginación por entidad federativa y municipio, 2010. CONAPO, México.

Consejo Nacional para Combatir la Discriminación (CONAPRED). (2010). *Encuesta Nacional sobre la discriminación en México/ ENADIS*. http://www.conapred.org.mx/redes/userfiles/files/Enadis-2010-RG-Accss-002.pdf

Etxeberria, X. (2004). *Sociedades multiculturales*. Ediciones Mensajero, Bilbao.

Etxeberria, X., Muñoz, M. R. and Vázquez, J. P. (coordinadores). (2012). *Pueblos indígenas, estados y derechos humanos: los nasa en Colombia y los tseltales en México*. Universidad Iberoamericana/Instituto de Derechos Humanos Pedro Arrupe, México.

Instituto Nacional de Estadística y Geografía (INEGI). (2011a). Censo de Población y Vivienda 2010. INEGI, México. Available in internet www.censo2010.o rg.mx/default.aspx?_file=Presentacion.pptx http://conapo.gob.mx/index.p hp?option=com_content&view=article&id=457

Instituto Nacional de Estadística y Geografía (INEGI). (2011b). *Perspectiva estadística de México*, 4º Informe trimestral, diciembre de 2011, p. 15. Available in internet http://www.inegi.org.mx/est/contenidos/espanol/sistema s/perspectivas/perspectiva-mex.pdf

Instituto Nacional de Lenguas Indígenas (INALI). (2008). Catálogo de las Lenguas Indígenas Nacionales. Variantes lingüísticas de México con sus autodenominaciones y referencias geoestadísiticas. Diario Oficial de la Federación, México, pp. 31–112.

La Jornada (2011). "Duplican magnates minero el oro extraído en la Colonia." *Minera. 500 Años de Saqueo*. Suplemento La Jornada, 14 de noviembre de 2011. Available in internet http://www.jornada.unam.mx/2011/11/14/minera.pdf

PIAI-UIA (2011). *Misión, visión y objetivos de trabajo*. UIA, México. Internal Document.

Santos, Boaventura de Sousa. (2009). *Una epistemología del sur*. México: Siglo XXI-CLACSO.

Schmelkes del Valle, S. (2013). "Educación y pueblos indígenas: problemas de medición." *Realidad, datos y espacio. Revista Internacional de Estadística y Geografía*. Vol. 4, no. 1, Instituto Nacional de Estadística y Geografía (INEGI), México, January-April 2013.

Vázquez Gutiérrez, J. (2012a). "La situación de los pueblos indígenas. Balance y perspectiva." En Salvador Martí i Puig editor. *¿A dónde chingados va México?* Los Libros de la Catarata, Madrid, 2012, pp. 213–227.

Vázquez Gutiérrez, J. (2012b). "Los dilemas del multiculturalismo: retos para la construcción de una perspectiva intercultural." *Vanguardia Dossier*, Número monográfico, *"México en la encrujiada."* No. 44. Barcelona, July-September.

Zolla, C. and Zolla Márquez, E. (2004). *Los pueblos indígenas en México. 100 preguntas*. UNAM, México.

Chapter 3:
Alternatives to Nostalgia for Colonial Ethnology in the African Postcolonial Theory

Léon-Marie Nkolo Ndjodo

Introduction

A century ago, the French ethnologist Lucien Lévy-Brühl proposed some intellectual characters which he named, designating Non-western people of Africa, Latin America, India and Oceania, "primitive mentality". This author considered the mentality of "primitive" people as governed by the refusal of generalization, the rejection of systematization and the priority given to intuition and to direct apprehension of reality. For these reasons, primitive mentality had the specificity to be essentially "mystic". By differentiating the "reason" of "primitive" people—with a type of causality based on the action of invisible forces—from the "reason" of "civilized" people of Europe—with the scientific principles of determinism, positivism, materialism and objective causality—, Lévy-Brühl did not, however, aim at the establishment of any kind of hierarchy between the two. His fundamental statement was the equivalence of forms of thought depending on the "collective representations" governing the spirit of each culture. We can see Lévi-Strauss giving a more precise name to that cultural a priori—the *structure*—from which primitive mentality became a mentality amongst or besides others, meaning with a specific internal coherence. It is precisely that idea of an African spirit structurally mystical, emotional, intuitive, and radically dealing with sorcery, malefic, magic, secrecy and religion that led, in Africa, to the ideas developed by thinkers like Tempels (ethno-philosophy) and Senghor (negritude). After a period of relative eclipse due to the influence of M. Towa's criticism of "cultural essentialism" (1971), that perspective has been reactivated recently by M. Hebga, P. Hountondji as well as thinkers of postcolonial theory like A. Mbembe, J.-G. Bidima, A. K. Appiah, etc. All of them insist on the Dionysian, paranormal, mythical and interstitial foundations of African intellectual and social practices. Carried by the generalization of *cultural studies* or *subaltern studies,* and the introduction of these disciplines inside certain African intellectual circles favorable to the rehabilitation of traditional forms of mind, the contemporary concept of "endogenous knowledges" seems to manifest a profound nostalgia for the colonial ethnology with its racialist categorizations of people and cultures.

1. Primitive mentality, mysticism and plurality of logics

Lévy-Brühl had clearly defined what he understood by "primitive mentality" and what status he gave to this mentality relative to the mentality of the man of modern society.

a) The characteristics of primitive mentality: the negation of objective causes

As he clearly mentioned it in the opening of his book, the great statement of Lévy-Bruhl is the following: "the mind of primitive man does not walk like ours. It follows a different road" (Lévy-Bruhl, 2010: 83). To the French ethnologist, the main character of "primitive mentality" is that instead of an object, nature is a *being*, a superior invisible *living being* which secretly guides and governs the visible flux of events. We then have two types of mentality. One based on the interpretation of *natural causes*, and another based on the quest of *unnatural causes*. The first type of mentality, the mentality of the man of the industrial and civilized society, is the European one: this mentality is rationalist, analytical, naturalist, positivist, empiric, materialist, and based on "secondary causes", meaning the effects; more generally this mentality obeys Aristotle's principles of identity, contradiction and universality; it seeks coherence, rigor, determination and transparency in each operation of the mind. The second type of mentality is primitive mentality: this mentality is mystical, intuitional, magical, emotional, and based on the knowledge of "primary causes", meaning the action of *invisible forces* operating beyond the natural facts (Lévy-Bruhl 2010: 85). According to Lévy-Bruhl, the mystical mentality tends

Chapter 3: Alternatives to Nostalgia for Colonial Ethnology 43

particularly towards the complete ignorance of "secondary causes", in other words that mentality is not interested in the phenomena that intervenes on the surface of things; it is necessarily then a "metaphysical" mentality. From there, the complete ignorance in mystical mentality of the determinism of facts, but also the definition of hazard as a variable of life through which the spirits use to act (Lévy-Bruhl 2010: 107).

According to Lévy-Brühl, there is no tangible separation between the visible and the invisible worlds in the mind of the natives of Africa, Asia, America and Australia. People can even communicate with the gods; they can converse with them and ask them for prosperity, happiness, peace, fertility for themselves, for their family or for their land. But they can also use the occasion given by this contact with invisible and supernatural forces to do evil, to attack the enemy, to make war, to provoke disease, death, dryness, etc (Lévy-Bruhl: 97).

b) The plurality of rationalities and the conviction of their equivalence

If the spirit of the primitives is fundamentally mystical, Lévy-Bruhl insists again on two crucial elements about it. Firstly, the insensitivity to conceptual forms of the mind is due to a "mental reflex" (Lévy-Bruhl 2010: 84) by which primitives make certain "logic pre-relations" permitting an invisible foundation to visible things. In other words, the mind of primitives is naturally, metaphysically and structurally pre-conceptual or a-conceptual. Primitives don't ignore the notion of cause, but to them this notion remains obscure, immediate and does not follow the circuits of western classical cause, meaning the cause based on a clear demonstration and a public argumentation or analysis. To Lévy-Brühl there are two "reasons" or two types of rationalities: on one side, the "logic rationality"; and on the other, the "prelogic rationality". But contrary to the majority of his colleagues, Lévy-Brühl formally contests the common opinion shared among the European public that the first type of rationality is superior to the second type. Lévy-Brühl didn't conclude the inferiority of the "pre-logic rationality" relative to the "logic rationality" (Lévy-Brühl, 2010). By using contemporary vocabulary, we can conclude from this point that the notion of "multiple rationalities", of "plurality of reasons" or of "plural reason", is effectively present in Lévy-Bruhl's ethnologic thought. Indeed, he seemed to turn his back on the original mission of ethnology science which was, responding to an imperial commandment, to classify people—on the basis of their race, tribe, color of skin or religion—in two great compartments: civilized and savages, rational people and irrational people. Levy-Brühl sustained the idea of an equivalence of rationalities. In appearance, his enterprise was full of good intentions and marked by a certain humanism (Deprez, 2010).

That is, for us, the occasion to rapidly precise that Lévy-Bruhl's ethnological conclusions are shared, in many aspects, by certain great tendencies of contemporary social sciences. That is the case with the hermeneutics of Hans Gadamer. This author begins with a severe critique of the pretention of social and historic sciences to say something about the human subject, knowing that that subject is not inert like matter and leaves, always open to the possibility of his proper permanent reinvention; Gadamer is led to reconsider positively the subjective power of traditions, myths, arts, mysteries, secrecy; he requires for all knowledge, an approach which is similar to the exegesis of sacred texts (Gadamer 1996). There are also some traces of Lévy-Brül's ethnological demarche in the structuralism of Levi-Strauss which considers that there are certain internal principles that guide the practices proper to each social and cultural group; he even goes so far as to qualify as "dialectical" the reason of indigenous people (Levi-Strauss, 1962). In the same manner, the various forms of post-structuralism in Michel Foucault, Jacques Derrida, Gilles Deleuze and even Georges Bataille carry the common conviction that the modern conception of science and of man is a simple parenthesis that needs to be closed very quickly to the benefit of the analysis of the structures of the language (Foucault, 1966, 1969, 1971, 1972, 2001; Derrida, 1967; Deleuze and Guattari, 1975). In the pragmatism of Richard Rorty appears the idea that truth is a matter of efficiency and faith, magic has the same validity as science if the objective is to solve pragmatically the problems of daily life (Rorty, 1994).

To finish, the eruption of *cultural studies* and *subaltern studies* led brilliant sociologists, anthropologists, linguists or philosophers like Richard Hoogart, Stuart Hall, Paul Gilroy, Ranajit Guha, Edward Said, Homi Bhaba, Dipesh Chakrabarty, Ashis Nandy, Arjun Appadurai, etc., to give a new status to the details of phenomena of daily life (toilets, kitchens, sex, airports, dustbins, metros...); to pose the problem of knowledge and social status of individuals in cultural terms (Spivak, 2009; Mattelart & Neveu, 2004); to recognize the chaotic, volatile, migrant and diasporic nature of the identities. The doctrines of post-modernity summarize perfectly these intellectual evolutions which they claim ended the era of western universalism with the principle of a high rationalist culture. Postmodernity announces a new anarchist and de-founded universe made of simulacra, irony, metaphoric and traditional beliefs (Vattimo, 1987; Maffesoli, 2010).

Postcolonial theory inherits this climate of cultural postmodernity. This theory symbolizes the *ethnologic turn* that has massively intervened in African contemporary social sciences. But two intermediate moments led by ethno-philosophy and the movement of negritude in literature played a crucial role in that conversion. To those moments we can add a third one represented by a certain interpretation of the ideas of Cheikh Anta Diop. Let us quickly say something about those three intermediate moments.

c) Three intermediate moments: ethno-philosophy, the negritude movement and a certain version of Cheikh Anta Diop's philosophy

The conviction that there exists a mystical mentality proper to Africans, but which has the same validity as the European logic mentality, has been strongly defended inside the African continent. The trend named later by the Cameroonian thinker, Marcien Towa, "ethno-philosophy" has been developed in Africa since the 1940s by a Belgian missionary, Placide Tempels.

The priest Tempels aimed to give an objective description of the mind of the Bantu people of Central Africa, knowing that that mind rests on an authentic philosophy which, nevertheless, has its proper "logic" principles. To Tempels indeed, the African Bantu philosophy rests on the principle of *vital force*. According to the "ontology" of vital force, Africans consider that each reality is invested by "invisible forces" charged with "energy" (Tempels 1947: 30). These forces or these energies are living and active "beings" that inhabit nature and society (Tempels 1947: 35). From those invisible and supernatural beings depend Bantu representations of cosmos, politics, economy, morality, art and religion. The entire life of the Bantu is then organized around the idea that each reality manifests a vital principle that determines its place and role in the architecture of the world and events. The dynamism of nature and society is then explained by the dynamism of the energies that conform both of them. The hierarchy between minerals, vegetables, animals, men and gods strictly depends on the charge of energy of vital force that constitutes each of these realities. And even inside minerals, animals, vegetables, men and gods, there exists a severe hierarchy upon which depends the place of each thing (Tempels 1947: 31). Because he is himself an ensemble of vital forces, humans can communicate and act with the other vital forces existing in nature. It is only thus that the course of history can be understood, meaning through the actions and interactions of supernatural causes (Tempels 1947: 41–43). In consequence, Tempels considered that the "Bantu philosophy" was the opposite of "Western philosophy". That philosophy didn't know the notion of argumentation; it was "unconscious" ontology and every Bantu had a direct knowledge of it (Tempels 1947: 51). Thus, that philosophy was "collective", meaning that the African way of thought avoids subjective reflection, conceptualization, experimentation and the principle of contradiction (Tempels 1947: 58–63)[1].

The necessity of finding a way of thinking for the African world radically distinctive from the rationalist and methodical European way took a particular resonance in Leopold Sedar Senghor. To this Senegalese poet, very influenced by the doctrines of Levy-Brühl, Placide Tempels, Leo Frobenius and Henri Bergson, *negritude* is the celebration of the "cultural, intellectual and spiritual values of the black world". Very close to the *vitalism* attributed by Tempels to the negro-Africans, these values are principally emotion, intui-

---

[1] It could be interesting to study the resurgence of the ethno-philosophical discourse in the approach of "paranormal phenomena" by an African thinker like Meinrad Hebga. The basis of his analyses is that contrary to western anthropology, which is dualist (body/soul), African anthropology is triadic (body/soul/shadow). From this point, it is perfectly conceivable for an African that the shadow of somebody leaves his body and his soul, and causes actions in very different places. Conforming to the ideologies of "New Age", Hebga tries to conciliate this mystical approach with the most advanced modern science (Relativity theory, quantum physics...). But as we can see, this is a manifest contradiction: African spirit cannot be presented as opposite to western science and at the same time converge in its results with the modern science.

tion and sensation. To Senghor, the black man is a "complex of sensations", a flux of energy characterized by a direct fusion with reality. Senghor uses the metaphoric figure of the feminine gender to show that in front of nature the African reacts with his body: his is total fusion, reception, love, desire, and intuition. Senghor seeks the nature of what he calls the "black soul". The latter has a biological ground that disposes the black man to rhythm, music, creativity, dance and esthetics (Senghor, 1964). Senghor finds in the biological soul of the black man the proof of the rejection of materialism, utilitarianism, pragmatism and technological domination of nature by Africans. The discovering of cultural differences based on racial differentiations, in other words the biologization of culture, pushed Senghor to the formulation of the concept of "Universal Civilization". This notion appeals the mix of both Negro and White natures with the final objective to create a hybrid universal culture made up of the alliance of emotion (Africa) and reason (Europe). We know that the hybridism of culture is at the heart of the postcolonial discourse.

To finish, it would not be uninteresting to notice the theoretical concessions made to this mystic vision attributed to the African cultures by the great African Egyptologist, Cheikh Anta Diop. A Camerounian researcher, Anatole Fogou, perfectly summarizes this strange situation. He uses the concept of "logical receptiveness" to show how the Cheikh Anta Diop ideas, like those formulated, for example, in the book *Civilisation ou barbarie,* prepared for the possibility of an African alternative epistemology aiming at the "decolonization of the African scientific discourse". Fogou shows, therefore, the way Cheikh Anta Diop has integrated notions like "vital force" in order to adapt them to notions of contemporary science like quantum physics (Fogou 2014: 63–85).

2. The ethnologic turn in postcolonial theory

The *ethnologic turn* of the postcolonial theory means the positive reconsideration of the outputs of ethnology, as a science put into the service of the imperialist and colonialist power, in African contemporary social sciences. In Cameroon, for example, this *return to the ethnologic age* has formed a great wave that has submerged all the domains of knowledge, to natural sciences (physics, mathematics, informatics, biology...) to the sciences of society and humanities (literature, history, anthropology, psychology, sociology, linguistics, political sciences and even philosophy). Imitating the postmodernist mode, consisting of a massive critique of the spirit and values of modernity (Lyotard 1979), African postcolonialists chose to question the concept of "universal reason". They came to the conclusion that "reason" is a cultural process and a historical construction of white and western societies. It is in that constructivist manner that the fundamental statement of "postcoloniality' encounters the main affirmations of the colonial ethnology carried by Levy-Brühl ideas, ethno-philosophy and the Senghor version of the negritude movement. At the age of globalization, two great passions guide African postcolonial doctrines: first, the passion for the micro-objects of African daily life; second, the passion for the fantastic world of images.

a) The passion for details of daily life

A major trait of postcolonial primitivism is its enthusiastic passion for the details of facts. Such a passion for nominalism is a legacy of the redefinition of the notion of culture that took place in England, mainly after the Second World War, with the displacement of culture from its official and academic expressions, or sites, to clandestine and non-official manifestations. Such a displacement transformed profoundly the notion of culture by giving to those informal phenomena the premier role in the social production. From there came the primacy given to the way that minor social groups, races, people, professional and sexual categories re-invent by themselves a new *style* or "culture" that escapes the tools of the classism generalization. Ethnography became fundamental in the studies carried out on the ancient colonized world of Africa, India, the Arab World, etc. By using instruments borrowed from ethnology and ethnography, postcolonial theory describes the marginalized people of the Third World in their proper, self and internal practices.

A neo-foucaldian strongly influenced by Antonio Gramsci's ideas, Jean-François Bayart, is a leader of African postcolonial studies in the francophone area. In Bayart, the reactivation of the link with ethnology is combined with the rejection of the western model of universalism through the conviction that one must approach "African societies through their banality" (Bayart, 1989). Taking into account the production of life by the African disfavored social cate-

Chapter 3: Alternatives to Nostalgia for Colonial Ethnology 49

gories, the concept of the "African banality" requires, in a manner that reminds Martin Heidegger phenomenology, to leave the sky of abstractions, theorizations, intellectualizations to the profit of a proximity observation of African contemporary practices. In their daily life, little people of Africa express themselves through esthetical forms like humor, rumor, dance, joke (joking or jokes sounds better), etc. According to Bayart, something appears from those daily attitudes, which is the fever for eating and drinking. To Bayart, the "proper rationality" of Africans, the explanation of their social behaviors and of their historic trajectory, in brief their "proper historicity", is a basic biological, organic, ordinary and primitive reflex revolving around food. As much as African societies are political, their politics are the "politics of the stomach". The discovering of such ventriloquism pushes Bayart to a long development that the key affirmation, considering the hedonism of some practices, is the existence in Africa of a cultural tendency towards corruption and economic crimes. While African official political practices or theorists imitate the attributes of universalism, coherence and unity for the African State, the officious African discourses, the discourses "from below", show a State mined by clientelism, affairism, tribalism, regionalism and ethnicism. The African political configurations are then chaotic and incoherent. Their type of "rationality" is typically opposed to the western model of the State with its norms of freedom, justice and law.

The Achille Mbembe's philosophy of history perfectly expresses the biological hedonism and the chaotic and indeterminate political constellations attributed to African societies by postcolonial theory. More ostensibly than Bayart, Mbembe recognizes the influence on his thought of the postmodern theories and assumes their beliefs to a new world order or a new *Zeitgeist* made of fragments, discontinuities and contingency. He clearly takes into account the contribution of the *cultural* and *subaltern studies* to the formation of a universal study that does not recover the modern western and linear model of science and knowledge led by rationalism, positivism and utilitarism. The exclusion of those corollaries of 19th century western imperialism demands the reconsideration of ways of producing knowledge, truth, morality, God, life, society, and history that are completely different from European methods. Mbembe is then convinced that other forms of human spirit exist, other trajectories of human mind and consciousness (Mbembe, 2000). He seeks those trajectories in phenomena which can even be found beyond classical social sciences, or modern esthetics and that embrace the dark world of sexualities, spectra, ghosts, magicians, sorcerers and manifest the powerfulness of intuition. African contemporary societies offer Mbembe the occasion to test how historic modern sciences fail to describe a postmodern African continent in full re-compositions and re-collections according to a process of *bricolage* or patchwork. This process of *métissage* doesn't give to the people of the continent any more chance than the possibility to make racial and cultural "juxtapositions". The Cameroonian historian speaks of the "concatenation of the world" (2010). He appears—certainly with Valentin Mudimbe and Mamadou Diouf (1999)——as one of the most talented theorists of hybridism in Africa.

The idea of a new political and scientific "cosmopolitism" impregnates considerably the theorizations of another Cameroonian philosopher, Jean-Godefroy Bidima. More influenced by Jacques Derrida and Theodor Adorno than by Michel Foucault, Bidima contests the power of western rationality to produce a truth discourse on African societies. He endeavours to use the demarche borrowed to the *critique theory* (*théorie critique*) which had allowed Adorno, Horkheimer, Benjamin, Marcuse and even Habermas to unmask the violence and the lie running behind a modernity that proclaimed its attachment to universality, liberty, justice, progress, equality, etc. Inspired by the works of Georges Bataille who had rediscovered the greatness of Dionysian faculties, Bidima tries to give another comprehension to the nature of the State in Africa by denouncing the dictatorship of so-called universal norms on African political and administrative practices and theories. In Africa, Bidima wants "to make public what is subtracted to the rational discrimination" (Bidima 1993: 14). He is engaged in the liquidation of the "ratio of identity" with its homogenizing and totalizing power. Bidima is attentive to the mobility, movement, contradiction of the African realm or life, in brief to what in that life obeys contingency and escapes the category. Bidima wants to think Africa is under the form of the "anti-category", of the "anti-method" (Bidima 1993: 23). To him, the discourse of political philosophy, political sciences, economic sciences, administrative sciences and juridical sciences doesn't grant enough attention to the anthropology of fragmentation in Africa which reconciles the mind with the fields of imagery, desire, sexuality, body (Bidima 1995). Bidima rediscovers the central role played in Africa by the manifestations of unconsciousness. In his quest of a "lateral universal" (Bidima, 2011), he underlines the top place of ethnology and tries to highlight the "sexual nature" of the African State. He gives a task to African philosophers: to describe the way they use their sex, their money, their administrative positions to produce power and domination.

In Bayart, Mudimbe, Mbembe, Bidima as well as Appiah, what we see is the manifestation of an African postcolonial theory that tries, in multiple ways, to emancipate Africa from the domination of the western model of science. It is in this manner that African post-colonial theorists have actively taken part in the debate about "endogenous knowledges". The reconsideration of traditional habits as a reminder of the ethnological age of African societies appears with more and more evidence if we consider the attention given by post-colonial authors to images and imagination.

b) The passion for images

The approach of colonial or postcolonial situations through imagination, arts, poetry, legends, popular traditions, music, dance, mysticism, narrative, literature, considered as non-objective and nonscientific instruments is very pregnant in post-colonial theorists. The recourse to the imaginary world is the typical signature of what we can call the *esthetic turn* of postcolonial studies. In fact, post colonialism is not a "theory" at all; it is an esthetical world vision that supposes the certitude of the superiority of sensible faculties on conceptual and intellectual faculties. The rehabilitation of imagination appears as a pertinent alternative to the illegitimate domination of the western model of science based on rationalism and pragmatism.

It is crucial not to forget that historically the arts, more precisely literature through the novel, were the first fields of expression of postcolonial doctrines in Africa. In Yambo Ouologuem's (1969) and Ahmadou Kourouma's (1970) works we can observe the emergence of a new stylistic form tending to paint Africa by exaggerating and deforming some of its features. This new style uses constant caricatures and presents Africa through a dark and obscene humor. In addition to this obscenity of African manners, the postcolonial novel develops a great historical and ontological pessimism that considers as totally negative the post-independence African evolution and presents these failures as the result of the weakness of the African metaphysical constitution. Imported by political scientists, historians, economists and anthropologists in the social science fields, the esthetical approach pushes a French theorist like Bayart (following the method of Michel de Certeau) to show strong interest in African vulgarity. He considers with particular attention new unusual micro-objects (libido, sex, money, stomach, mouth, food, the recourse to sorcery...) and reveals the fundamental role played in contemporary African processes by attitudes like humor, rumor, popular beliefs, the recourse to mysticism, etc (Bayart, 1983). He contests the opinion sustaining the inertia of African political formations and suspects that this wrong point of view is simply the consequence of the usage of tools borrowed from the western rationalist social sciences. On the contrary, he remarks upon the internal movement inside those societies and suggests that it is the movement of the inferior social classes that fight the monopole of a brutal African State upon society. Bayart speaks of "the revenge of African societies under the State". To him humor, caricature, irony and dance appear as a manner for the little people of Africa to disqualify their political and economic elites (Bayart, Mbembe, Toulabor, 2008).

Mbembe doesn't approve of Bayart's oppositions: State/Society, political society/civil society, institutions/popular habits. On the contrary, he radicalizes the presupposition of the "banality", the "vulgarity" and the "obscenity" of African lives by extending them to the official institutions. In Africa, the State and the populations of civil society share the same *ethos* which is the *ethos* of consumption. There exists connivance and even complicity between political elites and the populations around a common agreement on a Dionysian way of life (Mbembe 2000: 141). "Postcolony" is a particular process of social zombification; it constantly produces death and its esthetics is an esthetics of death. In postcolonial social formations, power plays a "*game*", the game of domination and command; meanwhile, the populations play another "game", the game of subordination and submission. The postcolonial subject is a *homo ludens* (Mbembe 2000: 144). The "postcolony" is a vast scene of production and reproduction of *simulacra, excess, games* and *parodies* (Mbembe 2000: 149). The postcolonial power *ima-*

gines its own power with ostentation and magnificence through *feasts, festivities, rejoicings, orgies*. It extends its control on African human *bodies* essentially through *copulation* and a *fantastic* violence. The "postcolony" is completely a "stylistics of disproportion" (Mbembe 2000: 163) where political power enters in trance and produces *fables* and *hallucinations* on itself; it is the regime of *falsification* and *re-invention*. The "postcolony" is a matter of telling stories (Mbembe 2000: 165). It is the reason why Mbembe uses metaphors, images, stories, imagination and convokes music and poetry to paint the new cosmopolite African world that emerges from the juxtaposition and the hybridism of cultures on the continent (Mbembe, 2010). This new Africa which is coming to be born out of African imagination has a name: "Afropolitanism".

Bidima shares the same attraction for hybridism of cultures and studies very attentively the incoherent and discontinuous lines of African social productions. To him, African contemporary arts represent the perfect prism of this new sensitivity that denies academic stylistic forms as well as offering a new *image* for the African future. This new esthetic utopia works with processuality, uncertainty, complexity, mediations, interstices, and finds the new Africa "possible" in the "shameful practices" of society laying on sex, dustbins, defecation, etc (Bidima 1997: 32). Bidima discovers in African contemporary art a scatological aesthetics that considers disgust as the fundamental category. From this point, Bidima is led to explore the abnormal aesthetic practices produced by people from below who in Africa represent marginal socio-economic categories like women, slaves, manual workers, women, children, homosexuals, poor people, etc. Through them, Bidima conceives an "esthetics of scraps" (Bidima 1197: 90–98) that prefers heterology, difference, transition, emptiness instead of an aesthetics of homology, identity, fullness. In Bidima, postcolonial aesthetics is an aesthetics of emptiness (Bidima, 1998).

What is remarkable in these postcolonial aesthetics is the way that they try not only to replace scientific explanations by aesthetic figurations, but to impose the return to ethnology and its biological, primitivist and aesthetic categories as the central moment in the new African social sciences. He lays the methodological basis of "endogenous knowledge" in Africa. However, combined with esthetics and even with the inflation of the "text" (textualization, textuality), the ethnologic turn of social sciences in Africa lends itself to some critical remarks.

3. Critical remarks about the ethnologic turn: for a new approach to endogenous knowledge

A different concept of endogenous knowledge, based on a radically different reception than the one imposed by colonial ethnology, is possible. Indeed, legends, myths, cosmogonies, imagery are effective productions of human spirit that are worthy of admiration, but they do not say anything by themselves. They need to be submitted to reflection and conceptualization in order to express the rationality existing inside them. This supposes indeed an alternative reading of the African past and the rediscovery of the Negro cultural heritage of science, art, technique and philosophy from antiquity until the present times. This approach has drawn the attention of many African thinkers like Cheikh Anta Diop, Théophile Obenga, Engelbert Mveng, Marcien Towa, Nkolo Foé, etc.

a) Reason in Ancient Negro Egypt

One of the main gains obtained by African Egyptologists was to show the common cultural heritage shared both by Ancient Egypt and negro-African traditional and contemporary civilizations. Clearly established by Cheikh Anta Diop and Théophile Obenga, this "*parenté génétique*" (Obenga, 1993) recovers all the aspects of African culture: language, religion, mythology, esthetics, philosophy, gender, science, political and social organizations, etc (Anta Diop, 1955; 1967; 1981). But most important is that after having demonstrated the "precedence of Negro civilizations", these authors led their gigantic intellectual efforts toward showing the rational character of the African Egyptian thought.

For example, Théophile Obenga presents an excellent manuscript named the *Philosophic Manuscript of Memphis*. In this treatise, the beginning of the world is due to an intellectual and autogenic cosmic principle, Ptah. According to this document, "Ptah stands in front of Râ every day" (Obenga 1990: 68) The document adds that Ptah "comes to existence through the heart"(Ibid). We can then see that the heart designates the same thing as language, and both are similar to the thought which governs each part of the body, of things, of the universe and even the gods themselves: "Ptah comes to existence through language (a thought) as a form of Atoum. Great and powerful Ptah, which has transmitted (his strength) to all (gods) and to their *kaou* (soul) though really that heart, that tongue from which Horus came to existence; from which Thot came to existence, as Ptah" (Ibid). Ancient Africans of Egypt considered that the premier principle of things is reason; however, reason is not static, immobile, inert, but dynamic. By conceiving the idea of a dynamic reason, ancient Egyptians founded the dialectical philosophy by which they gave a magisterial attempt to solve the great metaphysical and social question of unity and multiplicity, self and the other, identity and multiplicity, same and difference, stability and change. We know how much this question had drawn the attention of ancient Greeks, from Heraclites to Parmenides, from Plato to Aristotle passing to sophists like Protogoras, Gorgias, Zenon, etc. To ancient Africans of Egypt, the question of being, which is definitely the question of reason and truth, must be posed in terms of *relation, tension, contradiction, conflict, opposition.*

The significance of this contradiction is not the radical impossibility of truth, but the necessity to formulate this truth at the end of a long and passionate *process* by which ideas circulate throughout all the human organs of knowledge, going from sensation, emotion, intuition, imagination to reflection, conception, meaning, thought. But only thought can give truth, because only thought has the power of judgment. Ancient Africans said: "The heart and the tongue had gained power over (all) the members in order to teach: Ptah exists (as heart) in each body and (as tongue) in each mouth of all gods, of all men, of all animals, of all worms and all things that have life; in order to think (as he is the heart) and to command (as he is the tongue) everything he wants" (Ibid). The dialectical nature of Ptah allows him to exist as an ennead, a group of nine gods which summarizes all the active forces working inside nature and culture: Atoum-Rê (the Sun); Shou and Tefnout (hot air and humid air); Geb (the ground); Nout (the sky); Osiris (fertility and vegetation); Isis (political power and governmental laws); Seth (the hurricanes); Nephtys (goddess of death). According to the ancient Africans from Egypt, only the positive and active confrontation of these forces can give birth to civilization.

The error of postcolonial theory can then clearly be seen. This error consists of a profound ignorance or incomprehension of African systems of thought. Apparently, Levy-Brühl didn't know anything about those complex systems from Africa. He contented himself to erect them into particular forms of "rationalities", the common opinions circulating in the imperialist countries about the "mentality" of so-called "primitives". In the name of the rediscovery of the "endogenous", postcolonial theorists reproduce the same fault. Like J.-G. Bidima, they consider that the interpellation of the Egyptian Negro's past is a form of "fundamentalism" (Bidima 1995: 78), which tends to give an "absolute assize" to African civilizations presented as governed by the paradigm of the One, or the "monotheistic model". (Ibid) To escape to this so-called "theology of the One", postcolonial theorists claim that—like one of their masters, Levi-Strauss—it is preferable to consider that History is after all a story that can be told by having recourse to fiction, metaphor, construction. Such is the case with Mamadou Diouf, who insists on the role of narration in the *bricolage* of African histories that are necessary, marginal, fragmented, plural, chaotic and hostile to any submission to the modern model of linearity and progress (Diouf 1999: 5–35). The emergence of alternative narrations of the African or Negro past also pushes Paul Gilroy to show a great resistance to the transmission of the glorious heritage of Ancient pharaohs; for him, that "history must not be transmitted" (Gilroy 2003: 247–291). By doing so, postcolonial theorists make the choice to turn their back on African facts to the profit of imagination, the imaginary, invention. The privilege given to a poetical and aesthetical approach poses many problems because it excludes from the analysis vast domains of knowledge of African societies.

In effect, how is it possible to sustain that African mentality is mystical and that, in consequence to that assertion, African contemporary societies are guided by a non-positivist rationality ignoring the principles of identity, of non-contradiction and of universality when the level of abstraction attempted for example by Egyptian mathematics is regularly underlined by specialists? The abstractive nature of this mathematics is brilliantly exposed by the Cameroonian epistemologist, Malolo Dissakè. He studies the method used by the Egyptian mathematician Ahmès, and he remarks on "the extraordinary rigor in the progression of the exposition" (Dissakè 2005: 60). This rigor in the reasoning is perfectly adapted to the spirit of modern science in the sense that René Descartes had defined this spirit: the identification of the "problem"; a step by step approach demanding to go from the simple to the complex; the necessity to create a link or to establish a bridge between the epistemological need to know things and the necessity to observe and to accomplish certain social obligations (Descartes, 1997). Long before Descartes, the African mathematician Ahmès, discovered the *rules of method* (Dissakè 2005: 60). He considered that mathematics as the science of numbers, the science of multiplication, division, subtraction and addition, was the privileged instrument in the process of penetrating the secrets of nature and the universe. But while the knowledge of these secrets was conditioned by the respect of the rules of methodic thought, Malolo Dissakè notes in Ahmès's approach the existence of a "philosophy of learning" (Ibid). The principle of this philosophy is the permanent training of the intellectual capacities of the student confronted by the scribe with diverse exercises or cases. From these individual facts or particular situations, the student must be able to identify the "problem", meaning the difficulty, and he must find the appropriate way to solve it or to eventually solve the highest difficulties. Ultimately, the scribe is also a pedagogue who teaches his student the correct way to lead his thought and the art of reflection by the establishment of the proof.

This art of proof is the true foundation of the African spirit. So when postcolonial theory pretends that African consciousness ignores demonstration, analysis, experimentation, the art of proof or the principle of a thought governed by laws and methodic rules, this theory is wrong. The history of African societies offers a formal denial of the proposition that nonwestern societies are principally led by uncertainty, indeterminism and immediacy. If mysticism, sorcery, popular superstition play a role in these societies, this role cannot be the major or determinant one. Mystical spirit normally occupies here—as in modern western societies—a minor and marginal place. As we will see below with Henri Brunschwig, Aimé Césaire and Frantz Fanon, only certain historic circumstances marked by domination—for example the colonial, neocolonial, para-colonial, or imperial situation—can explain the inflation of irrational attitudes in non-western societies. Unfortunately, postcolonial theory shows a real incapacity to consider the concept of domination.But let us end our demonstration about the extreme modernity and the rationality of the African Egyptian spirit with a few remarks about morality and politics. A text entitled *Instructions given to Vizir Rekhmiré* gives precious elements on the formation, during the XVIIIth dynasty (1550–1292 B.C.) at the apogee of Egyptian civilization, of *public space* regulated by the principles of reason. The modernity of this text is due to the fact that we can see the central place taken by the sovereign principle of Maât (Truth-Justice) in ancient Egypt through it. According to the text "it is not an easy and smooth thing to be a vizir, it could be even very bitter (...). You will be attentive to make things conform to law, to make them conform to what is right for the people, by insuring justice for each man (...) The vizir must live being known from everybody, by acting openly, because water and wind bring back each of his acts and no one ignores his actions" (Lalouette 1984: 182–184). This text underlines the need to apply justice rightly and publicly. Here the principle of publicity of justice is the unique guarantee of its rationality; it prevents arbitrariness and the rule of force; it provides the proof that the magistrate makes his decision without any pressure other than the pressure of truth and fairness: "Partiality is an abomination of God (...) You must conform yourself to this instruction. Consider the person who is familiar to you in the same manner that the person you don't know (...). Don't be hostile to somebody before given the ear to what he wants to say" (Ibid). The exigency of impartiality is the corollary of the necessity of rationality on the part of the judge who must not be impatient and gained by subjectivity when he leads a trial: "The dignity of the judge is to practice justice (...). If a judge lies, he will come out as he merits" (Ibid). Because objectivity, impartiality and equity are his main characters, the goal pursued by the judge is finally the truth. It is the reason why he will take his audiences in the room called the "room of the two Maât": Truth on one side and Justice on the other side (Ibid).

After having read this ancient text, we can see how the postcolonial hypothesis of African political societies ruled by chaos, arbitrariness and incoherence is false. Ancient Egyptians didn't only build a homogeneous rational State; they have also formulated the idea, the concept and the theory of such a State.

This explicit reference made by ancient African political societies to rational principles of truth, justice, equity, probity, equality, also appears clearly in a period which remains insufficiently studied in the history of Africa: the medieval age. Let us rapidly present some of the fundamental characteristics of these historic sequences from the points of view of epistemology, cosmology, cosmogony, philosophy of environment and aesthetic. What we will discover is very far from the conclusions drawn by Levy-Brühl and postcolonial theorists about the "mystical" spirit of Africans—even if "mysticism" is presented by them as a form of "alternative" or "lateral" rationality with its proper laws.

b) Reason in the African medieval period and in traditional African texts

Let us start with an interesting text drawn from the cosmogony of the Fang people, a Bantu ethnic and cultural group living between five countries in the centre of Africa: Cameroon, Equatorial Guinea, Gabon, Republic of Congo and Sao Tome and Principe. The account of the birth of the world given by the *Mvett* is a fascinating one in terms of complexity, but also because it furnishes an extraordinary testimony of the part that the "mechanic analogy" plays in certain cosmogonies in traditional Africa. Below are some lines from this myth as we have translated them:

> "Oyono Ada Ngono, great musician and great warrior,
> In his coma entered into the nothingness.
> He did not see anything; there was nothing.
> Eyo engendered Ngos Eyo,
> Ngos Eyo engendered Akii Ngos
> Which took form with four angles.
> He got bigger in an exaggerated way in front of Oyono Ada Ngono, who was astonished.
> He exploded and gave birth to Minkur-Mi-Akii;
> Minkur-Mi-Akii engendered Biyem-Yema-Bi-Nkur;
> Biyem-Yema engendered Dzob-Biyem-Yema;
> Dzob-Biyem-Yema engendered Bikoko-Bi-Dzob;
> Bikoko-Bi-Dzob engendered Ngba-Bikoko (...)
> Mebege engendered Zame-Ye-Mebege, Kara-Ye-Mebege et Zong-Ye-Mebege"
> (Tsira Ndong, 1970)

In the language of the Fang populations of central Africa, *Eyo* designates the foyer of the forge; *Ngos*, copper; *AkiiNgos*, the copper-egg; *Minkur-Mi-Akii*, coopery clouds; *Dzob*, the sky; *Bikoko*, the planets, the stars; *Mebege*, the blowtorch of the forge; *Zame*, a character associated to metallurgy; *Kara*, either a crab or a bellows.

What is fundamental with this myth sung by a poet named *mbomo mvett*, is the over-representation of elements belonging to the craft of metallurgy. As Ptah in the antic city of Memphis, the demiurge of the Fang people emerges from the primitive ocean of chaos by its own force or its proper action. It is an autogenic god. But more significantly, this demiurge emerges in the form of an egg made of copper. According to the Fang people, copper is the central element in the genesis of the cosmos. We must remark that the reference to this matter—copper—is recurrent in some other African cosmogonies like the one that forms the world vision of Africans from the Sahel, the Fali for example. Their cosmogony as well as the cosmogony of the Fang is then very similar to the Memphite cosmogony. We know that Ptah, is the figure of *copper man*. For this reason, he is the master of techniques and of architects. All the aspects of culture derive from his creation and from his creative work: cities, the sciences, the arts, law and religion. Like Ptah, who is at the beginning of the human civilizations and cultures, *Zame* is also the figure of the *copper man*. He is himself the result of a process of auto-engenderment. But it is important to notice that this process of self-production implies also, for the demiurge, the capacity to be a mathematician (Elimane Kane, 1992; 2007)[2]. We must always remind ourselves that *Akii-Ngos* "formed himself with four angles". In the dialectical metamorphoses of his beings, the god, one but multiple, conserves the aptitude to draw and form geometric figures. He, himself, is a mathematical figure. And he forms—not creates as we can see in the Judeo-Christian cosmogony—things through this geometric process which is completed by a technical practice: the god uses his reason, his *is reason*; but he also uses his technical instruments, he *is those technical instruments*: the hammer, the bellows, the blowtorch, etc. They constitute the origins of everything: cultures, civilizations, States, laws, moralities, arts, sciences, gods, mountains, plants, animals, rivers, stars, etc.

As we can see, in the cosmogony of *Mvett* the world results from the action of a technician working in his factory and making ob-

---

[2] This author reveals the fundamental place of mathematics in African cultures, principally in the structure of languages like Poular and wolof.

jects with his hands. The "technomorphy"of the myth of *Mvett* presents a demiurge that is an authentic builder. But the great lesson drawn from this myth is the presence, inside traditional African cultures, of a philosophy of technic. The evocation of mechanic tools is a reminder that traditional Africa had perfectly assimilated the spirit of modernity and that it was engaged in a process of modernization that was stopped. The crucial question is then the following: for what reasons and by what historic forces—internal and external—was this process of modernization broken? Postcolonial theory shows a real incapacity to pose and solve this question positively. Following wrongly certain ideas defended by Levy-Brühl, Placide Tempels, Sedar Senghor and Meinrad Hebga, this theory fails to see the perfect conformity of certain African cosmogonies with the spirit of modernity. Postcolonial theory shows a deep inaptitude to study the Fang cosmogony, for instance, the eyes fixed to the most advanced scientific theories about the formation of the universe. In effect, when *Akii Ngos* gets bigger and bigger, and then explodes, this clearly reminds us of the "big bang" theory about the concentration and the explosion of primitive matter in the origin of the world. To the Fang people, *Ngos*, copper, is this exploded primitive matter. In consequence, a veritable project aiming to come back to "endogenous knowledges", or to revitalize African "*ancestralités*" would necessarily take the true way of exploration of African traditional systems of thought (Towo-Atangana, 1966)[3]—instead of limiting the analysis to bizarre tales about vampires, demons, sorceries, handicrafts, mystical cannibalism, ghosts, zo-anthropy, multi-location, etc[4].

Another aspect of postcolonial discourse is the claim of the existence of a "proper political historicity" in Africa, a "proper rationality". This claim turns around a presupposition that in contemporary Africa political power comes from two main sources: on the one hand the "ancestral authoritarianism", and on the other, the

---

[3] This text is regularly quoted by the Cameroonian philosopher Marcien Towa, who concludes, after having studied it, that Fang mythology refuses the idea of a Providence, of a God creating everything, almighty and absolutely good.

[4] Submitted to the influence of senghorism, this is the error generally committed by afro-descendants, meaning the African Diasporas throughout the world (USA, Latin America, Caribbean islands, Indian ocean, Europe), who have the tendency to identify the magico-religious attitudes with the authentic African spirit.

legacy of colonization with its brutality on the bodies of colonized men. This presupposition is the extension, in the field of politics, of the postmodernist principle of the "plurality of rationalities". Achille Mbembe perfectly theorizes that position (Mbembe, 2000), which finds its first intellectual expression in modern Africa in the esthetical work of Yambo Ouologuem at the end of the 1960s. This novelist marks the beginning of the postcolonial movement in literature and social sciences in the African circles of the post-independence period. He goes very far into the past, more precisely to the Middle Ages, and he discovers African political societies marked by tyranny, violence, arbitrariness and murder. In his work, aesthetics is put to the service of scientific truth in order to reveal the essence of an African culture intensively turned around crime, corruption, rape, anthropophagy, lubricity, frenetic and savage hedonism. The incarnation of this moral depravation running into African genes from immemorial times is King Saïf (Yambo Ouloguem, 1968). In Ahmadou Kourouma's work, African evil culture is represented by the character of Fama. The incapacity of this man to convert the recovered freedom into liberty and progress symbolizes the failure of African powers to domesticate modernity. It is the only way by which one can understand the vulgarity and obscenity of African cultural productions (Ahmadou Kourouma, 1970). This vulgarity, according to African postcolonial theory, is due to a "specific rationality", an "endogenous cause" that predisposes Africans to economic and political failure.

It is important, however, to notice that such statements advanced by postcolonial aestheticians and political theorists are made in perfect continuity with the arguments used by colonial racism in order to justify the economic exploitation of non-European populations in Africa. African chiefs were endlessly presented as abominable tyrants practicing ritual crimes and human sacrifices. But in truth, that description reposes on pseudo-scientific explanations that ignore the true past of African political societies. Our pretention is not to impose the idea of perfect African liberal societies which were ruled by goodness and practiced justice everywhere and every time. We just want to show, as we saw with ancient Egypt that traditional and medieval African societies had clearly formulated the principle of an open society tending to the protection of human rights. A magnificent text, *La Charte du Mandé: la déclaration mandingue des droits de l'Homme*, written in 1236 after the victory of Soundjata Keita over king Soumaworo Kanté and which was at the origin of the Mali Empire, gives an excellent illustration of that view. The *Charte* says:

> The children of Sanéné and Kontron declare: each human life is a life.
> It is true that a life comes to existence before another life,
> But a life is not "older", more respectable than another life,
> The same as a life is not superior to another life.

We assist here to the proclamation of the sacred character of human life. This sacred character means the absolute dignity of that life. The consequence of the sacred dignity of human life is then the affirmation of the universal equality between human beings. All men are equal and no one is superior, or inferior, either in nature or in rights to another one. For this reason, human life must be respected, protected and preserved from any aggression or violation. If the contrary were the case, justice must be done:

> The children of Sanéné and Kontran declare: because each life is the same than every other life, any harm caused to any life requires reparation.
> In consequence, may no one take it out without reason on his neighbour;
> May no one cause harm to his close kin;
> May no one martyrize his fellow man.

By putting emphasis on the need for each one to protect his close relatives, to venerate his progenitors, to educate his children, to satisfy the needs of his family, the *Charte* considers the right to be fed as one of the fundamental human rights. According to the Malinké, hunger pushes people to slavery and condemns them to be submitted to exploitation. It is the reason why hunger must be fought. This double denunciation of hunger and slavery is one of the most enriching discoveries of traditional African legacy:

> The children of Sanéné and Kontron declare:
> Hunger is not a good thing,
> Slavery also is not a good thing;
> There is no worse calamity than those things,
> On this earth.
> As much as we would dispose of the quiver and the arc,
> Hunger would not kill anybody in the Mandé.
> If by extraordinary circumstances starvation comes,
> War will not destroy a village ever
> To take slaves;
> It means that from now on, no one will put the bit between fellow's teeth,
> In order to sell him;

Equally no one will be beaten in the Mandé,
A*fortiori*, no one will be killed because he is the son of a slave."

Since the 13th century, around the time that the *Habea Corpus* was edited by Jean-Sans-Terre in Europe, the Empire of Mali had given in to the indignity of slavery. Africans had understood that this practice was an infamy which needed to be abolished. This institution was a horrible crime and aggression against values of freedom, equality and dignity. Slavery was the complete rejection of the essence of human nature: liberty. This humiliating and abominable treatment could not be maintained:

> The children of Sanéné and Kontron declare:
> The essence of slavery has become extinct today.
> "From a wall to another", from a border to another of Mandé;
> The raids are banished from today in Mandé,
> The torments due to these horrors will disappear from today in Mandé.
> The famine, what a horror! A starving man ignores any decency, any restraint.
> What an appalling suffering for the slave and the starving,
> Mainly when they don't have any means to avoid famine;
> The slave is deprived of his dignity whatever the place in the world.

The *Charte of Mandé* proclaims the dignity of a man as a man. The *Charte* particularly stresses the obligation to nourish not only his body, but also his soul. It is only in that condition that man can be *free*: free to learn; free to study; free to be informed; free to express his opinions and his judgment; free to come and go. Once again, the *Charte of Mandé* is clear in this aspect:

> Man as an individual, made of bones and chair,
> Of marrow and nerves, of skin covered by coats and hairs, is fed with food and drinks;
> But his "soul", his mind lives for three things:
> Seeing what he desires to see,
> Telling what he desires to tell,
> Doing what he desires to do.
> If one amongst those things came to be subtracted to the satisfaction of the mind,
> It would be suffering,
> It would surely wilt.

The *Charte of Mandé* ends with a magisterial declaration full of an incontestable modernity. This declaration anticipates the spirit of the Declaration of Human Rights of the American, the French, the

Russian, the Chinese and the Cuban Revolutions. We know that this spirit was codified universally by the United Nations (U.N):

> In consequence, the children of Sanéné and Kontron declare:
> Each one disposes from now on his person,
> Each one is free of his acts, in the respect of the "interdicts", of the laws of his country.
> That is the oath of Mandé,
> At the attention of the world (Tata Cissé et Sagot-Duvauroux, 2003. My translation).

The modernity of this text means two things. Firstly, it is a vibrant contestation of the so-called "African primitive and non-civilized political habits" proposed by postcolonial theorists; this text proves once again that in the field of politics, just as in many other fields, Africa was building a solid and coherent modernity that had brutally stopped near the 16th-17th centuries; the same true question remains: for what historical reasons, by which historic forces and through which historical events was that modernity hindered? Secondly, the *Charte of Mandé* teaches us the road that must be followed if we seek to pose in Africa the essential question of a *new modernity*; effectively different, this modernity is certainly inseparable from the current disputations about the "opening of reason", the "local knowledges", the "clandestine wisdoms", the "endogenous knowledges". But by remaining prisoner of the postmodernist conception of the "opened reason" in the sense of absolute fragmentation and uncertainty, postcolonial theory fails to seize the true concept of notions as "endogenous", or "local".

For us, those notions don't have anything to do with a so-called authentic "African" reason which would be essentially, metaphysically or by nature different from the "European reason". This essentialism, hidden behind the argument of diversity or *métissage*, is perverse and unacceptable (Towa, 2010). It fixes the differences and artificially organizes a "global apartheid" at the level of science between individuals, people, races and nations (Lefebvre 1975; Nkolo Foé, 2008). For us, this notion of "plural reason" involves the rigorous study of African texts, may they be written or oral, with the universal tools of the most advanced scientific techniques and methodologies in the domains of anthropology, psychology, philosophy, mathematics, linguistics or literary analysis. The attentive study of cosmogonies, tales, proverbs, myths, sculptures, songs, dances, scientific treatises, birth or death rituals, military games, political Charts, etc., will allow seizing the active and universal reason in those African cultural productions, as they are part of human creativity.

c) Some challenges for modern reason in contemporary Africa: beyond the obstacle of nostalgic romanticism

The important effort made by postcolonial theory in the reinvestment of fields such as myths, legends, arts, superstitions, imaginations, handicrafts etc., has the merit of having massively re-explored wide domains of African creativity that had been rejected without regard by so-called "rationalist" and "modernist" African thinkers. But postcolonial theory made a mistake, having erected without any critique of scientific systems of thought, data that, however, could not speak for themselves. Postcolonial theory did not capitalize the lesson learned from Hegel for whom the value of the symbol comes from the concept which leads its life (Hegel, 1997). Postcolonial theory commits the fault that Marcien Towa considered as the main fault, the original sin *(péché originel)* of "popular philosophy": this "philosophy" appeals for "tolerance", insists on the supreme right of intuition, sensation, imagination, the sacred, faith, common sense, enthusiasm to tell the absolute, and strongly contests the pretention of conceptual reason to get the monopole of judgment; but while ready to judge reason, "popular philosophy" is not ready to be judged by the concept, it shows real intolerance vis-à-vis conceptual reason. Critical of the intolerance of conceptual thought, "popular philosophy" turns itself into intolerance by the imposition of the unique right of the "subjective arbitrary" (Towa 1971: 64–65).

In a completely different plan, it could be interesting to notice that the destiny and the trajectory borrowed by reason in modern Africa are similar to the process that had guided the access to modernity of a country like Germany. Henri Brunschwig describes the apogee of romanticism in Prussia between the 18th and 19th centuries as marked by the growth of all kinds of the miraculous, illuminism and irrationalism. This author explains this irruption by the deception felt by the ascending German young bourgeois class vis-à-vis the ideals of the French Enlightenment. In effect, under the reign of Frederic II, Prussia had launched an ambitious program of modernization of German society in such areas as the economy, religion, science and art as well as the political and philosophical domains. Despite a more liberal society, young bourgeois intellectuals found difficulties to get access to social recognition. They had the knowledge, the scientific culture, but they did not have the political leadership. In fact, the old nobility continued to keep society under its grip. The emergent young bourgeoisie was in despair. Incapable of changing its society, this bourgeoisie lost faith in the ideals of the French revolution. Under the pressure of economic crisis at the end of the 18th century, young bourgeois did not believe that reason could change life at all. In Schelling, Schiller, Hölderlin, Novalis, Kleist, etc., poetry, religion, art and mythology, magic appear as the unique solutions to tyranny, poverty and illness. They thought that there was a mystical law (made of illusions, metaphors, hallucinations, dreams, trances, esoteric movements like free-masonry...) superior to the rational and positivist laws of nature. In other words, they thought that there was an *invisible* reason situated beyond the *visible* and material reason of modern society (Brunschwig, 1973). The System of Reason developed by Hegel, who established a rigorous hierarchy of faculties, appears as the monumental response to this romantic mysticism.

It seems that postcolonial theorists face a similar mysticism and skepticism nowadays. Confronted with African tragedies (poverty, unemployment, disease, corruption, wars, sexual violence against women and children, economic crisis, economic austerity measures imposed by neoliberal institutions like IMF and WB, religious fundamentalisms led by sects like Boko Haram...), they are not able to question the *historical causes* of those failures. They believe that African processes are ruled by chaos, hazard, incoherence and indeterminism. In Africa, they discover a totally different "reason" at work which responds to phenomena like fragmentation, disorder, elementary factors, primitivism, etc. In Africa, they explain tragedy through tragedy. In consequence, they do not explain it at all. And the reason for this absence of a pertinent explanation comes from the forgetting of postcolonial theory of the enriching lessons of Aimé Césaire, Frantz Fanon, Amilcar Cabral or Marcien Towa.

To those authors the first and main cause of the actual African failures is the colonial, para-colonial, semi-colonial, neocolonial and imperial situation of the Negro-African people throughout the world (Césaire 1956: 190). Culture is the "soul" of each society or of each people, it is the subjectivity of a people, the identity that this people gives to itself through historic productions like science, art, religion, technique, law, etc. In summary, culture is the living substance of a people (Césaire 1956: 191), the level where the people express their "*particular will, unique, making choices between different options*" (Césaire 1956: 192). Culture is the instance where people have the experience of freedom. But this freedom cannot flourish without a solid and free stable material, with an economic and political base. In Africa, this base has been destroyed by the colonial system. At this time, the "passion of life" in African cultures has been broken. Incapable of making choices by their own will, African people entered a profound cultural crisis. The end of self-determination led to the death of the "creating powerfulness" of African cultures, which then lost their "faculty to renewal" (Césaire 1956: 194). Petrified by colonialism, indigenous culture offers a spectacle of heterogeneous cultural elements. Such a juxtaposition of fragmented and partial cultural elements coming from everywhere, called "*métissage*" or hybridism, is the symbol of the "anarchy" that governs the dominated culture. Césaire speaks of "*Barbarism by cultural anarchy*" (Césaire 1956: 201).

One of the symbols of this cultural anarchy is the return of indigenous people to irrational aspects of tradition (magic, sorcery, ritual murders, etc.). To break the development of this "primitive mentality" which is incompatible with the objectives of liberation, Césaire, as well as Fanon and Towa, pose the necessity for African people "*to re-conquest the historic initiative*" (Césaire 1956: 201). The rediscovery of the "dialectic of our proper needs" commands Africans to fight against the world capitalist system of domination.

To Fanon this fight means principally the rupture with racialism, the biologism and the culturalism of Senghor's version of *negritude* in its ignorance of the question of national independence (Fanon 2002: 202–211). Once the colonized people enter in a struggle for their emancipation, their entire culture changes. Fanon brilliantly describes the dynamism that seizes this traditional culture, mainly in the spheres of esthetic productions like music, sculpture, poetry, myth, literature, dance, song, etc. To Fanon, the revolutionary struggle disrupts indigenous culture which, therefore, can express its modernist potential of *creation*. The liberation struggle provokes the "complete revolution of the actual state of

African cultures" (Towa, 1971), and leads them to a new humanism and a new universalism based on reason and liberty.

Conclusion

The *ethnographic* and *ethnologic turn* in African social sciences and humanities is the direct legacy of the ideas of Lévy-Brühl about a so called "primitive mentality" proper to the non-European people throughout the world. Based on the hypothesis of ignorance of materialism, determinism, objectivism and rationalism of causes by those populations, the thesis of a primitive mind supposes the existence of a mystic spirit, proper to indigenous peoples which gives priority to the action of invisible beings. This mysticism would form a particular type of "rationality" that functions with its internal rules. Re-affirmed inside the African continent by intellectual movements like ethno-philosophy, whose *negritude* version was presented by Senghor and certain readings from the Cheikh Anta Diop texts, the recourse to colonial ethnology and its racist presuppositions about the biological nature of the African mind has been perfectly prolonged by the African postcolonial discourse helped in that task by post structuralism and postmodernism, but the concept of "endogenous knowledges" it gives suffers from too many insufficiencies. Hidden behind the mode of "esthetization of the realm", postcolonial theory principally ignores the true history of reason in Africa; it ignores the rational and dialectical way in which, from antiquity to contemporary times, African mathematicians, geometers, political thinkers, estheticians, cosmologists and metaphysicians have posed the questions relative to the origin of existence, truth, goodness, justice, morality, State, culture, civilization, techniques, arts, gods, etc. By rehabilitating archaic forms of consciousness, the postcolonial approach produces a false concept of the "endogeneity" of knowledge. More interesting, that theory is unable to see that only a historic situation marked by political and economic domination pushes societies in the peripheries of global capitalism towards superstition and irrationalism.

References

Anta Diop, C. (1955). *Nations nègres et cultures.* Paris : Présence Africaine.

Anta Diop, C. (1967). *Antériorité des civilisations nègres.* Paris : Présence Africaine.

Anta Diop, C. (1981). *Civilisation ou barbarie.* Paris : Présence Africaine.

Bayart, J.-F. (1983). La Revanche des sociétés africaines. *Politique africaine*, No. 11, pp. 95–127.

Bayart, J.-F. (1989). *L'Etat en Afrique. La politique du ventre.* Paris : Librairie Arthème Fayard.

Bayart, J.-F., Mbembe, A., and Toulabor, C. (2008). *Le politique par le bas en Afrique noire.* Paris : Karthala.

Bidima, J-G. (1993). *Théorie critique et modernité africaine. De l'Ecole de Francfort à la « Docta Spes Africana ».* Paris : ouvrage publié avec le concours du Conseil scientifique de l'Université de Paris I (Panthéon Sorbonne) et de l'Institut de Missiologie de Aechen.

Bhabha, H. (2007). *Les Lieux de la culture. Une théorie postcoloniale.* Paris : Editions Payot.

Bidima, J-G. (1995). *La Philosophie négro-africaine.* Paris : PUF.

Bidima, J-G. (1997). *L'Art négro-africain.* Paris : PUF.

Bidima, J-G. (1998). Art de la critique, critique de l'art : pour une théorie critique des arts africains. *Art et philosophie.* Paris : ENS Editions.

Bidima, J-G. (2011). Philosophie, démocraties et pratiques : à la recherche d'un "universel latéral". *Critique (Philosopher en Afrique).* TOME LXVIIX-N° 771772, pp. 672–686. Paris.

Brunschwig, H. (1973). *Société et romantisme en Prusse au XVIIIe siècle. La crise de l'Etat prussien à la fin du XVIIIe siècle et la genèse de la mentalité romantique.* Paris : Flammarion.

Chakrabarty, D. (2009). *Provincialiser l'Europe. La pensée postcoloniale et la différence historique.* Paris : Editions Payot.

Césaire, A. (1956). Culture et colonisation. *Présence Africaine.* No. 8–9–10 : Paris.

Deleuze, G. and Guattari, F. (1975). *Capitalisme et schizophrénie I. L'Anti-Œdipe.* Paris : Editions de Minuit.

Deprez, S. (2010). *Lévy-Brühl et la rationalisation du monde.* Paris : Presses Universitaires de Rennes.

Derrida, J. (1967). *L'Ecriture et la différence.* Paris : Editions du Seuil.

Derrida, J. (1967). *De la grammatologie.* Paris : Editions du Seuil.

Elimane Kane, A. (1992). Structure linguistique et structure mathématique des énoncés en numérotation orale. *Revue sénégalaise d'histoire, sociologie, philosophie des sciences et techniques*, No. 3, 89–97.

Chapter 3: Alternatives to Nostalgia for Colonial Ethnology 71

Elimane Kane, A. (2007). Mathématiques sauvages et rationalité. In P. Hountondji (dir.), *La rationalité, une ou plurielle?* Dakar : CODESRIA-UNESCO, pp. 218–219.

Fanon, F. (2002). *Les Damnés de la terre.* Paris : Editions La Découverte&Syros.

Fogou, A. (2014). Cheikh Anta Diop et la décolonisation du discours scientifique en Afrique. In F. Renucci and S. El Mechat (dir.) *Les décolonisations au XXe siècle. Les hommes de la transition ; itinéraires, actions et traces.* Paris : L'Harmattan, pp. 63–84.

Foucault, M. (1966). *Les Mots et les choses. Une archéologie des sciences humaines.* Paris : Editions Gallimard.

Foucault, M. (1969). *L'Archéologie du savoir.* Paris : Editions Gallimard.

Foucault, M. (1971). *L'Ordre du discours.* Paris : Editions Gallimard.

Foucault, M. (1972). *Histoire de la folie à l'âge classique.* Paris : Editions Gallimard.

Foucault, M. (2001). *L'Herméneutique du sujet. Cours au Collège de France 1981–1982.* Paris : Editions Gallimard.

Gadamer, H.-G. (1996). *Vérité et méthode. Les grandes d'une herméneutique philosophique.* Paris : Editions du Seuil.

Hebga, M. (1997). *Rationalité d'un discours africain sur les phénomènes paranormaux.* Paris : L'Harmattan.

Hegel, G.W.F. (1997). *Esthétique I.* Paris : Editions Livre de poche

Kourouma, A. (1970). *Les Soleils des Indépendances.* Paris : Editions du Seuil.

Lalouette, C. (1984). *Textes sacrés et profanes de l'ancienne Egypte. Des pharaons et des hommes.* Paris : Editions Gallimard.

Lefebvre, H. (1971). *L'Idéologie structuraliste.* Paris : Editions Anthropos.

Levi-Strauss, C. (1962). *La Pensée sauvage.* Paris : Plon.

Lyotard, J.-F. (1979). *La Condition postmoderne. Rapport sur le savoir.* Paris : Editions de Minuit.

Lévy-Brühl, L. (2010). *La Mentalité primitive.* Paris : Flammarion.

Mattelart, A. and Neveu, P. (2004). *Introduction aux cultural studies.* Paris : Editions La Découverte.

Malolo Dissakè, E. (2005). *Mathématique pharaonique égyptienne et théorie moderne des sciences.* Paris : Editions Dianoïa

Mbembe, A. (2000). *De la postcolonie. Essai sur l'imagination politique dans l'Afrique contemporaine.* Paris : Karthala.

Mbembe, A. (2010). *Sortir de la grande nuit. Essai sur l'Afrique décolonisée.* Paris : Editions La Découverte.

Nkolo Foé, (2008). *Le Postmodernisme et le nouvel esprit du capitalisme. Sour une philosophie globale d'Empire.* Dakar : CODESRIA.

Obenga, T. (1990). *La Philosophie africaine de la période pharaonique. 2780–330 avant notre ère.* Paris : L'Harmattan.

Obenga, T. (1993). *Origine commune de l'égyptien ancien, du copte et des langues négro-africaines. Introduction à la linguistique historique africaine.* Paris : L'Harmattan.

Ouologuem, Y. (1968). *Le Devoir de violence.* Paris : Editions du Seuil.

Rorty, R. (1994). *Objectivisme, relativisme et vérité.* Paris : PUF.

Sédar Senghor, L. (1964)> *Liberté I. Négritude et Humanisme.* Paris : Editions du Seuil.

Spivak, G. C. (2009). *Les Subalternes peuvent-elles parler ?* Paris : Editions Amterdam.

Tata Cissé, Y. and Sagot-Duvauroux, J. (2003). *La Charte du Mandé et autres traditions du Mali.* Paris : Editions Albin Michel.

Tempels, P. (1947). *La Philosophie bantoue.* Paris : Présence Africaine.

Towa, M. (1971). *Essai sur la problématique philosophique dans l'Afrique actuelle.* Yaoundé : Clé.

Towa, M. (1979). *L'Idée d'une philosophie négro-africaine.* Yaoundé : Clé.

Towa, M. (2010). *Identité et transcendance. Examen d'un dilemme de la pensée africaine moderne.* Paris : L'Harmattan.

Tsira Ndong Ndoutoume, P. (1970). *Le Mvett.* Paris : Présence Africaine Editions.

Vattimo, G. (1988). *La fin de la modernité. Nihilisme et herméneutique dans la culture pos-moderne.* Paris: Editions du Seuil.

Chapter 4:
The Interlinkages between Western and Indigenous Psychology in 20th- and early 21st-century India

Christiane Hartnack

In colonial India indigenous knowledge systems and practices were suppressed, but not completely destroyed. As part of the resistance efforts against British cognitive hegemony, in the early 20th century, members of the Western-educated Indian elite even revived pre-colonial concepts and practices. In a similar dialectic, globalization in India today is being accompanied by a wide range of efforts toward an appreciation of Sanskrit scripts and a return to Hindu practices.

British colonialism and globalization are but the most recent influences impacting India. Mughal and earlier invasions also shaped India's diversity. These complex layers of dominance and resistance led to manifold indigenous systems of knowledge and practices. As these cannot be reduced to one homogeneous type, in (British) India the "indigenous" does not exist in the singular, but needs to be conceptualized in the plural.

Moreover, South Asian social structures are anything but homogenous. Instead, they consist of hierarchical social layers with little or no mobility between them. The respective knowledge systems–specific to the so-called 'castes'—thus contribute further to the plurality of the notion "indigenous".

This contribution presents examples from the fields of the psychology, psychiatry and psychoanalysis during the last hundred years in (British) India, whereby the focus is on the political, economic, social and cultural dynamics that allowed indigenous knowledge systems and practices to break through Western cognitive hegemony. The interlinkages between Western (colonial and global) and indigenous concepts and practices in the psychological sciences in British India will be examined within three time frames from the past hundred years 1) the last three decades of British

India (1917–1947), 2) the postcolonial era (1947–1991) and 3) the current neo-liberal era beginning in 1991.

1. The psychological sciences in British India (1917–1947)

Although the British colonial administration made use of European as well as Indian scientists to better exploit this colony, the acquisition of knowledge in Western science was not forced upon the colonized subjects. Instead, since the late 19th century, members of the Western-educated urban Hindu and Moslem elites on their own initiative enthusiastically followed scientific developments in Britain, in the United States of America and to some extent also on the European continent. In the first decades of the 20th century, the long-time vice-chancellor of the University of Calcutta (now Kolkata), Sir Asutosh Mukherjee, procured financial support from well-to-to Bengali factory owners, businessmen and aristocratic landowners to shape the university's educational agenda more in accordance with the interests of the urban Bengali elites. His goal was to make science at the University of Calcutta—one of the world's largest universities of that time—relevant for the Indian people, and not for the colonizers. The 1920s, during which several postgraduate departments flourished at the University of Calcutta, became a golden age of research activities, culminating in the 1930 Nobel Prize in physics being awarded to Bengali scientist, Chandrasekhara V. Raman.

On the surface, scientific research as done in British India seemed to be the same as in Europe or North America. A closer look, however, reveals a creative interweaving with indigenous traditions. As Ashis Nandy pointed out, the plant physiologist Jagadish Chandra Bose formulated his research questions around Hindu concepts regarding the essential unity of all matter. In his case, even the research laboratory reflected a cultural amalgamation: on top of the room with the experimental equipment was a specially created space, a Vedi or "sight" room, where Bose meditated to help him gain clarity about (among others ideas) his research questions and methodological procedures.

Girindrasehkar Bose's practical and theoretical work in psychoanalysis also exemplifies how the acquisition of state-of-the-art

European knowledge could be combined with Bengali Hindu knowledge and practices. Moreover, it illustrates that there was no essential dichotomy between Western conceptual imports and indigenous concepts. Like Jagadish Chandra, Girindrasehkar Bose was a Western-educated Bengali Hindu from the high social stratum (sub-caste) of writers. He studied medicine at University of Calcutta and obtained an additional doctorate in psychology from there in 1921. Soon thereafter, he founded the Indian Psychoanalytical Society (IPS) and, from then on, split his time between research and teaching at the University of Calcutta and psychoanalytic treatment of patients in his private practice and at an outdoor clinic he had founded and financed with the help of his wealthy and famous brother Rajsehkar.

While Bose made no secret of his sympathies for the Indian independence movement, his British colleagues Owen Berkeley-Hill and Claude Dangar Daly—also active members of IPS—openly defended colonial rule with the help of psychoanalytical theories. This might have served to further motivate Bose to avoid mimicking a European model and instead to use a conceptual import (in this case psychoanalysis) as a basis for creatively developing his own concepts and practical work, which reflected his priming in upper caste (Kshatriya) Bengali Hindu culture. Instead of following post-Darwinian linear Freudian concept of developmental stages, he employed more circular and fluid modes of thought; instead of conceptually separating "subject" and "object", he considered all that exists to be interconnected. In his correspondence with Sigmund Freud between 1922 and 1936, he avidly disagreed with Freud's view on the Oedipus complex and on women and femininity. Regarding the latter, Bose emphasized the importance of female goddesses in Bengali Hindu culture (as opposed to the notion of the one male god in monotheism).

While head of the department of psychology at the University of Calcutta, Bose also established yoga as part of the psychology curriculum and published widely on the psychological content of Vedic scripts. Suhrit Mitra, his successor as head of the department of psychology, was similarly interested in indigenous Hindu psychological knowledge. But unlike Bose, who creatively combined Western psychoanalysis with Bengali Hindu thought and practices, Mitra never tried to combine these two strains of thought into one unified theory. Instead, he—like his colleagues Manmatha Nath

Banerjee and N.S.N. Sastry—compartmentalized these two forms of knowledge and dealt with them separately. It is revealing that in his publication 'Growth of Psychology in India' Shastry devoted the first thirty-five pages to reviewing the psychological content of ancient Indian texts and only the last five pages to academic psychology.

All these activities were carried out by members of the so-called Bhadralok (privileged Western-educated urban high-caste Bengali Hindu men), who not only had access to international literature, but lived in sprawling extended family structures with well-functioning support systems based on large numbers of servants. This lifestyle granted them the leisure time to acquaint themselves with newly imported ideas and to discuss their insights at length with their peers. As Kancha Ilaih pointed out, the vast majority of the Indian populace worked and lived differently. Their insights were not derived from various indigenous traditions or from the latest Western texts, or from the study of Sanskrit texts or meditations, but rather from hands-on reflection about how to improve their daily lives and work practices.

At the end of the British rule in India, we thus have—roughly speaking—three different groups that contributed to knowledge systems in India: 1) the majority of India's population which survived on their physical labour, 2) a small urban elite consisting primarily of high-caste Hindus with access to Western education and Sanskrit learning and 3) an even smaller number of British colonial subjects whose agenda it was to assure the smooth and efficient rule of this "Jewel of the Crown". This changed in 1947 when India gained independence and left British India divided into India and Pakistan (which split in 1971 into the Islamic Republic of Pakistan and Bangladesh).

2. The psychological sciences during the postcolonial era (1947–1991)

After India gained independence in 1947, the Indian National Congress Party (INC) dominated the country's politics for about 60 years. The INC was primarily shaped by the anglicized Brahmin Jawaharlal Nehru and his descendants, who held a virtual dominion over the position of Prime Minister of the Republic of India.

The first postcolonial decades were marked by dire poverty. As a consequence, some psychologists worked on issues relating to poverty. Due to the country's economic isolation, it was extremely difficult to negotiate attendance at international congresses or even to get access to publications in the field. This might have been an additional motivation for employing indigenous methods like yoga in practical psychiatric and psychotherapeutic work. By referring to the interactions between psychiatrist and patient as a guru-chela relationship, Jaswant Singh Neki articulated another form of the return to culture-specific traditions. At that time the most prominent psychologist interested in indigenous contributions to psychology was Indra Sen, who drew inspiration from the writings of Sri Aurobindo. Yet in this political and social context, in contrast to the colonial context at the beginning of the 20th century, Western-educated Indian elites showed less enthusiasm for questioning Western influence and countering it by posing their own research questions. Once out from under British colonial rule, intellectual resistance against "the West" appears to have lost its target.

Instead, many social scientists decided to pursue lines of research that might be rewarded by their colleagues in the West (which had by then almost become synonymous with the U.S.). The Cold War situation helped Indian social scientists to receive funding from abroad, most generously from the U.S., and when the U.S. lifted emigration restrictions from South Asia in the mid-1960s, many resourceful young scholars tried to emigrate. To increase their chances of landing a job at a US-American university, Indian social scientists not only proactively tended to reproduce US-American research, but also offered to play auxiliary roles collecting data for Western scholars to use for their publications (and advancement), which were often rewarded with a scholarship.

Another option for gaining a reputation outside of India was to leverage Western academia's and the public's interest in exoticism. Because of their language skills and cultural and religious knowledge, Sudhir Kakar and other members of the Western-educated Indian elites were able to obtain access to knowledge not available in Europe and North America. As India's old and rich culture provided enough resources for fascinating descriptions and narratives of the tropical "other", this turned out to be yet another kind of intellectual conveyor belt between India and the West.

With research questions formulated in—or in anticipation of—Cambridge/Mass., Stanford or New York, research in the psychological sciences in 1960s and 1970s India was often but a stale imitation of the work being done at Anglo-American institutions of higher learning. As such, it was not responsive to local needs. These developments did not escape criticism: Among the most prominent Indian intellectuals to complain about the lack of relevant and original research being done in the social sciences in India was the social psychologist Ashis Nandy. As early as 1974, he passionately questioned the relevance of much of the work done in his field and complained that Indian psychology has become not merely imitative and subservient but also dull and replicative. In a later contribution entitled "Towards an Alternative Politics of Psychology", Nandy became even more radical in his criticism: "... modern psychology has served as the ethnopsychology of a small part of the world and peddled itself as a universal psychology on the basis of the political, economic and cultural dominance of precisely that part".[1]

In the last decade of his life, Durganand Sinha, the doyen of academic psychology in India in the late 20th century, also questioned the relevance of much of the work done by psychologists in India. While he typically did this in a soft-spoken manner, at the end of his life, he ventured to openly criticize Western experimental psychology and called for a research agenda that concerned itself with the needs of people in Asian, African and Latin American countries.

During all those years in which the post-colonial state was still raw and India was trying to consolidate itself, attempts to revive indigenous systems of knowledge and practices were hardly part of the official academic discourse. This revival only materialized with the political, economic and cultural changes occurring in the early 21st century.

---

[1] Nandy, A. (1983) 'Towards an Alternative Politics of Psychology.' *International Social Science Journal*, Vol. 35(2), pp.323–338, here: 329.

3. The psychological sciences in today's neo-liberal era in India

In order to save the Indian economy, Manmohan Singh, the finance minister of the socialist-leaning Indian National Congress Party let India open its markets in 1991 and allowed foreign investments and capital into the country; but the party still lost the elections in 1998 and again in 2014. In May 2014 the Hindu nationalist Bharatiya Janata Party (BJP) under the leadership of Narendra Modi won an overwhelming victory to become the sole ruling party of India. Although the BJP won these elections with the promise to develop India's economy and infrastructure with the help of a neo-liberal economic agenda, it is first and foremost a Hindu nationalistic party. Its ideology "Hindutva" is a nationalism based on Hindu cultural, religious and ideological dominance. Hindutva ideologues conceptualize and propagate the idea of the pre-colonial and pre-Mughal eras in India as the glorious Hindu past and envision the country as a pure Hindu realm untainted by Muslim and other non-Hindu (including Western) influences.

The spread of Hindutva ideology has been promoted and defended on many levels. The government of the National Democratic Alliance, a major partner of the BJP between 1998 and 2004, introduced Vedic astrology as a subject in college curricula. The application of Vastu Shastra, Hindu concepts about the unity of architecture, space and nature, then also led to architectural changes of government buildings. In December 2014, Sushma Swaraj, India's Minister of External Affairs elevated the Bhagavad Gita to the status of the national scripture, thereby challenging the importance of the nation's constitution. Based on an initiative by India's Prime Minister, Narendra Modi, from 2015 onward June 21—the longest day of the year (summer solstice in the Northern hemisphere)—has since become the International Yoga Day.

As a result of Hindutva's growing influence, Non-Hindus are no longer allowed to teach about Hinduism at Indian institutions of higher learning. In 2011, an essay entitled "Three Hundred Ramayanas: Five Examples and Three Thoughts on Translations" by A.K. Ramanujan, a well-known poet and linguist, was removed from the history syllabus at Delhi University because it contained readings of the Ramayana in non-Brahmin texts, thus also reflecting the lower classes of India's population. In early 2014 an Indian reprint of the book "The Hindus: An Alternative History" by Wendy Doniger, an eminent scholar from the University of Chicago, was withdrawn by Penguin India, and the remaining copies pulped, because her academic work contained passages that were considered to be disrespectful of Hinduism.

These political and cultural developments are echoed in the social sciences. In 2002, over 150 Indian psychologists supported the "Pondicherry Manifesto of Indian Psychology", which was basically a declaration of intent to turn to Hindu conceptual traditions. Several volumes about indigenous Hindu psychology were published in the first decade of the 21st century. Among other topics, these publications deal with the interpretation of Sanskrit texts on emotion, the self, perception and cognition, and meditation. Some of these are quite voluminous: K. Ramakrishna Rao's work on "consciousness" runs to more than 900 pages.

The BJP' agenda has two sides: it is culturally Hindutva and economically neo-liberal. The growing GDP that came along with foreign investment and capital flowing into the country also meant fewer restrictions on imports, including literature, and more possibilities for travelling. For social scientists, the most significant change, however, was increased access to the Internet and thus to international literature and discussions. Indian psychologists committed to social improvement and those belonging to minorities also benefitted from these changes.

Although the first woman to study psychology in India did so in 1918, women's voices remained silent in psychology until around 2000 when Bhargavi V. Davar brought attention to the embarrassing situation of women in psychiatry. She also criticized the work of Girindrasehkar Bose and Sudhir Kakar, the eminences of psychoanalysis in India, as being the work of male elitists. Undurti Vindhya published widely on women's concerns including violence against women and Manasi Kumar questioned the relevance of much of the research done in the field of psychology in postcolonial India and worked on combining psychoanalysis with socially relevant issues.

Parallel to India's entry into the globalized market, "reservations", the Indian version of affirmative action for members of less privileged sections of the society, began to bear fruit. More students from poor families and even from families with a Dalit ("untouchable") or tribal social background have been able to enter academia and become lecturers and researchers. As a result, other indigenous knowledge systems and practices have begun to break through the cognitive hegemony of upper-caste Hindu knowledge. The political scientist Kancha Iliah, for example, pointed out that he became conscious of a divide within Indian society when, as a low-caste schoolboy from a rural family background, he realized that the Sanskrit playwright and poet Kalidasa was as alien to him as Shakespeare. In his numerous publications he proudly proclaimed that the lower castes, the Dalits ('Untouchables') and Adivasis (Tribals)—unlike the Brahmins and Kshatriyas—possess profound theoretical and practical knowledge not only about soil, water and animals, but also about a host of other issues essential for survival.

Though verbally powerful, these are currently only marginal voices, however. The majority of the Indian population, such as women, members of the Hindu lower castes, Dalits or Adivasis are hardly ever <u>subjects</u> of social science activities in India in the sense of being in a position to propose research questions and lead the research agenda. If they are included at all, they are but <u>objects</u> in this process and thus, more or less, deprived of agency.

Conclusion

The many invasions into India led to a long history of cultural dominance, resistance, co-existence and hybridization. As a result, there is no clear or static dichotomy between "foreign" and "indigenous", but rather an intricate dynamic of negotiations and re-negotiations. These were and are embedded in political, economic and ideological contexts: Under colonial domination, indigenization was a form of resistance, a form of anti-colonial nationalistic self-assertion. In the context of globalization it is similarly a retreat into a realm that belongs to the Sanskrit-educated elite and contributes to Hindutva ideology. Whereas upper-caste Hindu elites have the opportunity to articulate their resistance to Western cognitive hegemony, this hardly applies to the less privileged majority of the Indian population consisting of roughly 85% of India's population, thus close to one billion people. It remains an open question whether their indigenous systems of knowledge can be more fully realized in the future.

References

Banerjee, M.N. (1930). The Psychological Outlook of Hindu Philosophy. *Indian Journal of Psychology*, 5, 119–46.

Banerjee, M.N. (1937). Hindu Psychology: Physiological Basis and Experimental Methods. *American Journal of Psychology*, 50, 328–46.

Chatterjee, P. (ed.) (1996). *Texts of Power: Emerging Disciplines in Colonial Bengal*. Calcutta: Samya.

Cornelissen, R. M.M., Misra, G., and Varma, S. (eds.). (2011). *Foundations of Indian Psychology: Concepts and Theories*. New Delhi: Pearson.

Dalal, A. K. (2010). The Core and Context of Indian Psychology. *Psychology and Developing Societies*, 22 (1), 121–155.

Davar B.V. (1999). Indian Psychoanalysis, Patriarchy and Hinduism. *Anthropology and Medicine*, 682, 173–193.

Doniger, W. (2009). *The Hindus: An Alternative History*. New York: Penguin Press.

Hartnack, C. (1990). Vishnu on Freud's Desk: Psychoanalysis in Colonial India. *Social Research*, 57, 921–49. Reprinted in T. G. Vaidyanathan and Jeffrey J. Kripal (eds.) (1999) *Vishnu on Freud's Desk. A Reader in Psychoanalysis and Hinduism*. Delhi: Oxford University Press, pp.81–106.

Hartnack, C. (2001). *Psychoanalysis in Colonial India*. New Delhi: Oxford University Press.

Hartnack, C. (2011). Colonial Dominions and the Psychoanalytic Couch: Synergies of Freudian Theory with Bengali Hindu Thought and Practices in British India. In A. Warwick, R. C. Keller, and D. Jenson (eds.) *Unconscious Dominions: Psychoanalysis, Colonial Trauma, and Global Sovereignties*. Durham: Duke University Press, pp.97–112.

Ilaih K. (1996). Productive Labour, Consciousness and History: The Dalitbahujan Alternative. In S. Amin and D. Chakrabarty (eds.) *Subaltern Studies IX*, Delhi: Oxford University Press, pp.165–200.

Kakar, S. (1982). *Shamans, Mystics and Doctors: A Psychological Inquiry into India and its Healing Traditions*. Delhi: Oxford University Press.

Kakar, S. (1985). Psychoanalysis and Non-Western Countries. *International Review of Psychoanalysis*, 12, 441–8.

Kumar, D. (ed.) (1991). *Science and Empire: Essays in Indian Context (1700–1947)*. New Delhi: Anamika.

Kumar M. (2006). Rethinking Psychology in India: Debating Pasts and Futures. *Annual Review of Critical Psychology*, 5, 236–256 www.discourseunit.com/arcp/5 (last accessed: August 25, 2015).

Mohanty A. K. and Misra, G. (eds.) (2000). *Psychology of Poverty and Disadvantage*. New Delhi: Concept Publishing.

Misra, G. and Mohanty, A. K. (eds.) (2002). *Perspectives on Indigenous Psychology*. New Delhi: Concept Publishing Company.

Nandy, A. (1974). The Non-Paradigmatic Crisis of Indian Psychology: Reflections on a Recipient Culture of Science. *Indian Journal of Psychology*, 49 (4), 1–20.

Nandy, A. (1974). New Responsibilities in Psychology: Experiences, Values and Alternatives. *Indian Journal of Psychology*, 49 (4), 337–342.

Nandy, A. (1980). *Alternative Sciences: Creativity and Authenticity in Two Indian Scientists*. New Delhi: Allied Publishers.

Neki, J. S. (1973). Guru-Chela Relationship: The Possibility of a Therapeutic Paradigm. *The American Journal of Orthopsychiatry*, 43, 755–766.

Neki, J. S. (1975). Shajada: An Indian Ideal of Mental Health. *Psychiatry*, 38, 1–10.

Pandey, G. (ed.) (2011). *Subalternity and Difference: Investigations from the North and the South*. New York: Routledge.

Prakash, G. (1992). Science 'Gone Native' in Colonial India. *Representations*, 40, 153–78.

Pondicherry Manifesto of Indian Psychology (n.d.). www.infinityfoundation.com/mandala/i_es_corne_frameset.htm (last accessed: August 25, 2015).

Raina, D. (1996). Reconfiguring the Centre: The Structure of Scientific Exchanges between Colonial India and Europe. *Minerva*, 34, 161–76.

Raina, D. (2003). *Images and Contexts: The Historiography of Science and Modernity in India*. Delhi: Oxford University Press.

Ramana, C. V. (1964). On the Early History and Development of Psychoanalysis in India. *Journal of the American Psychoanalytic Association*, 12, 110–34.

Ramanujan A. K. (1991). Three Hundred Ramayanas: Five Examples and Three Thoughts on Translations. In V. Dharwadker (ed.) *Collected Essays of Ramanujan A.K.* Delhi: Oxford University Press, pp.131–160.

Rao, K. R., Paranjpe, A. and Dalal, A. K. (eds.) (2008). *Handbook of Indian Psychology*. New Delhi: Cambridge University Press.

Sen, I. (1958). Teaching of Psychology in Indian Universities. *Indian Journal of Psychology*, 33, 129–133.

Sinha, D. (1986). *Psychology in a Third World Country: The Indian Experience*. New Delhi: Sage.

Vahia, N. S., Vinekar, S. L. and Doongaji, D. R. (1966). Some Ancient Indian Concepts in the Treatment of Psychiatric Disorders. *British Journal of Psychiatry*, 112, 1089–1096.

Vindhya, U. (2007). Quality of Women's Lives in India: Some Findings from two Decades on Psychological Research on Gender. *Feminism and Psychology*, 17 (3), 337–356.

Chapter 5:
Knowledge as Interaction: An Alternative Epistemology from Rural Mexico[1]

Roger Magazine

> "One gains alterity from attachments, not from the radical difference between the liberated and the alienated, the uprooted and the rooted, the mobile and the fixed."
>
> Bruno Latour, *On the Modern Cult of the Factish Gods*, p. 60.

Socio-cultural anthropology appears to be ideally situated to contribute to a discussion on multiplicity though our empirical data drawn from research among "others". In addition, a theoretical side to our science can also make a contribution to such discussions. This theoretical side I am referring to is practiced more like anti-theory. Our contact with alterity in the field allows us to redirect our gaze back upon theory and science themselves to see them as just one other socio-cultural variation. In other words, anthropological "theory" is often aimed at revealing the "localness", the ethnocentricism and thus the limits of established theory. However, this methodology does not limit us to destructiveness. We can be creative as well. The ideas or theories of the people we study can also be incorporated into scientific theory in an attempt to move beyond our own conceptualization of the world. This is what I will attempt to do here even though it is important to remember that such conceptual innovations are still small steps in the dark; mere glimpses beyond our own limits, far from final, universal solutions.

---

[1] I wish to thank the Universidad Iberoamericana's Dirección de Investigación for generously financing the research upon which this article is based. I am indebted to the participants in the Thinkshop on "Multiple Epistemologies," held the 21st and 22nd of February, 2013 at the Universidad Iberoamericana, for their comments on an earlier version of this article.

Multiplicity has been gaining ground in social and scientific thought recently. While this would seem to be good for anthropology (and just when we had gotten used to talking about globalization), it also sparks our anti-theoretical, suspicious side, ever on the lookout for ethnocentric, false universalisms. To talk of multiple anything implies variation but also the singularity or universality of whatever is multiplied. To speak of multiculturalism, for example, implies variation, but a specific kind of variation: cultural variation. And cultural variation implies the universality of human nature, the common base upon which we supposedly create culture or cultures. American anthropologist Roy Wagner critiques the idea of a universal human nature or any kind of nature for that matter. He posits that as humans we create our own realities, although we must also create the illusion (for ourselves) that part of that reality was already there, that it is innate (1981). Thus, nature is just as much a human creation as culture even though we misrecognize it as innate. Further, Wagner suggests that not all human groups share an idea of what is innate and what is created. Drawing on his ethnographic research in Melanesia, he shows that the kind of practices we usually see and study as "culture" (e.g. marriage prescriptions and prohibitions, community organization, division of labor, exchange, etc.) are in fact conceptualized by many of the peoples we study as innate or universal. Meanwhile, these peoples direct human action and creativity toward what we would see as innate and unmalleable: human nature. In these contexts, human creativity means, for example, transforming oneself into other kinds of beings such as animals with particular capabilities.

To speak of multiple epistemologies, as we do in this issue/volume, confronts us with a problem analogous to that of multiculturalism. Epistemological variation implies an ontological universality upon which this variation can occur: different ways of knowing the same reality. Can Wagner's argument about the human creation of supposed universals be applied to "ontological universality"? According to traditional Western philosophy it cannot because ontology is by definition universal. However, Brazilian anthropologist Eduardo Viveiros de Castro provides ethnographic data that forces us to confront the possibility of ontological multiplicity. He cites the example of indigenous Amazonian peoples, who begin with the assumption that there are multiple ontologies. Different points of view create different realities or different natures; what he refers to as perspectivism. "[T]he notion of matter as a universal substrate seems wholly absent from Amazonian ontologies" (2004:466–467). According to Amazonians, certain animals and other types of non-human beings, with whom humans must relate, were originally human and still maintain at their core "an intentionality or subjectivity formally identical to human consciousness" (2004:465). Since these apparently non-humans have different bodies, they see and exist in a different reality. Or, more accurately, they exist in the same reality as humans but they live it through different bodies and material objects. So, for example, when a jaguar looks at another jaguar it sees a human and when it sees a human it sees an animal that humans hunt and eat. The jaguar also lives in a village with houses and has social relations and cultural practices identical to humans although these are imperceptible to the human eye as such. Only certain beings, such as shamans, can transform their natures to see and communicate with other species and safely return to their original form.

This possibility brings us to another question: if there are multiple ontologies, then what is the universal base upon which they are multiplied? Or, in other words, if interaction or communication occurs among beings in multiple ontologies, what is the common ground that makes this possible? Viveiros de Castro suggests that for Amazonians it is this human consciousness or subjectivity shared by different species: "Reflexive selfhood, not material objectivity, is the potential common ground of being" (2004:467). This common ground makes it possible for ontologically distinctive beings to come into contact and communicate. By subjectivity or reflexive selfhood, I understand that he is referring to the potential for interaction.

According to Viveiros de Castro (2004), the Amazonian shaman is in a sense like the modern specialist in knowledge: the scientist. It is his job to reveal the unknown, to know the other. However, the approach he must take is the opposite of that of the scientist. While the scientist must objectify—that is, strip away all subjectivity and intentionality—to get to the truth, the shaman must personify or subjectify. He must find the human subjectivity and intentionality in animals or objects that appear not to have them. For the shaman, "[a] good interpretation, then, would be one able to understand every event as in truth an action, an expression of intentional states or predicates of some subject" (2004:469). In contrast, "[a]n exhaustive scientific interpretation of the world would for us be able to ideally reduce every action to a chain of causal events and to reduce these events to materially dense interactions" (2004:470). Thus, in our project of objectification, "the form of the other is *the thing*" (468), while in the Amazonian work of subjectification, "the form of the other is *the person*" (2004:468). In other words, for Amazonians, there are multiple ontologies, with the potential to be connected by a single human epistemology.

Linguist-philosopher Carlos Lenkersdorf's work among indigenous Tojolabal speakers in the southern Mexican state of Chiapas provides useful suggestions for further conceptualizing a subjectivizing mode of knowing [2]. More specifically, he demonstrates what knowing looks like and how it works when both the knower and the known are subjects. According to Lenkersdorf (2002), the Tojolabal language reflects a distinctive philosophy or world-view, with its most significant feature being the predominance of sentences with two subjects, instead of a subject that acts upon an object. A sentence such as "I told you" in Tojolabal would be expressed as "I told; you listened", where "I" and "you" are both subjects (2002:46; my translation). He goes on to explain: "Thus communication is not imposed as in the Spanish sentence, but rather complementary. If one of the subjects does not do his part, the communication cannot occur" (2002:46; my translation). Lenkersdorf connects this linguistic form with a world-view of "We" ("*Nosotros*") that he describes as intersubjective since it involves the "meeting of equals that complement each other . . . without denying the diversity of the functions of each" (2002:46; my translation). The equality of the participants has important political manifestations since it obviates the expression of inequality inherent to the grammar of Spanish and related languages. He continues: "In the intersubjective cosmovision, beginning with the key-word 'we', we are all subjects that need each other and that complement each other" (2002:48; my translation).

Intersubjectivity among Tojolabal speakers also has epistemological implications. Knowing, like other actions, is in fact

---

[2] I am indebted to Miguel Hirsch Soler for recommending Lenkersdorf's work to me.

an interaction that requires two knowing subjects. As Lenkersdorf states, drawing a comparison with scientific knowledge practices: "In physics, anatomy and other sciences, phenomena are usually divided into their component parts to know, understand and explain them. The Tojolabales, evidently take another route. They know by conjointly approaching the 'subject to be known.' The knowledge is achieved by dialoging with this living subject.... We do not know wild horses because we do not speak their language. To do so we would have to learn from them. No *analysis* of the Equus species or of horses will provide us with that knowledge" (2002: 89; my translation; emphasis in the original). Thus, Tojolabal speakers force us to imagine an epistemology that does not assume a single objective reality waiting to be known. Rather, it is an epistemology that involves interaction with an acting and thus changing subject; what we might call *interactive knowing*.

The ethnographic example I wish to expound upon here comes from my own fieldwork research in a village[3] on the outskirts of Mexico City's urban sprawl. This village, Tepetloaxtoc, hardly appears to be a model of Mesoamerican indigenous alterity. It counts among the many supposed success stories of the state's assimilation policies carried out during much of the 20th century. Its inhabitants are currently all monolingual Spanish-speakers (they do not speak the region's indigenous language, Nahuatl), the vast majority are wage-earners or small-business owners rather than peasant-farmers, and they do not even categorize themselves as indigenous. However, after getting to know some of their most cherished values and practices, I believe that their assimilation into Mexican national culture and society is superficial. Further, they insist on the existence of a significant contrast between themselves and "city people", which was key to my own learning process and which I will draw upon shortly.

My intention in having touched upon Viveiros de Castro and Lenkersdorf's work is not to draw a comparison among Amazonian, Tojolabal, and Central Mexican peoples (although such a comparison is not inconceivable), but rather to introduce the concepts that these two authors employ in their contrasts between

---

[3] While its population of about 6,000 is more what we would think of as a "town," I use the term "village" in an attempt to more accurately translate the local social category "pueblo".

indigenous and modern knowledge practices in order to imagine distinctive manners of conceptualizing and relating to an "other." There are also some significant differences among our data and conclusions. What Lenkersdorf and I describe is more "democratic" than Viveiros de Castro's case. By this, I mean that in our descriptions this mode of knowing and relating to an other is practiced by most everyone on a daily basis rather than being reserved for specialists such as shamans with their inter-species communication. And if Lenkersdorf introduces us to what I term interactive knowing, then in the case I describe, I trace the results of such interactions. I argue that they could be described as productive in the sense that the subjects act upon each other resulting in transformations in subjective states and in further actions. As with the concept "knowledge", it is necessary, as we shall see, to expand our understanding of "production" to include the participation of multiple subjects; what might be thought of as *interactive production*.

The Production of Action and Subjectivity in Tepetloaxtoc, Mexico

I will attempt to propose here that people in Tepetloaxtoc are linked together by their actions; they need each other to be able to act. This is because actions involve two subjects rather than one: the first who motivates and the second who performs the action. To put this another way, an important form of production in Tepetloaxtoc is the production of action and subjective states in others. This production takes the form of motivating others to act and to have them do so with an attitude of willingness or, in local terms, "*con gusto*." However, in contrast to the production of things in most contexts of modern capitalism, the product (the action and the subjective state) does not belong to the producer but rather to the actor. Put in other words, this relationship between persons and actions contrasts sharply with the form that this relationship usually takes in the modern West in which individual persons are naturally endowed with the ability to act (Strathern 1988). In the modern West, someone who cannot or does not exercise this ability is in a position of subordination to another and lacks the ideal human state of individual freedom. If one person acts upon another, there is a singular subject (the former) and an object (the latter). And if one person causes another to act—paying them to do a job, for example—the action and its products belong to the former and not the latter.

To illustrate this alternative relationship among persons and their actions ethnographically, I will describe the practice in Tepetloaxtoc of putting on celebrations or *fiestas* for patron saints. Throughout much of rural Mesoamerica, villagers take turns holding rotating posts known as *cargos*. Cargo holders are in charge of organizing different community projects such as building or maintaining roads, schools, cemeteries and water systems. Fiestas for patron saints are organized through a particular type of cargo known as a *mayordomía* (the cargo holder is the *mayordomo*). The cargos and in particular the mayordomías have played an important role in anthropological understandings of Mesoamerican villages because the so-called "cargo system" has been seen to constitute the internal social structure of the community as well as the boundary defining the community itself. According to common anthropological wisdom on the subject (e.g. Cancian 1965; Wolf 1955), villagers who take on mayordomías spend a considerable amount of time and money putting on the fiesta. This is conceived as a sacrifice for the community and in turn the person who holds the mayordomía consolidates himself as member of the community, gains prestige and moves up in the village hierarchy. Further, the "cargo system" is said to direct spending toward the community and away from the individualistic interests of the outside world. The cargos and fiestas have thus been interpreted not only as constitutive of the community's social structure and indigenous culture, but also what keeps the modern world at bay. This disciplinary focus is not surprising if we consider the fact that the anthropological object of study is assumed to be the community organization, social structure and culture that each human group constructs and reproduces upon what is supposedly universally given: nature, including human nature. Fixated on studying the social relations and cultural practices their informants have produced, anthropologists have found them in the cargo system and fiestas.

In Tepetloaxtoc, I observed and was taught that the mayordomía works quite differently. The mayordomo's principal task is not to put on the fiesta himself but rather to cause his fellow villagers to act; that is, to motivate them to participate in the fiesta. In more abstract terms, the mayordomo's task is not to produce community, social structure or local culture but rather to act upon other persons to produce their actions. Thus what people create or produce in this context—and consequently what we as anthropologists should focus on—is not a *thing*, inert, de-subjectified and ready to have its singular objective reality revealed once produced, but rather subjectivity and action, which continue to transform themselves and others after their creation.

The mayordomo and his team of helpers go door to door to ask fellow villagers for a *cooperación* (a cooperation; a cash donation) for the fiesta. Potential donors always begin by expressing their reluctance to give a cooperación, either because they say that times are hard and they do not have the cash or they say that they are concerned about whether the mayordomía will work sufficiently to put on a good fiesta. The mayordomo and his team's work basically consists of persuading these potential donors. They do this by talking about all they are doing to put on a beautiful fiesta and reminding the potential donor of the joy of contributing to such an effort. They do not in any way oblige the potential donor to give; they must convince or motivate him with their enthusiasm. They must also repeatedly visit the potential donor's house over the year leading up to the fiesta. Eventually, the potential donor's reluctance turns into "gusto" and he willingly, even enthusiastically, gives the cooperación, at which point he too is putting on the fiesta. In other words, the mayordomo does not produce a thing—the fiesta or cooperaciones—but rather active subjects who put on the fiesta. Donors participate in the fiesta through their cooperación, which is inalienable and is never possessed by the mayordomo. In Tepetloaxtoc this important fact is expressed through the phrase: "*la fiesta se hace entre todos*" ("the fiesta is put on among everyone"; "everyone puts on the fiesta"). This fact, rather than the qualities of the fiesta itself (the fireworks, music, food or other entertainment), is indicative of a good fiesta. Or, better said, the qualities of the fiesta itself are seen to reflect whether it was put on "entre todos," something for which, of course, the mayordomo cannot take credit. This double subjectivity (counting the mayordomo and the donors) or in local terms, to act "con gusto" is even important to the saint, who will be angered by anyone who acts unwillingly ("*con mala gana*") and will punish them in consequence. The mayordomo's work is considered difficult and it is highly valued, but it cannot be converted into social status or prestige because he does not own what he has produced—rather, the fiesta was put on "entre todos" and it belongs to everyone. A person who performs well as mayordomo is said to be "*conocido*" (known) or "*reconocido*" (recognized; renowned), but this cannot be converted into anything like power over others, although it will mean that he will be sought after for other cargos: more unpaid work. The only compensation for doing such work is the "gusto" that it brings to oneself and to others.

I will not get into here whether this contrast between traditional anthropological understandings the mayordomo's role versus what I describe here represents a difference between Tepetloaxtoc and other Mesoamerican villages or equivocations in anthropologists' understandings. However, I suspect that it is at least partially the latter since we anthropologists have tended to note and then promptly dismiss mayordomos' efforts aimed at getting others involved as simply one possible means for achieving what really matters—the fiesta or collective life. We have not been able to imagine the possibility that what needs to be produced are active subjects rather than *things* such as fiestas or social structure. We are blinded to this possibility because of our own culturally-based assumption that persons are naturally endowed with the ability to act and thus this aspect of humanity is defined as laying beyond the object of study ("society"; "culture") of the socio-cultural anthropologist (Magazine 2012).

I should also mention that the double subjectivity or interactive production I am attempting to describe here is, for people from Tepetloaxtoc, a general life principal. The fiestas are only one of many instances where people direct their efforts toward motivating action and subjective states in others rather than toward the production of *things*. The same interaction involving convincing, reluctance, motivation and enthusiastic acceptance occurs, for example, when the mayordomo finds his replacement for the following year. Cargo holders in charge of civil duties such as the maintenance of the water works, cemetery, roads or schools also succeed by motivating their fellow villagers to action. When a family puts on a life cycle fiesta for one of its members, it is considered inappropriate to hire help and to purchase what is needed for the fiesta. Instead, the celebrating family motivates others to help put on the fiesta by participating in the cooking and serving of food or through donations of objects needed for the fiesta (López Millán 2008). Within families parents provide their children with nourishment and care, which motivates their children to work to provide "*ayuda*" ("aid"; "help") to their parents (Magazine and Ramírez Sánchez 2007). In turn, it is sons' and daughters' provision of ayuda that motivates their parents to act as such. And while parents motivate their children to work, they do not obligate or control them. Further, they do not appropriate the products of their children's labor. Sons' and daughters' ayuda goes to their parents but is still recognized as theirs, and just like the fiesta is put on "together," sons' and daughters' contributions to the family economy are fully recognized. Even dying requires and motivates others. Having lived life as a good, interdependent neighbor causes fellow villagers to bear the deceased's casket. In contrast, a casket borne by the deceased's own family members is the sign of a life lived individualistically and selfishly.

According to many villagers, people who move from the city to Tepetloaxtoc in search of inexpensive housing as well as people originally from Tepetloaxtoc who have spent all or most of their lives in the city before moving back understand the fiestas in a manner analogous to anthropologists. As if they had read traditional ethnographies to prepare themselves for village life, when these people take on a mayordomía for a fiesta, they tend to try to pay for and put on the fiesta by themselves. Of course, they would not have to read an ethnography to think in this manner. The experience of life in the city or in the dominant society more generally is enough. They think they are acting in a morally correct manner since they are contributing to the community. They are, in their terms, acting independently and being productive in a way that contributes to society by creating things such as a fiesta, traditions and community. Villagers, however, see such behavior as immoral, arrogant or at least incompetent. They see such "city people" as individualistic, not because they do things to benefit only themselves, but rather because they think they can act on their own—that they do not need others. Even if the mayordomo buys enough fire works, music and food to make the fiesta look good, it is in fact a complete failure since he has not motivated others' participation. Interdependence is valued, but independence is not.

On one occasion a villager explained to me why she thought that another resident would do a poor job as mayordomo for the upcoming fiesta. She said that it was because he was not "*conocido*" (known). I had heard that this mayordomo was born in the village but had spent much of his life in Mexico City before returning to the village in recent years, so I asked her if she was referring to the fact that people did not know him because he had spent most of his life away from the village. But she answered that she did not mean "known" in this sense, adding that all of the villagers know each other in this sense, except for perhaps the children. She explained that she was referring to the fact that he was not known for his participation in community life and activities since his participation in the past had been minimal. He had not previously held other mayordomías or cargos nor was he known for responding enthusiastically to other cargo holders' efforts at motivating his participation. In other words, he was not known because he had not been involved in interactive production. Plus, he was seen as being "*presumido*" ("arrogant") and taking the attitude of someone who thinks they are superior and does not need others. Afterwards, I observed that the fiesta was in fact considered by many villagers to have been poorly done, since the mayordomo did not involve many of them in the fiesta. He also had to repeat as mayordomo the following year since he did not succeed at motivating a replacement.

This kind of approach to the mayordomías by city people or villagers influenced by city ways is seen to reflect city people's immorality or foolishness in general. According to many villagers, one of their main preoccupations is the migration of urbanites to the community. They explained to me that they did not want these migrants in the village because they are drug addicts and thieves. When I tried to get more details about the migrants' drug use and thievery, villagers seemed unable to respond and instead noted that they were talking about a more general attitude of individualism and of thinking they did not need others. I began to understand that taken to the extreme, this individualism was imagined as drug use and theft: actions that either waste one's resources on oneself or waste someone else's, not allowing these resources to enter into the exchanges through which people can be productive, producing actions and subjectivity in others.

In an effort to keep these people and their individualism out of the village, many community members discouraged outsiders from buying property (even though there was no established prohibition like in some neighboring communities and some owners were willing to sell) by telling them that they would have to pay dearly for a water connection. If this did not scare off a potential buyer, the community's Water Committee would in fact charge them more than ten times the usual price for the connection, following the logic that the villagers and not the government had constructed the water system "entre todos" and neither the newcomers nor their ancestors had contributed to that effort. I find it important to note that when these efforts at discouraging the migrants from settling in the village failed, the villagers did not attempt to exclude them from community life. Rather, they actively, patiently and courteously attempted to encourage their participation in fiestas and in the community's public works projects. This was done in the same manner that they coaxed the participation of their fellow villagers; it was not enacted as an imposition upon the newcomers. I believe this was the case because more important than forcing the newcomers' integration into collective community life to preserve community and tradition, was the need to produce them as active subjects and to have them do the same. The concern was to "know" the newcomers, in the sense described above, and this meant not a subject to object relationship but rather an interaction with them as subjects. To put this another way, this treatment of newcomers amounts to attempts to see or know them as persons or to personify them. In modern Western law and everyday thought, individuals are naturally and universally endowed with personhood as well as the obligations and rights that are perceived to go along with it. As innately complete beings, ready to individually produce things, including objectified knowledge, Western persons do not generally seek out the kind of interactive production practiced in Tepetloaxtoc. In contrast, persons in Tepetloaxtoc only exist as such as active subjects, and personhood is only recognizable through interaction with others. Villagers' portrayal of city people as drug addicts, thieves and sometimes, in extreme cases, as child snatchers reflects the latter's lack of interest in interactive production. This then results in their unrecognizability as persons to community members and the uncertainty and even fear that such unknowable beings provoke.

However, the villagers continue to attempt to interact with the newcomers, which I think has to do with the former's incredulity regarding the latter's individualism: villagers cannot help imagining that, deep down, newcomers are waiting for their personhood to be drawn out and known. So they keep trying to interact with them as subjects. Villagers could try to impose their practices, as if they were rules, upon newcomers. However, this would be missing the point which is that the important thing is not the practices themselves or conserving cultural traditions, but rather that the actions are motivated by others and performed willingly, with gusto. To sum up this contrast in another manner: if actors representing modern urban society stubbornly insist on the universality of naturally endowed human rights, people from Tepetloaxtoc obstinately attempt to interact with everyone, including urbanites, as active subjects. It is important to note that if the contrast I am proposing appears to be between two different realities, it only looks that way to the first set of actors, including myself, which is why I set it up in this manner. To people from Tepetloaxtoc, there is no such contrast between separate objectified others: alterity can only be gained from attachments (Latour 2010:60).

Is "alternative epistemology" an appropriate manner of describing this mode of knowing in Tepetloaxtoc? My worry is that the term epistemology will obscure how distinctive this mode of knowing really is compared to the usual variations found in philosophical discussions on the topic. In other words: will it convey that this is not simply another way of knowing but rather a completely distinctive manner of conceptualizing what it is to know? As I have suggested here, this example obliges us to imagine what might be called *interactive knowledge* since it involves two knowing subjects rather than a knowing subject and a known object. Further, since through this interaction the subjects bring about other actions and subjective states in each other, it cannot be reduced simply to a case of knowing. The subjects do know or recognize each other through the interaction but they also produce action and subjectivity in each other. I have suggested that this might be referred to as *interactive production,* with the reminder that actions and subjective states produced belong not to the producer but to the actor him- or herself.

This example also pushes us to rethink what we mean by multiplicity, variation or otherness. We usually expect or recognize multiplicities that are discrete, objectifiable, and comparable. For example, multiple cultures or multiple epistemologies that are imagined to exist individually or independently and that can be studied and represented. In contrast, in Tepetloaxtoc, otherness or multiplicity exist as subjects. This is why villagers value city people not for their distinctive culture but for the possibility of interacting with them as subjects. The other-as-subject is difficult to grasp, study or represent since he or she exists only in interaction. Thus it is hard to separate and distinguish subjects and to know where one ends and the other begins. And further, such active subjects are constantly in motion, transforming and being transformed through their interactions with others.

I have described this alternative mode of knowing here because I believe that it contributes, in a few ways, to the advancement of our conceptualization and practice of science. First, it contributes to the important and ongoing task of reminding us of the falsity or the "local-ness" of our supposed universalisms. In this same vein, it upsets the usual hierarchy and separation between science and local knowledge, truth and belief. It also offers an alternative to a currently dominant form of knowing that, like capitalism, objectifies and alienates. This alternative constitutes an epistemology of productive interaction among subjects, that may even extend beyond persons to include "things," such as land, water, plants and animals. This alternative, however, also presents a challenge that I do not even begin to face here: it is a mode of knowing that suggests that instead of limiting ourselves to the production of science as a thing, we start to imagine what it would mean to practice science as productive interaction.

References

Cancian, F. (1965). *Economics and Prestige in a Maya Community*. Stanford: Stanford University Press.

Latour, B. (2010). *On the Modern Cult of the Factish Gods*. Durham: Duke University Press.

Lenkersdorf, C. (2002). *Filosofar en clave tojolabal*. Mexico City: Miguel Angel Porrúa.

López Millán, Minerva (2008). "Sin ayuda no hay fiesta": Relaciones de reciprocidad en Santa Catarina del Monte. Ph.D.dissertation. Mexico City: Universidad Iberoamericana.

Magazine, R. (2012). *The Village Is Like a Wheel: Rethinking Cargos, Family, and Ethnicity in Highland Mexico.* Tucson: The University of Arizona Press.

Magazine, R. and Ramírez Sánchez, M. A. (2007). Continuity and Change in San Pedro Tlalcuapan, Mexico: Childhood, Social Reproduction, and Transnational Migration. In J. Cole & D. Durham (eds.) *Generations and Globalization: Youth, Age, and Family in the New World Economy.* Bloomington: Indiana University Press.

Strathern, M. (1988). *The Gender of the Gift: Problems with Women and Problems with Society in Melanesia.* Berkeley: University of California Press.

Viveiros de Castro, E. (2004). Exchanging Perspectives: The Transformation of Objects into Subjects in Amerindian Ontologies. *Common Knowledge*, 10(3), 463–484.

Wagner, R. (1981 [1975]). *The Invention of Culture.* Chicago: University of Chicago Press.

Wolf, E. R. (1955). The Types of Latin American Peasantry. *American Anthropologist*, 57(3), 452–471.

Chapter 6:
Indigenous knowledge in the social sciences: *comunalidad* and the challenge to Western categories

Claudia Magallanes-Blanco and
Leandro Rodriguez-Medina

1. Introduction

Indigenous knowledge (IK) is already a central category in our understanding of knowledge, its production, circulation and use. Yet, it is a vague category, which entails a specific genealogy, at least in the developed world. For Harding (2011), there is a series of circumstances that has contributed to give visibility, in the Euro-American academia, of postcolonial claims about science and technology. These are (1) the failure of West's development programs, (2) the appearance of new, original and sound empirical and theoretical works in English (originally published in other languages), (3) intellectual activism within and beyond the university, (4) the increase in the number of faculty, in metropolitan academia, who were born in developing countries, (5) the growing interest of scholars and students in travelling to developing areas, and (6) the proliferation of conferences, sponsored by organizations such as UNESCO, in which heterogeneous actors (from intellectuals to activists to government officials) have expressed concerns about the consequences of the universalization of Western(ized) notions of knowledge. Thus, it seems that 'gone are the days when it could appear uncontroversial to assume that Western sciences are or ever have been autonomous from society, value free, and maximally objective, or that their standard for rationality is universally valid' (Harding 2011: x).

Harding's account of this rise of interest in indigenous knowledge(s) lacks other important reason that also explains on which indigenous knowledge the West has focused. For the most part, Western interest in knowledge produced beyond its geographical area and its epistemological rules focuses on natural knowledge. This knowledge not only complements Western theories about natural resources but also illustrates ways of using them that Westerners usually call 'new' or 'original' although they are based on ancient practices and traditions. As Colin Scott puts it,

> Insofar as (indigenous knowledge systems) do explain aspects of nature's regularities and underlying causal tendencies that modern Western sciences have not yet considered, and use conceptual frameworks that reveal more than modern Western ones have so far been able to understand (such as how distinctive cultural practices both preserve biodiversity and enable successful interactions with environments), they already have scientific value (2011: 173).

An indicator of this narrow interest can be found in the list of organizations that, since the 1990s, have recognized indigenous knowledge as a valuable (i.e. profitable) resource. According to Warren, this list includes

> The Consultative Group on International Agricultural Research, the International Labor Organization, the United Nations Environmental Programme, the Food and Agricultural Organization of the United Nations, the International Board for Plant Genetic Resources, the International Plant Genetic Resources Institute, the United Nations Development Programme, the U.K. Department of International Development, the World Bank, the International Development Research Centre, the International Center for Living Aquatic Resource Management, the U.S. National Research Council, and UNESCO (2011: 248).

As it seems clear, agricultural and economic organizations have been pioneers and UNESCO appears as an exception (one, however, intimately connected with the debate about knowledge and intellectual property). Different notions of indigenous knowledge have exemplified one of the most pressing issues in relation to this economic appropriation. On the one hand, the recognition of IK as situated and intimately embedded in cultural practices. 'Communities that live in close contact with the natural environment,' Warren argues, 'have extensive knowledge of their natural resources... they are the true managers of in situ conservation of biodiversity' (2011: 253). On the other, even when good will might be involved, some state that IK should be codified and preserved for future generations, which in reality implies that it has to be translated into Western-style publications, databases and archives.[1] 'If indigenous knowledge has not been documented and compiled, doing so should be a research priority of the highest order. Indigenous knowledge is being lost at an unprecedented rate, and its preservation, preferably in data base form, must take place as quickly as possible' (National Research Council 1992: 45). Not surprisingly, when natural resources are involved, the interest of the West is accentuated because research and innovation paves the way for economic profitability.

Some scholars have attempted to widen the notion of indigenous knowledge to (1) overcome the narrowest approaches, which link IK with cultural and technological delay and (2) embed IK into a broad social, political, economic and cultural context. For Dah-Lokonon (1997) IK should take into account management techniques, while for Doussou (1997) it must comprise indigenous learning and knowledge transmission systems. Morever, Odora Hoppers and Makhale-Mahlangu (1988) have argued that IK also includes knowledge used in the liberation struggles. Thus, IK is related to a variety of disciplines, from forest resource exploitation, fishing and climatology to architecture and pharmacology. Therefore, IK must be thought of as having

Tangible and intangible aspects that... can be identified as those that:

- have exchange value and that, with support, can be transformed into enterprises or industries;

- perpetuate social, cultural, scientific, philosophical, and technological knowledge, that can provide the basis for an integrated and inclusive knowledge framework for a country's development;

---

[1] For example, Hayden (2011) has conceptualized this translation in the case of ethnobotany and chemistry. In that regard, she argues that 'engaged ethnobotanists and plant chemists have long used their field studies and laboratories precisely like court-rooms; that is as staging grounds for proving the veracity of "indigenous knowledge." In this sense, ethnobotany has been figured by some activist practitioners as a form of what I call "epistemological advocacy"—a commitment to translate "indigenous knowledge" into the language of biochemical efficacy, and to use these assertions of the scientific rationality of indigenous knowledge as an axis of political mobilization and even court-room defense' (2011: 347–348).

- represent major sociocultural institutions and organizational systems. (Odora Hoppers 2011: 397).

Within this broader context, it is easier to think of the social sciences as being part of the disciplines potentially confronted by indigenous knowledge. Nevertheless, as mainstream Western natural scientists are strongly imbued by some scientific myths (such as science's universalism), they also have been deeply influenced by another myth, modernization theory, which, during most of the 20th Century, thought of certain regions of the world as traditional, primitive or under-developed. As Catherine V. Scott puts it, 'modernization theorists viewed tradition, and the values associated with tradition... as absolutely incompatible with modern institutions' (2011: 291). Since these latter institutions were indispensable for development and democracy, traditions were conceptualized as obstacles, experiences to be removed in order to set up modern (i.e. Western) institutions. Hence, IK was the best representation of what had to be ignored or suppressed (Santos 2009).

Even though modernization theory is no longer fashionable in current social sciences, its influence has transcended. New social theories, from risk society (Beck) to information society (Castells) to actor-networks (Latour) and liquid modernity (Bauman) have questioned linear notions of progress as well as the very possibility of grand theories to explain the complete assemblages of (post)modern societies. However, they rarely, if ever, have relied on—or taken consideration of—theoretical contributions from parts of the world other than the Euro-American hemisphere. The centrality awarded to Western social knowledge (see Alatas 2003, Keim 2014, Rodriguez-Medina 2014, Suárez 2014, Vessuri 2011) is the visible side of this phenomenon of metropolitan ignorance. The other side has to do with indigenous knowledge and how it is produced, diffused and used, often only locally. This rather narrow and peripheral circulation is partially due to the scarcity of available material and symbolic resources in many areas of the world, which undermines the opportunity for local researchers, activists, and intellectuals to engage in a meaningful and productive international dialogue. Mainstream social sciences have much to gain from theoretical and methodological developments undertaken in the periphery. The remaining sections of this chapter are an attempt to exemplify the richness of a local contribution to our understanding of community media as well as the need to in-breed some Western(ized) knowledge about societal relations with theoretically-sound and empirically-relevant ideas coming from the South.

2. On *Comunalidad*

The concept of *comunalidad* is the result of a series of personal and community processes of struggle that took place in the Southern state of Oaxaca, México, during the 1970s and 1980s. From the beginning, the conceptual contribution is entangled with the lives and trajectories of the anthropologists who developed it. When Jaime Martínez-Luna and Floriberto Díaz returned to their communities (Ben Gwlahx and Ayuujk respectively) after separately having studied anthropology in Mexico City they joined local organizations that "explicitly reaffirmed ethnic identities" (Aquino, 2013:8) in their struggles to defend their territory, tradition and culture. From these experiences, both men developed a harsh criticism of anthropology and the way the discipline interpreted indigenous peoples. They, individually, reached the conclusion that the notion of *comunalidad* was best fitted to think about themselves as societies that are different (not opposed to) to the "western" ones (Aquino, 2013).

Martínez-Luna acknowledges that "*comunalidad*, which is our thought, has its origins in the history of dispossession, in the forced relation we have kept with the territories left by the Conquest and the far-fetched exploitation of the land. This is to say, *comunalidad* is too the product of colonial history" (2003, in Aquino, 2014:9).

According to Maldonado Alvarado (2013), *comunalidad* has three main elements: structure, social organization and mindset. They are anchored in local and ancient historic and cultural roots that set the course of the ways of living as indigenous peoples. Floriberto Díaz considers that *comunalidad* defines several key concepts of the indigenous reality as it expresses universal principles and truths of an indigenous society (in Nava, 2013). To him, the basic elements that guarantee the comprehension of *comunalidad* are: 1. Land as a mother and as a territory, 2. Consensus in Assembly as a way for decision making, 3. Free of charge service as a way to exercise authority, 4. Collective work as an act of recreation, and 5. Rites and ceremonies as a manifestation of the communal gift (in Robles Hernández & Cardoso Jiménez, 2007:49).

For Jaime Martínez-Luna, the communal power must be vouched by concrete work, which implies a practical concern about community imbricated into the daily activities and rooted in the traditions. This work, however, is not reduced to the actions involved, but embedded in the cultural purpose of reproducing organizations. As he puts it, "*comunalidad*—as we call the behaviors resulting from the dynamics of the reproduction of our ancient and current organization—rests on work, never on speech. That is to say, work for decision-making (assembly), work for coordination (*cargo*), work for construction (*tequio*), and work for amusement (*fiesta*)" (2013:251).

Although it is not the main objective of this chapter, it seems clear that the notion of *comunalidad* defies several assumptions and claims of mainstream Euro-American social sciences. Against modernization theorists and some of the scholars who still think of nature as resources, *comunalidad* raises land, as the fundamental source of life, to the category of a person (the mother). This seems perfectly in line with current trends in several parts of the world to grant rights to what was seen until recently as passive actors (i.e. subjects to modify/ignore/suppress in order to modernize). A beautiful example is the Whanganui River, in New Zealand, which "under a landmark agreement, signed (...) earlier this summer, has become a legal entity with a legal voice"[2]. Similarly, "Argentine courts study four orders of *habeas corpus* on behalf of apes to recognize their rights to life, freedom and not to be abused"[3]. Second, against rational choice theorists and much of liberal political science, *comunalidad* rescues the idea of free of charge service to be done under the principle of reciprocity. That is, no free riders and the preeminence of communitarian needs over individualistic responsibilities. In turn, this seems to be an alternative way of understanding volunteering, not necessarily linked to the volunteering work vs mandatory volunteerism

---

[2] See http://www.huffingtonpost.com/2012/09/18/new-zealand-whanganui-river_n_1894893.html, accessed September 2015.
[3] See http://www.lanacion.com.ar/1725226-personas-no-humanas-el-pedido-por-los-chimpances-que-analiza-la-justicia, accessed September 2015.

dilemma, as exemplified in debates in the United States' public education sector[4]. Third, the exchangeability of positions proposed by the concept of 'cargo' aims to re-think what politics (as a public service) is all about. Against Weberian traditions of bureaucratization and its derivatives, such as new public management, *comunalidad* challenges a basic understanding of political life, its institutionalization and professionalization. Under this approach, unpaid, volunteering work, such as political staffers in campaigns[5] and interns in the Executive Branch[6], can be reconceptualized. They are not betraying capitalist commandments, but bringing about circulation of public servants, which in many ways is a better instrument to deal with, family political inheritance, patronage, and corruption, longstanding problems of many societies. In a nutshell, the notion of *comunalidad* is not useful only to understand ancient practices in Mexico, or other peripheral regions, but also, and perhaps more important for its circulation, to explain phenomena of other societies in alternative, enlightening ways.

In order to see the utility of *comunalidad* we now turn to a case study: Ojo de Agua. We want to show that the concept, rooted as it is in traditional cultures, has been used to organize collective work in media. Moreover, we will introduce some of Ojo de Agua's works to illustrate how this organization ends up influencing its outputs, because *comunalidad* transcends procedural mechanisms and translates into ways of seeing the world.

3. Ojo de Agua Comunicación and *comunalidad*

> We are an organization of communicators born in Oaxaca, Mexico in 1998. In our work we apply and encourage the principles of comunalidad, cultural diversity, dignity of peoples and individuals and the values of life and reciprocity.

---

[4] See http://www.nytimes.com/2003/03/23/nyregion/the-logic-of-mandatory-volunteerism.html, accessed September 2015.
[5] See http://www.theguardian.com/us-news/2015/jun/13/hillary-clinton-unpaid-summer-intern-campaign, accessed September 2015.
[6] See http://thefederalist.com/2015/05/11/unpaid-internships-do-as-congress-says-not-as-it-does/, accessed September 2015.

(Ojo de Agua Comunicación A.C.)

Ojo de Agua Comunicación is an organization devoted to foster community and indigenous communication projects and products. They made the conscious decision to explicitly incorporate *comunalidad* into their everyday work and as a goal of the organization. Although not all members[7] are indigenous they found in the indigenous worldview, way of life, and organization something to reflect upon that could be applied to their *reason de étre* as a community and indigenous communication collective that aims at using communication as a way to challenge and resist side by side with first nations. Ojo de Agua asserts,

> We believe that media production makes full sense when we understand it as a set of tools that transform social conditions we find oppressive and unjust by way of fostering participative, democratic, harmonic and sustainable lifestyles. In so doing first nations have important lessons to teach about their social organization, the way they relate to the environment, how they name a territory, how they value situations and undertake transforming actions. We believe that community communication can help us to get to know us and appreciate us better as a society and to find better ways to live life (Ojo de Agua Comunicación, A.C.).

Throughout the history of Ojo de Agua we can find that they have made or encourage workshops, trainings, audiovisual productions, radio productions, seminars, participation in social movements, supervision, among other activities. What lies at the heart of these communication actions is a commitment to service and to enhance indigenous identities and cultural diversity using communication tools to challenge and resist the dominant media system. Ojo de Agua has two roots that sustain their work: *comunalidad* and a work ethic.

Following Díaz and Martínez-Luna we consider that the main elements of *comunalidad* are territory, assembly, *tequio*, *cargo*, and *fiesta*. Territory is both the geographic space as well as the

---

[7] Currently Ojo de Agua Comunicación has eight full-time members: Guillermo Monteforte, Sergio Julián, Juan José García, Clara Morales, Héctor García, Seberino Hipólito, Tonatiuh Ramírez and Roberto Olivares. Five of them are from indigenous communities in Oaxaca, two are from Mexico City but refer to themselves as oaxaqueños and the last one is Italo-Canadian but also identifies with Oaxaca as his place in the world.

political and cultural inhabitable space. It also embodies the relationship with Earth as a life source and as a central axis of existence. Assembly is the way to make decisions for the communal life. At the assembly every person from a community has the right, and the obligation, to participate. The goal is to reach consensus for making decisions. *Tequio* is a work donated as a service to the community. This work (ploughing, building, cooking, teaching, and so on) is done reciprocally, willingly, joyfully and free of charge. *Cargo* is a job within the community traditional activities that is undertaken as a way to serve the community. *Cargos* are both civil and religious positions that change every year. *Fiesta* is a collective process derived from history and tradition that gives cohesiveness to the community and reinforces its identity and values and allows to give continuity to traditions. All elements of *comunalidad* are present in the ways Ojo de Agua functions; nonetheless three of them are more easily identifiable.

3.1. Assembly

Ojo de Agua makes all decisions regarding the organization collectively and via consensus of all its members. "We have a weekly meeting where we make all decisions and assign all responsibilities" (collective interview, 2014a). They believe that the collective process of decision making they have used to work throughout the years is an important characteristic of the organization. They explicitly refer to the weekly meeting as an *asamblea*.

3.2. Cargo

All the tasks that have to be dealt with in Ojo de Agua (financing, grant applications, coordinate the use of and maintenance of equipment and infrastructure, yearly general coordination of the team, among others) must be shared by everyone and should rotate yearly. Since there are only eight people in Ojo de Agua throughout the years they have had to take the same *cargo* more than once. What they have learned from this rotation is that some people are better at fulfilling the responsibilities of a particular *cargo* than others. That is why the same person has been re-elected by the members of the collective in his *cargo* as financial administrator.

The decision has not only been based on the person's skills but also as a way to keep the finances of the organization sound as having different people taking care of this task led to economic and financial turmoil in the past. The rest of the members of the collective have taken different responsibilities that might not necessarily be the best suited to their skills, nonetheless the members of Ojo de Agua believe that there is a learning process that benefits the individuals and the organization in the rotation of the *cargos*.

3.3. Tequio

The work done inside and outside of the organization is assumed by the members of Ojo de Agua as *tequio*, a service work done with joy and a genuine desire to contribute to community and indigenous communication. Nonetheless, to consider work as *tequio* does not eliminate the need of economic and material subsistence. This is a delicate point that worries the members of Ojo de Agua who refer to the subject in the following manner:

> I do not like money but the world does not function any other way. We are denying how it works and this is affecting us by not having certainty about what we are doing because we are always worried about money.
>
> It is not that we are not clear about income distribution, I believe it is a bad distribution. We do not take care of ourselves. With Ojo de Agua's work logic if one gets sick s/he does not have a place to go to. This reveals our logic. We are not concerned about us, but about Ojo de Agua, as an abstract entity.
>
> ... We cannot go as far as to say we do nothing without pay, because then we would be acting as a business...
>
> We prefer to endanger the economic stability of Ojo de Agua to collaborate with or do work for something/someone we disagree with or that is not close to our political or ideological position. And that is fine, I believe it is one of the things we must value because that is something many other organizations have not accomplished (Ojo de Agua workshop, 2014b).

In spite of the economic difficulties that solidarity work (or *tequio*) has, members of Ojo de Agua are convinced that what they do contributes to the community and indigenous communication, strengthening a solid work ethics. In the words of Roberto Olivares (a member of Ojo de Agua):

> I believe people [we work with] quickly understood, maybe clearer than us, that there were things that Ojo de Agua would do and would not do. For example, a government institution would approach us to commission a video production and we always were able to clearly state that we could work with them as long as we had editorial and creative freedom. They could not demand us to make propaganda of any kind, of any individual or political figure. I believe that allowed us to accept commissions that were important for our financial sustainability but we never betrayed the principle that we are a social communication collective. Although we have been offered to produce very attractive and lucrative videos, if they do not agree with our goals we do not make them. I believe that even at the worst times we have respected that, regardless of risking the financial stability of the organization (2013).

There are many tensions between a communal living philosophy and the need to live a dignified life in an urban setting (city of Oaxaca) with an individualistic and commercial philosophy. Nonetheless, Ojo de Agua has held strong in its convictions, ethics and has made meaningful contributions to community and indigenous communication through teaching/training, video and radio productions, seminars, conferences, networks and so forth.

3.4. Fiesta

Ojo de Agua does not have a celebration of its anniversary or any particular rites that belong only to them as an organization. Nonetheless, they do participate in the *communal* life of the people they work with via the *fiesta*. The members of the collective have incorporated in their training workshops, in productions, in projects developed with the communities the celebratory elements of the *fiesta* as a form to reinforce identity and to contribute to the cohesiveness of the community and of them as collective. For example, the community radios they have worked with celebrate their anniversaries with a big *fiesta* to which Ojo de Agua attends, contributing with *tequio*. Also, as part of a project focused on defense of the territory they designed with the communities a song contest. The participating songs about the defense of the territory and the resistance against mining companies were sung live and the whole event became a *fiesta*.

Jaime Martínez-Luna (2013) considers that resistance is an important element of *comunalidad* that is expressed in all aspects of life including music, songs, food, clothing, color, all present in the *fiesta*. Ojo de Agua has a celebratory way to go about their work which is tuned in with the celebratory approach to identity and the (re)construction of the social fabric on *communal* life.

3.5. Territory

The territory as a place is a key element of *comunalidad* and the members of Ojo de Agua have an important connection with Oaxaca (both the City and the State) as their place in the world. According to Maldonado Alvarado (2013), currently, most people from Oaxaca still have a social relation and identify with a community. Some of them participate in the *communal* life even though they do not live in the community anymore and their mind set prioritizes the communal over the individual. Juan José García, for example, lives in the city of Oaxaca, is a full time member of Ojo de Agua and by September 2015 he has a *cargo* in his community as substitute major, so he travels constantly between both places. Other members of the collective refer to themselves as people from a specific town, for example Severino is from Santa Ana, and Tonatiuh refers to himself as "chilango-oaxaqueño"[8].

Another important aspect of the territory as a cornerstone of *comunalidad* is the relationship with the land, with mother earth as a living being. All members of Ojo de Agua have decided to live a sustainable life that takes care of the land. For example, they have kitchen gardens in their homes in an attempt to seek food self-sufficiency, others buy food from local farmers and in general they all have lifestyles that are respectful of the environment. Thus, they recycle (in a city that does not have recycling policies), have composts at their homes, use bicycles to move inside the city, and use rain water at their homes.

As an organization they have plans for moving their office to a house they own (currently they lease) where they can have a collective kitchen garden, a compost, and a rain farm.

---

[8] *Chilango* is the way to name a person from Mexico City. Oaxaqueño is a person from the city of Oaxaca.

4. Ojo de Agua's productions: *comunalidad* in action

Several audiovisual productions have been key to the history of Ojo de Agua because of their content, their social relevance, exhibition success, etc. A common element to most of them has been their role as nodes, as meeting points for diverse individuals, collectives and institutions as well as the way they embody the ideas and principles of *comunalidad*.

4.1. Pueblos de México (television series, 2002)

Pueblos de México is a documentary series Ojo de Agua produced in 2002. It was the first big commission production they had which consists of twenty three short films that narrate the everyday life, achievements or challenges of different indigenous peoples. What Ojo de Agua did was to focus on testimonies from peoples about current issues in their communities such as Community organization, health, education, language, migration and ecology.

The series is meaningful to the members of Ojo de Agua because it allowed them to learn about and from indigenous peoples while at the same time it presented an opportunity to communicate stories about indigenous peoples from their points of view. They recall,

> [...] A thing about the Ojo de Agua team [related with the production of Pueblos de México] is that we increased what we know about indigenous communities, regions, their problems, lifestyles. That made Ojo de Agua grow and it strengthened everything because if we lack that sensibility then we do not have the chance to set a course about where we have to head on to. The responsibility we had was to communicate the things people wanted. For example, the first thing we were told about the series was that we had to produce video monographs of indigenous peoples in Mexico, which is very pretentious because you cannot discuss a people and its culture altogether, and also, it is very boring. So we said, why don't we discuss very concrete experiences? And from there we can tell that there is a village with this name, that there is a tiny place of this village that lives an unknown reality. Our responsibility when communicating that was to respect the point of view of the community, so we were not only observers (García, 2013).

By allowing people to tell their stories from their points of view Ojo de Agua emphasized the relevance and richness of the daily practices of indigenous communities, which are an element of their identity and their thought. It is precisely this kind of narratives that materialize the embeddedness of IK knowledge into culture, and Ojo de Agua plays the role of helping people to narrate as well as diffusing the stories beyond its context of production. In this way, Ojo de Agua's project is vital to conceptualize IK not merely as a locally-grounded know-how but rather as knowledge potentially moved to different settings. To Maldonado Alvarado (2013) *Comunalidad*, takes into account the historic and cultural roots of the indigenous peoples from ancient times but also from current everyday practices as they shape the life of indigenous peoples. Pueblos de México shows how indigenous peoples live, feel and think, and how that is precisely what makes them indigenous.

4.2. "Mal de Ojo" (grassroots video collective, 2006)

In 2006 in the city of Oaxaca a grassroots social movement emerged to confront Governor Ulises Ruiz, known for its authoritarian and corrupt regime. A social protest movement emerged gathering different groups from around the State of Oaxaca such as teachers, students, union workers, artists, indigenous communities, among others. Ojo de Agua convened and participated with other communication collectives, social organizations and individuals in the production of audiovisual reports to inform what was happening. They called this collective participatory media project Mal de Ojo TV. The video productions they made offered an alternative discourse to that of mainstream media which presented the official side of the story leaving aside what was happening at the city's barricades, camps and assemblies.

Tonatihu Ramírez, a member of Ojo de Agua remembers the social mobilizations of 2006 as an experience that marked him and the collective deeply. To him, Ojo de Agua was able to reinforce and re-shape their collective work in a way that allowed them to respond to the needs of the moment. He recalls, "We did a very intense and immediate work to produce and distribute what was taking place. We organized in a way that we could report what was occurring throughout the city every day. That experience, beyond the results of 2006 and what we produced, taught me a lot about what the media are capable of" (2013).

Through the video productions they made, Mal de Ojo TV was able "to amplify the voices, the claims and the struggles of the

Chapter 6: Indigenous knowledge in the social sciences

people from Oaxaca at that time of protest, resistance and defense against State repression" (Ojo de Agua, 2007: 83). This was an exercise of resistance against repression from the armed forces, the State authorities and the mainstream media. It was also a way to exercise autonomy. Floriberto Díaz (in Nava, 2013) considers that autonomy and self-determination are deeply related to the practice of *comunalidad* as they are ways to exercise individual and collective rights and to exercise power.

4.3. "Community Communication with a Gender approach for Life and Territory in Mesoamerica" (training and media production project, 2014–1015)

Facing state reforms geared to take away the land and territories of indigenous peoples and communities to exploit their natural resources for mining, oil drilling, electric or Eolic energy production, tourist complexes and so on, indigenous men and women throughout the Mesoamerican region have got organized for the defense of their territories and their legal and human rights. They have done marches, protests, fora, and symposia, produced radio and video contents and fought to defend their individual and collective rights as well as life in their communities and the environment they inhabit.

A major element in these struggles is the production and distribution of information and knowledge for people to understand the complex dynamics of the major transnational projects as well as the reasons for resistance and confrontation. Nonetheless, mainstream media corporations concentrate almost the totality of the radio-electric spectrum thus controlling the flow of information and the way reality is shaped, by focusing only on the official version of events, atomizing popular movements. By the same token, the relationship between culture, society and development that mainstream media propose is harmful to social transformation processes promoted from diverse social sectors to democratize family relations and eliminate gender stereotypes, violence and discrimination.

Taking this complex reality into account Ojo de Agua obtained a grant from the government of the Basque Country to implement the project "Community Communication with a Gender approach for Life and Territory in Mesoamerica." The project aims at implementing community communication processes to promote women's rights to political participation and non-violence as well as the exercise of collective rights to land and territory of indigenous peoples in four localities of Oaxaca: Santo Domingo Zanatepec, San Francisco Ixhuatán, Magdalena Teitipac y Santa María Jicaltepec.

Ojo de Agua coordinates the general efforts of the project and supports the different activities in each of the four communities, which are defined, organized and executed by local actors. A last feature of Ojo de Agua that is worth mentioning is its capacity to develop networks with different individuals, organizations and institutions. According to Laurel Smith (2005), many of the everyday working strategies of Ojo de Agua are based on networks and have the intention to support individuals, communities and indigenous organizations. Networks are both human and technological and operate at local, regional, national and international levels, always in the service of those who need them. Some of the networking has been oriented to financing, the biggest and more generalized challenge for community and indigenous communicators throughout the world. Ojo de Agua has played an important role in this task since the beginning while functioning as a node for indigenous video makers to get grants or scholarships from the Rockefeller Foundation, Ashoka and other organizations.

5. Final thoughts

The organization Ojo de Agua and its works provide teaching and training to community and indigenous communicators, to produce and distribute media messages using video, radio and digital resources to challenge mainstream media discourses. In this way, it promotes self-representation and acknowledges media as fields of struggle to confront political and economic powers that continue the domination and oppression of indigenous peoples.

The collective has put its know-how and work to the service of different media and communication collectives and has helped expand training, production and distribution of indigenous voices using media platforms. It has also positioned itself as an authorized organization in community and indigenous communication mainly because the way to go about their work in a communal way working and sharing their work with others. Ojo de

Agua starts from *comunalidad* as both a principle and a practice that shapes how they understand community and indigenous communication, how they organize as a communication collective and what they want to accomplish.

At a theoretical level, what informants have stated resonates with Anibal Quijano (2000) and other authors of the de-colonial turn who consider that modernity and colonialism are inextricably bound. Arturo Escobar argues that colonialism is constitutive of modernity and that there is no modernity without colonialism. Modernity is the bright, visible side of the history of global-eurocentric-capitalism; whereas colonialism is its dark, hidden, unvisibilized side (in Veronelli, forthcoming).

To Quijano, Mexico as other former colonies did not reach de-colonization with Independence, instead there was a "re-articulation of the coloniality of power on the basis of new institutions" (2000:36). Grosfoguel states that currently, "peripheries remain in a colonial situation even when they have stopped being under a colonial administration" (2006, 29). The coloniality of knowledge is a principle that undermines and silences different forms of knowledge of subaltern peoples (Mignolo in Aquino, 2013). Boaventura de Sousa (2009) refers to cognitive injustice, which is the product of oppression and exploitation processes that exclude certain groups and suppress, make invisible and exterminate their knowledge.

According to Aquino, the main contributions of *Comunalidad* are strongly bound to the struggle against the coloniality of knowledge and cognitive injustices. To her, *comunalidad* "makes visible the legacy of colonialism in relation to indigenous peoples, the Nation-State and national society", while at the same time it is a "counterhegemonic category to think about indigenous peoples" and is an "example of knowledge for emancipation" (2013, 8–9).

Freya Schiwy (2009) in *Indianizing Film*, discusses how mass media work as instruments of capitalism and neocolonial domination, mainly by way of stereotypes and caricatures of indigenous peoples who are portrayed as inferior, ignorant and uncivilized. Schiwy also analyses how indigenous media have contributed to de-colonization. To her the struggles that take place in the realm of indigenous media are to create new epistemes that are based on self-representations and the use of technology challenging the notion that indigenous peoples are pre-technology or that using technology makes them less "authentic". Schiwy states that de-colonization though indigenous media is about rescuing indigenous culture as well as transforming and reinventing the present.

Magallanes-Blanco, Parra Hinojosa, Atala Layún and Flores Solana (2013) have highlighted the relevance of indigenous media in Mexico as they have a strong relationship with social and political movements, they have helped overcome historical tensions and prejudices while at the same time they have reinforced indigenous cultures, ways of knowing and forms of transmitting social memories; hence, making a contribution to the de-colonization of knowledge.

What is worth to point out, as a concluding remark, is that indigenous knowledge is valuable not only because of its cultural and geographic roots, its embeddedness in ancient traditions, but also because of its explanatory power. Before anything else, IK is useful knowledge and its capacity to deal with phenomena beyond its context of production will depend more on the actors sensitive to it than intrinsic properties that allow for universalization. Mainstream scholars will understand not only peripheral zones but their own societies better if they are open to what, so far, have considered primitive and obsolete. Because, as Comaroff and Comaroff (2013) have argued, many Southern countries are no longer peripheral but central to late capitalism. However…:

> Still being highly polarized within, they are geo-escapes in which enclaves of wealth and order feed off, and sustain, large stretches of scarcity, violence, and exclusion. This is also true, increasingly, of Euro-America. In short, there is much south in the north, much north in the south, and… more of both to come (2013: 20).

Perhaps, if there is much South in the North, more *comunalidad* can be expected in mainstream social sciences. To what extent this notion, and others coming from the periphery, will defy the dominant theories of the North is something to be studied. Nevertheless, it seems clear who will be the main losers if the dialogue cannot take place.

References

Alatas, S. F. (2003). Academic Dependency and the Global Division of Labour in the Social Science. *Current Sociology*, Vol.51(6), 599–613.

Aquino Moreschi, A. (2013). La comunalidad como epistemología del Sur. Aportes y retos. [Comunalidad as an epistemology from the South. Contributions and Challenges], *Cuadernos del Sur. Revista de Ciencias Sociales*, Year 18. No., 34, 7–19, January-June.

Comaroff, J. and Comaroff, J. (2013). Writing Theory from the South: The Global Order from an African Perspective. *World Financial Review*, Sep-Oct 2013, 17–20.

Dah-Lokonon, G.B. (1997). Rainmakers: Myth and Knowledge in Traditional Atmospheric Management Techniques. In P. Hountondji (ed.) *Endogenous Knowledge: Research Trails*. Oxford : CODESRIA.

Doussou, F.C. (1997). Writing and Oral Tradition in the Transmission of Knowledge. In P. Hountondji (ed.) *Endogenous Knowledge: Research Trails*. Oxford : CODESRIA.

García, J. (2013). *Personal communication*. Oaxaca, Mexico.

Grosfoguel, R. (2006). La descolonización de la economía política y los estudios postcoloniales: Transmodernidad, pensamiento fronterizo y colonialidad global. [The de-colonization of political economy and postcolonial studies: Transmodernity, border thinking and global coloniality], *Tabula Rasa*, No.4, 17–48, January-June.

Harding, S. (ed). (2011). *The Postcolonial Science and Technology Reader*. Durham and London: Duke University Press.

Hayden, C. (2011). Bioprospecting's Representational Dilemma. In S. Harding (ed.) *The Postcolonial Science and Technology Reader*. Durham and London: Duke University Press.

Keim, W., Çelik, E., Ersche, C. and Wöhrer, V. (eds). (2014). *Global Knowledge Production in the Social Sciences: Made in Circulation*. Farnham: Ashgate.

Magallanes-Blanco, C., Parra Hinojosa, D., Atala Layún, A., & Flores Solana, T. (2013). Memoria e Imaginarios en el Discurso Mediático Indígena: Producciones Radiofónicas de Oaxaca. [Memory and imaginaries in the media indigenous discourse: Radio productions from Oaxaca]. *REALIS. Revista de Estudos AntiUtilitaristas e PosColoniais*, 3(2), 156–177. jul-dez.

Maldonado Alvarado, B. (2013). Comunalidad y responsabilidad autogestiva. [comunalidad and self-produce responsibility]. *Cuadernos del Sur. Revista de Ciencias Sociales*. Año 18. No., 34, 21–27, January-June.

Martínez Luna, J. (2013). *Textos sobre el camino andado. Tomo 1* [Texts about the road taken. Volume 1]. CSEIIO, IEEPO, Centro de Apoyo al Movimiento Popular Oaxaqueño, Plan Piloto-CMPIO, Congreso Nacional de Educación Indígena Intercultural, Coordinación Estatal de Escuelas de Educación Secundaria Comunitaria Indígena; Oaxaca de Juárez, Mexico.

National Research Council. (1992). *Conserving Biodiversity: A Research Agenda for Development Agencies*. Washington DC: National Academy Press.

Nava Morales, E. (2013). Comunalidad: semilla teórica en crecimiento. [Comunalidad theoretical seed in growth]. *Cuadernos del Sur. Revista de Ciencias Sociales*. Año 18. No., 34, 57–69, Janurary-July.

Odora Hoppers, C.A. (2011). Towards the Integration of Knowledge Systems: Challenges to Thought and Practice. In S. Harding (ed.) *The Postcolonial Science and Technology Reader*. Durham and London: Duke University Press.

Odora Hoppers, C.A. and Makhale-Mahlangu, P. (1988). *A Comparative Study of the Development, Integratino and Protection of Indigenous Systems in the Third World. An Analytical Framework*. Document. HSRC.

Ojo de Agua Comunicación, A. C. web site: http://ojodeaguacomunicacion.org/quienes-somos. Retreived September 2015.

Ojo de Agua. (2014a). Collective interview. Oaxaca, Mexico.

Ojo de Agua. (2014b). Workshop. Oaxaca, Mexico.

Ojo de Agua. (2007). *Raíz de la Imagen y el movimiento social en Oaxaca* [Raíz de la Imagen and the social movement in Oaxaca]. Ojo de Agua: Oaxaca, Mexico.

Olivares, R. (2013). Personal communication. Oaxaca, Mexico.

Quijano, A. (2000). Colonialidad del poder, eurocentrismo y América Latina. [Coloniality of power, eurocentrism and Latin America]. In Edgardo Lander (comp.). *La colonialidad del saber: eurocentrismo y ciencias sociales. Perspectivas Latinoamericanas [Coloniality of knowledge: eurocentrism and social sciences. Latin American perspectives]*. Buenos Aires, Argentina : CLACSO, Consejo Latinoamericano de Ciencias Sociales.

Ramírez, T. (2013). Personal communication. Oaxaca, Mexico.

Robles Hernández, S. and Cardoso Jiménez, R. (2007). *Floriberto Díaz. Escrito. Comunalidad, energía viva del pensamiento mixe* [Floriberto Díaz. In writing. Comunalidad, living energy of the Mixe thought]. Mexico, DF : Universidad Nacional Autónoma de México.

Rodriguez-Medina, L. (2014). *Centers and Peripheries in Knowledge Production*. New York and London: Routledge.

Santos, B. S. (2009). *Una Epistemología del Sur. La Reinvención del Conocimiento y la Emancipación Sociali*. México: CLACSO and Siglo XXI.

Scott, C. (2011). Science for the West, Myth for the Rest? The Case of James Bay Cree Knowledge Construction. In S. Harding (ed.) *The Postcolonial Science and Technology Reader*. Durham and London: Duke University Press.

Scott, C.V. (2011). Tradition and Gender in Modernization Theory. In S. Harding (ed.) *The Postcolonial Science and Technology Reader*. Durham and London: Duke University Press.

Schiwy, F. (2009). *Indianizing Film. Decolonization, the Andes and the Question of technology*. USA: Rutgers University Press.

Smith, L. (2005). *Mediating Indigenous Identity: Video, Advocacy and Knowledge in Oaxaca*, Mexico. Unpublished doctoral thesis. University of Kentucky.

Suárez, M. (2014). Movimiento de asimetría en las redes. Nuevas formas de entender las relaciones entre el Sur y Norte Global. In P. Kreimer, H. Vessuri, L. Velho and A. Arellano (coor) *Perspectivas Latinoamericanas en el Estudio Social de la Ciencia, la Tecnología y la Sociedad*. México: Siglo XXI and Foro Consultivo Científico y Tecnológico.

Veronelli, G. (Forthcoming). Sobre la colonialidad del lenguaje. [On the coloniality of language]. *Revista Universitas Humanística. Prácticas Comunicativas, Creatividad y Nuevos Desafíos*. No. 82. January–June 2016.

Vessuri, H. (2011). La actual internacionalización de las ciencias sociales en América Latina: ¿vino viejo en barricas nuevas? In A. Arellano Hernández and P. Kreimier (dir.) *Estudio Social de la Ciencia y la Tecnología desde América Latina*. Bogotá: Siglo del Hombre Editores.

Warren, D.M. (2011). The Role of the Global Network of Indigenous Knowledge Resource Centers in the Conservation of Cultural and Biological Diversity. In S. Harding (ed.) *The Postcolonial Science and Technology Reader*. Durham and London: Duke University Press.

Chapter 7:
What can Science and Technology Studies do with and for Latin America?[1]

An anthropophagic response and some examples[2]

Ivan da Costa Marques[3]

In Latin America, as in other parts of the world, the evaluation of the work of a scholar working on sciences and technologies studies (STS), be she a senior or a newcomer in the field, often faces the question "what is the contribution of your work for STS?" This question, which enjoys hegemonic academic legitimacy, is "slick" for politics and for the life of the researcher.[4] As it does not situate STS and ignores local ties, the question naturalizes STS and endows them with a universal character that they themselves problematize. If handled without care, this question acts to thrust the researcher into a universalist trench. If somewhat rudely, however, an outstanding result of STS themselves could be synthesized in

---

[1] As a Brazilian, I have always felt somewhat obliged to have an answer for his question. Maybe the novelty is the "with" added to the "for". Presently I feel that somehow the question is in the air. In the 2014 4S conference, held in Buenos Aires together with a Latin American STS conference, the opening plenary composed of 24 scholars was entitled "What is STS for? What are STS scholars for? Making and Doing in STS."

[2] I am especially grateful to Michel Christie (Charles Darwin University, Australia) for his comments and critics, which greatly improved the manuscript. I am also grateful to Antonio Arellano Hernández (UAEMEX), Yuri Carvajal Banhados (Universidad de Chile), and Gary Downey (4S/Virginia Tech) for the opportunities they have provided to discuss this text outside Brazil. Many thanks also to my students and Brazilian colleagues who provided opportunities for discussions at Brazilian universities.

[3] Graduate Program of History of Sciences and Techniques, and Epistemology, Universidade Federal do Rio de Janeiro, Brazil.

[4] In his broad framework of education and co-construction of knowledge, Paulo Freire denounces a game "slick" of words that "appears or wants to appear as the one that defends freedom and not as the one that is afraid of it". Freire, P. (1978). Pedagogia do Oprimido. Rio de Janeiro, Paz e Terra.

the assertive "the universal is a particular in power". But which particular? Universalist trench of whom? Of what?

The fantasy of the universality of modern science that came into shape around the middle of the last millennium makes answering the question a difficult task. At that time a new set of practices, attitudes and mentalities, today called modern, based on a set of ideas known as rational in respect of man, of nature, of morality and of society, which, in its origins, were, ordinarily of "Europe", was configured. The dawn of modernity is distinguished by an intricate geographical, social and intellectual expansion of the European borders. Geographically and socially, the opening of new shipping routes between continents considerably increased the basis of the accumulation process in Europe and established permanent contacts between the contemporary civilizations. Intellectually, the Reformation and the Renaissance performed the expansion. In this general framework, what is perhaps more surprising and certainly more relevant for the purposes of this chapter is that, in the centuries following this historic event, a common technological base became an axis of attraction and capture of all cultures. European, so called Western, sciences and technologies have managed to establish themselves as a universality through the work of a planetary construction.[5] This is the sense of the modern universal. Therefore, briefly explained, this is a first historic and technoscientific link that situates the question "what is the contribution of your work for STS?" The universalist trench is a trench for the defense of ways of being, knowing and building modern knowledge of Western Europe, whose particular is in power.[6]

Emblematically, we can find the exclusionary appropriation of universality by the European particular in the opening paragraph of Max Weber's consecrated work that makes respectable "the fact of Western Civilization, and only in Western Civilization, have appeared cultural phenomena have (as we believe) of a universal de-

---

[5] See also in this respect Mignolo, W. D. (2003/2000). Histórias locais/Projetos globais: colonialidade, saberes subalternos e pensamento liminar. Belo Horizonte, MG, Editora UFMG., especially session V of the Introduction (The gnosis and the imagination of the world system colonial/modern), pag. 48 to 61.

[6] "Western science is a philosophical artefact which may become a veritable epistemological obstacle when it comes to making a historical and social study of the sciences in the Latin American context."Polanco, X. (1985). "La ciencia como ficción. Historia y contexto." Cuadernos de Quipu 1(1): 41–56.

velopment in its value and meaning". (Weber 1987/1904) (Emphasis in the original)[7]

By highlighting the fact that modern European sciences and technologies have come to constitute an axis of attraction and capture of all cultures, we take one-step further in the direction of the desired standpoint for this chapter. The standpoint I am adopting here is that in the encounters of our region with European modernity, Latin Americans have not succeeded in overcoming their minority in their relations with modern European sciences and technologies. For the Indian intellectual Partha Chatterjee, this would mean a continued subjection to a world order that only lays down our tasks, over which we have the least control:

> Why is it that the non-Europeans colonial countries have no other historical alternative but to try to approximate the given attributes of modernity when that very process of approximation means their continued subjection under a world order which only sets their tasks to them and over which they have no control?(Chatterjee 1986:10)

In the contemporary global scale, the question "what is the contribution of your work for STS?" resonates Chatterjee's question. However, if it applies to the Latin American countries, how this is so? What are the alternatives in Latin America to face (to negotiate with) Europe? Today, are Latin Americans modern? Moreover, if they are not modern, or they are modern in a peculiar way, how is this so? How close have they come to the attributes of modernity?

According to Walter Mignolo, a difference distinguishes Latin America in the panorama of "subaltern studies of South Asia, or

---

[7] The subtlety is in the surreptitious delivery of the power to define and decide on the "universal" to modern epistemology, restricted to analytical philosophy and the philosophy of science, without mentioning this delivery (Rorty, R. (1982). Consequences of pragmatism : essays, 1972–1980. Minneapolis, University of Minnesota Press. in Mignolo, W. D. (2003/2000). Histórias locais/Projetos globais: colonialidade, saberes subalternos e pensamento liminar. Belo Horizonte, MG, Editora UFMG.). Weber said that only in the West there is "science" in a "valid" stage of development. He argued that, although knowledge and observation of great acuity also existed in other civilizations, mathematical reasoning lacked to Babylonian astronomy, as well as the rational proof, the experimental method and the biological foundations respectively to geometry, to the natural sciences and medicine in India. Weber, M. (1987/1904). A ética protestante e o espírito do capitalismo. São Paulo, SP, Livraria Pioneira Editora.

Edward Saïd's *Orientalism*" as these have the 18th century and the
Enlightenment as the chronological border of modernity:

> "Since my feelings, education, and thinking are anchored on the colonial legacies of the Spanish and Portuguese empires in the Americas, 'to begin' in the 18th century would be to put myself out of the game" (Mignolo 2003/2000:43) (Mignolo 2000:19)

Mignolo rejects the idea that the Latin American region has undone or surpassed the colonial relations, as the term *post*-colonial may suggest. Instead, the understanding that colonialism in Latin America transformed throughout the time prevails. Power passed from European colonizers to the "Creole" elites and to those with connections to the metropolitan centers and global markets. It is possible, from different angles, to identify ambivalences of position in relation to European civilization in the plurality of the Latin American intellectual life, including in the STS field.

Ambivalences between simultaneously copying and rejecting the models of European civilization often lead many Latin American researchers to a hindrance. They both mimic and are hostile to the models they imitate. They copy to the extent that they accept standards, even if different standards, disseminated by modernity. However, Latin Americans who are approaching modernity are also involved in at least two rejections pointed out by Chatterjee in post-colonial studies,

> both of them ambivalent: rejection of the alien intruder and dominator who is nevertheless to be imitated and surpassed by his own standards; and rejection of the ancestral ways which are seen as obstacles to progress and yet also cherished as marks of identity(Chatterjee 1986:2)

Similarly, contemporary Brazilian intellectuals indicate different nuances of a feeling that Roberto Schwarz identifies as a "*malaise* that has remained in the minds of educated Latin Americans since the 19th century":

Chapter 7: What can Science and Technology Studies do? 127

> Brazilians and Latin Americans constantly experience the dummy, inauthentic, imitated character of the cultural life that we carry on ... a given trace of our critical reflection since the time of Independence ... [which] involves the feeling of contradiction between the national reality and ideological prestige of the countries which serve us as model ... (whose) manifestations range from the harmless to the horrifying ... (from) Santa Claus using a sled with a dog team to travel over the land in a tropical country ... (to) the Human Rights policy of the Montoro government benefited prisoners causing manifestations of popular discontent: why should one give assurances to the sentenced, if outside of the prisons they are missing to a lot of people? From this perspective, Human rights would be false in Brazil ... Before committing one more explanation, let us say that the mentioned malaise is a *fact*. (Schwarz 1987:29–30)

What is the relationship between this malaise and doing STS with and for the Latin America? In recent decades, STS convincingly argued that *all knowledge is situated*. All knowledge is historically contingent, has its place and its time, its *situation* and, let us not forget, all knowledge also configures its *situation*. Knowledge enacted by stories of the winners, a criticized but still hegemonic way of narrating, suggests pure territories with scarce contact zones. These narratives demarcate the world, create winners and losers, create and assign values to asymmetries and undermine the dialog between the various collectives. The almost naturalized aim to almost exclusively focus the work at answering the question "what is the contribution of your work for STS?" tends to throw the knowledge that the Latin American researcher builds and, as a consequence, to throw the researcher herself into spaces of being, living and knowing that I call "bubbles of pseudo-winners". Yes, they are "pseudo-winners" if one compares the respectability that they may succeed to achieve to that of their imagined peers in the North. This is nothing new. In the 1980s, Xavier Polanco used the expression "inside brain drain", to show that this bubble of pseudo-winners is the destination (not rarely desired and sought, I regret) of many Latin American researchers.

It is also worth noting that, in addition to being detectable as a fact, the bubble of pseudo-winners, at least in Brazil, precedes the 20th century, once that

> [t]aking advantage of an "illustrated" State policy, believers in the power of a single and universal reason and the pragmatic function of science at the service of the material progress, the Brazilian scholars of the late 18th century and the beginning of the 19th century sought to include Brazil in western culture, reflecting, learning and, above all, trying to apply. That was, in the words of Arruda Camera, the purpose of the *Areopagus of Itambé*, "make the current state

of Europe known in Brazil", as well as that of the magazine *O Patriota*, "the lights are spread in the world for all; we must take advantage of them". (Dias 2005:78)

The Latin American researcher lives in an academic community that very problematically seeks its place in the West. Hence, the importance of addressing questions that vibrate in frequencies that are different from those of the western hegemonic sounds. Frequencies that will shake knowledges and researchers into other situations. This paper will crucially try to intervene contributing in seeking more symmetry and amplification of the dialogical capacity in knowledge construction, distancing itself from the (epistemologically) asymmetrical and anti-dialogue division of knowledges so that winners have science and truth and losers have beliefs and mistakes. In the bubbles of pseudo-winners in Latin America, where one, mistakenly, tries literally and thinly to follow the catechism of European construction of knowledge, and attributes beliefs to non modern, non civilized people, Latin American intellectuals throw Latin American local knowledges and their own people into spaces of worthlessness.

In the open space of possibilities STS create, seeking greater analytical *symmetry* to open dialogs to collate European scientific knowledges and other knowledges, I suggest questions to reverse the original questions, such as, "what is the contribution of the STS **for** Latin America?", or "what is the contribution of STS for Brazil?" The explicit formulation of these questions, even if at this point they still remain in their "reductionist generality",[8] is legitimate from the point of view of both academic life and the life of the researcher and, moreover, it is politically crucial. Such questions seek to situate the research and open a line of flight from the universalized space. They are exposed to the accusation of "being utilitarian". Thanks to STS, this accusation is today epistemologically untenable given the collapse of the fantasy of a science that would be universal and neutral.[9] To defend against the accusation of be-

---

[8] "Reductionist generality" refers to the fact that Latin America or Brazil are too big or complex to be local if one takes a more rigorous theoretical STS stand. I will come back to this point.

[9] Greater analytical symmetry allows us to counter the accusation of "being utilitarian". STS provide the tools to show that "pure", that is, non utilitarian, scientific research is not pure; it is in fact utilitarian for Europeans. It is as if all scientific activity is somehow utilitarian for specific interests and so there

ing utilitarian, it is important to emphasize that the utilitarianism of western science is surreptitiously present in scientific activity of those who appear as "winners", that is, of the Europeans:

> "After the 16th century, the western expansion was not only economic and religious, but also the expansion of hegemonic forms of knowledge that have shaped the very conception of economics and religion. In other words, it was the expansion of a representational concept of knowledge and cognition (Rorty 1982) that has imposed itself as epistemic, political and ethical hegemony." (Mignolo 2003/2000:48)

In other words, the questions that situate and resonate the research activities *in the particular of the winners, which is presented to us as universal,* are already subtly embedded in the entities of knowledge that come to us. They are already present in proto-negotiations or in the ontological policies that configure the universal quality of modern science. So the question "What is the contribution of the STS for the West?" does not need to be made. Western Science is born already sequestrated by the interests of Western Europe, one might say. Up to the 1970s and 1980s, when the ethnographic laboratory studies showed the sciences as they are made, modern epistemologies had succeeded in granting "universality" to the scientific western particulars, freeing them from the accusation of "utilitarianism" guided by demands from Western Europe.

Alternatively, the explicit formulation of questions that resonate with "what is the contribution of STS for Latin America?" reverberate around as "utilitarianism" in the ears of those who are trapped in the edifice of modern knowledge as a universal, natural entity, the shade of which assists the bubble of pseudo-winners, final destination of the "inside brain drain". The deconstruction of the naturalized universality of science and technologies of European civilization is crucial so that STS may fulfill a political role, that of participating in a decolonization process. This does not mean to discard knowledges of western science in a space of worthlessness. That, in addition to everything else, would be impossible today.

---

no sense in the accusation of utilitarianism. Neutrality or purity are gone, or better said, they were never present (though some people believed and still believe in such fantasies as advancing knowledge of/for humankind).

However, it does mean enacting the question "what can STS do with and for the networks in which you chose to live?" [10]

How can one escape from hegemonic universalism that is, in fact, particular western knowledges in power? How do we escape from a hegemony that even STS, in its "banking" forms, reinforce?[11] We can see that several Europeans have indicated lines of flight that initiate around the so- called Actor-Net Theory (ANT). This wave led Europeans to give back to the particulars, including the particulars outside Europe, the respectability that the universality admired by Max Weber had withdrawn from the particulars. This is a good thing and helps us. Nevertheless, we can also juxtapose another potential of respectability. Paulo Freire would say that Brazilian STS would be those forged with Brazilians and not for Brazilians (by Europeans). Paulo Freire would say that the malaise to which Roberto Schwarz refers installs itself into Brazilian scholars when they host universality, making themselves "inauthentic, dual beings". With my apologies for the lack of license to adapt, Paulo Freire would say that the "great problem is how can Brazilian scholars who "host" universalism participate, as inauthentic, dual beings, in the elaboration of STS with and not for Brazilians." (Freire 1978:32)

In their trade with the "moderns", Latin Americans, and especially Latin American scholars, import not only themes and solutions but also the problems and the research questions. It is precisely at this point that, in fact, the bubble of pseudo-winners becomes the final destination of the "internal brain drain" of Latin American scholars in their search of palliatives for their "malaises".

> By this expression ("inside brain drain") I mean a cognitive position taken by the scientists of the Third World and Latin America who without emigrating from their country—a sense that is commonly associated to the expression "brain drain"—direct their scientific work in terms of research fronts, reward and publishing systems of the developed countries. The "internal brain drain" is the result of the exogenous orientation of local scientific work, by a voluntary and professional subordination to issues and research programs defined and rewarded in scientific centers in the developed countries. (Polanco 1985:46)

---

[10] The question is now free from a "reductionist generality".
[11] Paulo Freire uses the word "banking" ("bancária" in Portuguese—activities that are bank-like activities) in his texts about education. It means a kind of teaching that supposes that the student is like a bank account where the teacher makes deposits of knowledge.

Nevertheless, since in the title I have "an anthropophagic response and some examples", how to respond to the question "what can STS do with and for the networks in which you chose to live?" It should be clear that any answer to this question must be a situated answer. So far, I have brought in "internal brain drain" and "bubbles of pseudo-winners" as elements that Paulo Freire would call "generators" in the construction of a response. [12] By undressing sciences and technologies of their western endowments of universality and neutrality, and by showing scientific facts and truths as temporarily stabilized juxtapositions of heterogeneous elements, STS opened up new ontological spaces and new possibilities of legitimations of knowledge.[13] STS showed that other bodies of knowledge, in addition to the entities backed by European sciences, deserve not only to exist or to resist, but also to acquire respectability. STS are a tool that can become powerful in constructions of new respectable stories, new ontologies and new worlds. Although the respectability of stories does not determine the resolution of the conflicts, STS can put knowledges that western sciences do not endorse in a new situation, with "stories sufficiently respectable to go to trial with", and if this may not be all what local knowledges need, it is certainly a novelty. Behold then the opportunity for responses. By deconstructing frontiers, STS can take the initial step, without guarantees of success, to grant ontological respectability to knowledges and practices that are situated, located, particular, and popular compared to western hegemonic epistemologies that go from mathematics and physics to philosophy and forensic sciences. Starting from here, the anthropophagic character of the responses that I seek to offer in the remainder of this text, somewhat paradoxically, first turns to the European Enlightenment. In terms of an anthropophagic metaphor, *the suggestion is to eat the European in an imitation, but a regenerative imitation.*

---

[12] Here comes Paulo Freire again. He says a word is a "generator" when it is meaningful in the life of a student. He claims that that kind of word is a good start, such as shovel or plow for poor peasant. I believe that "internal brain drain" and "bubbles of pseudo-winners" may be "generators" for Brazilian academics.

[13] For a detailed understanding of scientific facts and truths as temporarily stabilized juxtapositions of heterogeneous elements, see Latour, B. (1987). Science in action : how to follow scientists and engineers through society. Cambridge, Mass., Harvard University Press..

Anthropophagy as a response

Let us see how one can provisionally juxtapose three heterogeneous elements—STS, European Enlightenment, and Anthropophagy—as a triple encounter to fulfill the promise of the title.

In 1784, Kant begins his famous essay "An answer to the Question: 'what is Enlightenment?'" with the following paragraph:

> *Enlightenment is man's emergence from his self-incurred immaturity. Immaturity* is the inability to use one's own understanding without the guidance of another. This immaturity is *self-incurred* if its cause is not lack of understanding, but lack of resolution and courage to use it without the guidance of another. The motto of enlightenment is therefore: *Sapere Aude!* Have courage to use your *own* understanding! (Kant and Reiss 1991:54)[14]

Walter Mignolo situates the Enlightenment in a Latin American history by claiming that

> [t]he Enlightenment comes second in my own experience of colonial histories. The second phase of modernity, the Enlightenment and the Industrial Revolution, was derivative in the history of Latin America and entered in the nineteenth century as the exteriority that needed to be incorporated in order to build the "republic" after independence from Spain and Portugal had been gained. (Mignolo 2003/2000:43) (Mignolo 2000:19)

I do not intend to explore Walter Mignolo's rich study that configures "modernity-coloniality" as a unit in the history of Latin America. What I have in mind is to be provocative claiming that STS, although of European origin, by pointing out ways to make anthropophagy legitimate, encourage Latin Americans to feed on European Enlightenment to become more symmetrical and emancipatory in their encounters with modernity. The incitement is to say that Latin American scholars should "dare to know". *Sapere Aude!* If the minority, which Kant referred to, was a minority in relation to the religious authority, the Latin American minority that I suggest here is in relation to Western sciences and technologies. I suggest that the triple encounter—STS, European Enlightenment and Brazilian anthropophagy—may be fruitful for Brazilians and Latin Americans. Of course, the audaciousness of the Enlightenment is inseparably cognitive and political, and it may inspire an anthro-

---

[14] Obviously, I am not attempting to assess the Enlightenment as a historical process, but rather just making use of its most known moto.

pophagical encounter of Latin Americans with western sciences and technologies. This happens if the boldness of Latin Americans prevails when and if they are determined to go after currents of local, situated Latin American experiences. That is, when Latin Americans direct their own understanding and their own wanderings, making their own choices within the edifice of knowledge of European modernity or even outside it. Latin Americans will then be empowered to compensate for the asymmetries enacted by European entities of knowledge, even if they are consecrated entities, devoted to the powerful in the Western world. In this way, the boldness of the European Enlightenment, adapted and transformed in the light of new knowledges of fact, truth, reason, theory and method brought by STS, opens to Latin Americans the possibility of a practice associated with the most eloquent decolonizing metaphor, Anthropophagy.[15]

Roberto Schwarz notes that the anthropophagic program launched in the 1920s in Brazil sought to give a triumphalist interpretation of the distance between Brazil and modernity, with the disharmony between the bourgeois models and the realities of rural patriarchate in Brazil's own heart. The novelty of the anthropophagic program was to consider this distance as a source, not of anxiety but of optimism, evidence of the innocence of the country and the possibility of an alternative, not bourgeois, historic development. Even more relevant for the purposes of this essay is that this *sui generis* cult of progress was accompanied by a technological bet: the innocence of Brazil (the result of a very thin varnish of bourgeoisification and Christianization) plus technology equal to utopia; the modern material progress would make possible a direct jump from a pre-bourgeois society to paradise.[16]

---

[15] Although Anthropophagy is quite famous in Brazil as a cultural movement, there are scarce references to it in English. For a quick general reference to Anthropophagy in English, see, for example, Jauregui, Carlos, A. "Antropofagia." Dictionary of Latin American Cultural Studies. Edited by Robert McKee Irwin and Mónica Szurmuk (eds.). Gainesville: The University Press of Florida (2012): 22–28, or yet, Yara Guasque, "Circularity and anthropophagic consumption as a metaphor. the body as currency?" on http://www.aprja.net/?p=833

[16] Schwarz, R. (1987). Nacional por subtração. Que horas são? : ensaios. São Paulo, Companhia das Letras: 29–48. reminds, "Marx himself in his famous letter to Vera Sassulitch (1881) ventured around a similar hypothesis according to which the Russian peasant commune would reach socialism without

Schwarz argues that the anthropophagic program presented a change in tone. The local primitivism would return a modern sense to the tired European culture, releasing it from the Christian mortification and capitalist utilitarianism. The Brazilian experience would become a landmark on the map of contemporary history. The Brazilian modernism thus brought about a profound change of values: for the first time it was said that the processes in Brazil had something to offer to the modern world. Oswald de Andrade defended cultural irreverence instead of obfuscation, using the metaphor of "swallowing" the stranger: a copy, certainly, but of regenerative effect. Schwarz notes,

> the historical distance allows one to see that the programmatic innocence of the *Antropófagos*, enabling them to bypass the malaise, does not prevent them from emerging renewed. ... "Tupi or not Tupi, that is the question!"—the famous formula of Oswald, with its contradictory use of English looking for a national identity, a classic citation and a pun, alone says a lot about the nature of the impasse" (Schwarz 1987:39)

"Programmatic Innocence"? Perhaps. Nevertheless, the questions posed by an autonomous approximation to modernity, and particularly the study of options for the construction of scientific and technological (reliable) knowledge, are precisely the ones that face opposition that is more consistent from Western colonizers. Few things tend to cause more opposition than "to denaturalize" the scientific and technological progress. Albert Hirschman observed that

> United Nations experts, authors of the report on the trade in goods, rather innovative in other instances, wrote: "We are strongly opposed to a retardation of technological progress to relieve the pain of adjustment that progress inevitably meets." And continued to encourage an attitude "daddy knows best" if the industrialized countries would encourage the production of substitutes through subsidies: "The industrial countries do not have the habit of moving in this direction unless there are reasons to much weight" (Hirschman 1971:167)

Among the moderns, in contemporary European civilization, there is an even more detestable prospectus than what they call "interfere in market prices": *interfere with the enshrined neutrality of*

---

the capitalist interregnum, thanks to the resources that the progress of the West made available to them. In the same sense, though intermingling jokes, provocation, philosophy of history e prescience (as one can find later in Glauber Rocha), Anthropophagy sought to jump over a stage."

the technical progress! They even do not hesitate to abandon their announced standards and established spaces if they consider necessary to do this, utilizing strength to sustain scientific reason. In one of his more pungent paragraphs, Bruno Latour emphasizes,

> Native Americans were not mistaken when they accused the Whites of having forked tongues. By separating the relations of political power from the relations of scientific reasoning while continuing to shore up power with reason and reason with power, the moderns have always had two irons in the fire. They have become invincible. (Latour 1993:38) (Latour 1991/1994:43)

In the 1920s, the group that launched the *Manifesto Antropofágico* did not have the ontological and epistemological tools to make the criticism of universality and neutrality, and consequently to find, locate, criticize, qualify and select the European sciences and technologies. Therefore, the "programmatic innocence" pointed out by Roberto Schwarz therefore is not surprising. Today Latin Americans can rely on STS to give respectability to their "daring to know", experiencing with anthropophagic practices and techniques. I conclude by indicating three examples of anthropophagy.

Labordireitórios: reverse engineering and respectful enough stories to go to trial with[17]

The concept of intellectual property is strongly linked to epistemological assumptions that are considered universal, especially the existence of: 1) stable natural borders in space, and 2) instants of discovery in time. The idea of natural stable borders makes it possible to conceive the existence of subjects and objects or things that are "pure", that is, completely defined and not problematic. The concept of discovery allows for highlighting a relative instant in time as the moment of recognition or creation of an entity (a thing, a stable form, a provisional juxtaposition of heterogeneous elements). The epistemological assumptions of stable borders and discovery intertwine with the "rule of origin." The rule of origin is equivalent to give precedence, priority, predominance, preference, privilege, right of way, and supremacy to the original over the copy, to the model over the imitated. Moreover, the rule of origin legiti-

---

[17] (Marques 2003) (Marques 2004) (Marques 2005) (Marques 2008) (Marques 2012)

mates the granting of intellectual property rights to those who "first" recognize or invent something. Through the intellectual property rights, the rule of origin is more or less surreptitiously evoked and translated to ensure the predominance of the center over the periphery, of Europe over Latin America, of the first over the third world or of the "colonizer" over the "colonized". Let us see an incarnated case.

In 1985, Unitron, a company based in São Paulo, Brazil, designed a "clone" of the Apple Macintosh 512 computer. Unitron installed the first version of the product in a hundred users. The machine won the nickname "Mac of the periphery". However, this fact was unacceptable for Apple and for the American government, which in retaliation threatened to impose trade barriers to exports of Brazilian companies to the United States. Under strong political pressure on the part of the United States, Brazil passed a new specific law to regulate the software industry in Brazil. Unitron's sales of the "Mac of the periphery" became conditional upon the provision of more information and, possibly, further developments.

What may come as a surprise is that Unitron reassessed the situation and decided to study/clone the Mac 1024, Apple's next model. Unitron attached a law office extending its laboratory. A new round of contacts, negotiations and contracts with governmental institutions, universities and an American company allowed Unitron to show confident in a court of appeals, claiming that its model 1024 could "legitimately be adopted in Brazil or in any other country, because it was the result of an invaluable work of reverse engineering of the original American machine." Unitron had made its "history sufficiently *respectable* to go to trial with it, and that was all that was needed", if we borrow Geoffrey Bowker's words of in his valuable study of the patents of Schlumberger.(Bowker 1994:124) In Unitron's case, that "all that was needed" was not enough for a victory. In December 1988, the court decided against Unitron in a vote of eight to seven. Unitron closed. Notwithstanding, Unitron had understood that it could not face or take a market share from Apple fighting only with engineers. Engineers alone were not enough to configure a computer. Unitron needed to juxtapose more heterogeneous elements to make its artefact a more robust artefact. Unitron needed lawyers as well, and lawyers had to work together with engineers to construct a respectful enough story to go to trial with.[18]

Market reserve and consequential research[19]

In its brief existence during the decades of 1970 and 1980 in Brazil, the National Policy for Information Technology—*Política Nacional de Informática*—was a sui generis experience. The development of a Brazilian industry of minicomputers in the decade around 1980 was not the result of a gradual or revolutionary ascension of the Brazilian industrial bourgeoisie. It was more the result of a cognitive rupture in a community of professionals who dealt with computers. From 1974 to 1980, this community of professionals, in their meetings called "SECOMU" and through a journal called "Dados&déias", collectively searched for and established new frameworks to situate and locate both their professional activities and the community itself, self-denominated a "community of informatics". Starting in 1977, that community achieved the political mobilization that was necessary to demarcate a pragmatic shortcut: to reserve a part of the computer market for products that would result from skilled work of Brazilian engineers, that is, products designed in Brazil.

The American sociologist Peter Evans portrayed the individuals of the "community of informatics" as "frustrated nationalist *técnicos*", for having traveled abroad to have a technical education that made them capable of carrying on computer design activities and returned to a country where the local industry did not design:

---

[18] Elsewhere I call this arrangement a "labordireitório", which would correspond to something like "laboratory-courtroom", expressing the idea that technological products come from labs and courtrooms simultaneously.
[19] (Marques 2000) (Marques 2002) (Marques 2002) (Marques 2003) (Marques 2005)

Their American educations and familiarity with the "Silicon Valley" gave them a sense of participation in an international process of development and a sense of frustration with their local environment. Brazil's computer industry as it was structured at the beginning of the 1970s denied them the jobs they had been educated to do. In Brazil they could become salespeople for IBM or they could process data for the federal government. If they wanted to engage in technological entrepreneurship—designing products, producing them, and then seeing whether the market validated their ideas—they would have to forsake Brazil and return to the Silicon Valley. Unless, of course, they could do something to transform Brazil's informatics industry.(Evans 1995:107)

In fact, Evans has assigned a "malaise" to these individuals. The "frustrated nationalist *técnicos*" have striven to find a way to change the position Brazilians occupied in the international division of labor. Somewhat surprisingly, they succeeded until the microcomputer wiped out the minicomputer market and completely changed the structure of the industry worldwide.

Multimixture:
truths of science and truths of beliefs[20]

The case of multimixture also points out more symmetrical and dialogical possibilities for relations between modern scientific knowledges and other knowledges. The multimixture is a food supplement used to feed hundreds of thousands of poor children in Brazil. In the 1970s, pediatrician Clara Brandão resorted to locally available ingredients to deal with poor children in a situation of extreme food shortage—ingredients of very low value, not consumed and discarded in other situations, such as the shell of the pumpkin, the straw rice and dark leaves. By mixing and crushing such kind of ingredients, she prepared a powder that she added to what else she could find to feed the children. She found that the children soon stopped to show the acute symptoms of hunger. Starting from there, Clara Brandão became an activist in the dissemination of multimixture—as the food supplement came to be known. By the end of the 1980s, multimixture reached the scale of millions of children, after its adoption by the Pastoral of the Children (linked to the CNBB—the National Confederation of the Bishops of Brazil) and a favorable report made by UNESCO. By the beginning of the 1990s, Clara Brandão had moved to Brasilia and

---

20 (Marques 2009) (Marques 2012) (Marques 2012) (Marques 2012)

Chapter 7: What can Science and Technology Studies do? 139

started to work on the possibility of multimixture be adopted in a nationwide school meals government program. However, it was also on this occasion that nutritionists—scientists established in Brazilian universities—have put samples of multimixture in their laboratory equipments to analyze its nutritional components, concluding that multimixture does not contain nutrients in quality and quantity to cause the effects reported and touted by Clara Brandão. There being no significant controversy among nutritionists over these laboratory results, "multimixture does not feed" went on to be a scientific fact. The Federal Council of Nutrition published a pamphlet attacking multimixture, enacting a world radically divided into fact X fiction, knowledge X ignorance, truth X fraud. From then on, the expansion of the use of the multimixture encountered difficulties. The receptivity of the Brazilian Government faded away and even the CNBB officially ceased supporting the multimixture, although the Bank of Brazil Foundation continues supporting the multimixture program to this day.

The activists, mothers, parents, relatives, friends of the children and other volunteers enact a world different from the world that results from a scientific ontology. Without the schooling that would enable them to open up a space to engage in theoretical discussions, these people keep the possibility of dialog with the scientific world. They live as if they knew that any scientific fact has a finite set of elements (in this case, inscriptions obtained in instruments) as its support and the life world happens in an infinite range of possibilities. For practical purposes, these people perceive that the "reality test" of modern science does not test reality but preconceived notions of reality. (Vitebsky 1993)

Final Comments

In each of the above examples, STS, enlightened, and anthropophagic elements are juxtaposed to enact a more symmetrical, dialogical and, why not say, inclusive world, by constructing "respectful enough" stories. In the three examples, in local and situated ways, the enlightened motto "daring to know" meets the anthropophagic motto "eat the stranger" around modern (western) scientific and technological issues.

The anthropophagic character of UNITRON is its strategy that would either 1) be victorious or 2) force the "enemy" (owners of the dominant technologies through patents) to show to external actors that the decision violated law and "justice".

The anthropophagic character of the "frustrated nationalist *técnicos*" is translating and situating the concept of what is a legitimate object of research. If Brazilian engineers did not master the knowledge to manufacture a computer, then computer design and manufacturing would be a legitimate object of research, even if one could buy a computer in the market. It involves to treat objects of Western sciences as "natural objects". If it is legitimate to research a mango to establish its aminoacids and vitamins, then it is legitimate to research a computer (or a cell phone) to establish its components.

The anthropophagic character present in the multimixture case is not taking for granted the applications of scientific truths. Multimixture enacts the knowledge that a scientific truth is a convention based on inscriptions. A scientific truth may have effects, and certainly it has effects, but the space and time where it is valid and serves as a good guide, are confined and a result of a convention upon a restricted set of elements (inscriptions). So there may be situations where and when, although a claim continues to be a scientific truth (because it has not been contested among scientists) it may not be a truth in a specific situation in the life-world.

STS of the last decades has adequate epistemological tools to build a common ontology for both sides in each of the three examples above. They can do well with and for the networks one chooses to live in.

References

Bowker, G. C. (1994). *Science on the run : information management and industrial geophysics at Schlumberger, 1920–1940*. Cambridge, Mass.: MIT Press.

Chatterjee, P. (1986). *Nationalist thought and the colonial world : a derivative discourse?* London, U.K.

Chatterjee, P. (1986). *Nationalist thought and the colonial world. A Derivative Discourse*. Minneapolis: University of Minnesota Press.

Dias, M. O. L. d. S. (2005). *A interiorização da metrópole e outros ensaios*. São Paulo: Alameda.

Evans, P. B. (1995). *Embedded autonomy : states and industrial transformation*. Princeton, N.J.: Princeton University Press.

Freire, P. (1978). *Pedagogia do Oprimido*. Rio de Janeiro: Paz e Terra.

Hirschman, A. O. (1971). *A bias for hope : essays on development and Latin America*. New Haven: Yale University Press.

Kant, I. and H. S. Reiss (1991). *Kant : political writings*. Cambridge [England] ; New York: Cambridge University Press.

Latour, B. (1987). *Science in action : how to follow scientists and engineers through society*. Cambridge, Mass.: Harvard University Press.

Latour, B. (1991/1994). *Jamais fomos modermos—ensaio de antropologia simétrica*. Rio de Janeiro: Editora 34.

Latour, B. (1993). *We have never been modern*. Cambridge, Mass.: Harvard University Press.

Marques, I. d. C. (2000). Reserva de mercado: um mal entendido caso político-tecnológico de "sucesso" democrático e "fracasso" autoritário. *Revista de Economia da Universidade Federal do Paraná*, 24(26), 91–116.

Marques, I. d. C. (2002). Liberalismo Democrático e Políticas Tecnológicas. Panorama dos Estudos sobre Ciência, Tecnologia e Sociedade na América Latina. In R. Dagnino and H. Thomas (eds.) Taubaté, SP, Brasil, Cabral Editora e Livraria Universitária. pp. 103–122.

Marques, I. d. C. (2002). A New Look at an Old Devil: The Computer Market Reserve in Brazil. In G. Széll and G. P. Cella (eds.) *The Injustice at Work—An International View on the World of Labour and Society*. Frankfurt am Main: Peter Lang. pp. 486–505.

Marques, I. d. C. (2003). Minicomputadores brasileiros nos anos 1970: uma reserva de mercado democrática em meio ao autoritarismo. *História Ciências Saúde MANGUINHOS*, 10(2):, 657–681.

Marques, I. d. C. (2003). Reverse Engineering and Other Respectful Enough Accounts: Creating New Spaces of Possibility for Technological Innovation under Conditions of Global Inequality. Aarhus, Denmark: The Centre for STS Studies, Department of Information & Media Studies, Aarhus University.

Marques, I. d. C. (2004). Uma História Suficientemente Respeitável sobre Novos Espaços de Possibilidade para a Inovação Tecnológica na América Latina. *Convergencia—Revista de Ciencias Sociales*, 11(35), 51–78.

Marques, I. d. C. (2005). Cloning Computers: From Rights of Possession to Rights of Creation. *Science as Culture*, 14(2), 139–160.

Marques, I. d. C. (2005). Novos espaços de possibilidade para a inovação tecnológica em condições de desigualdade global. Brasil em desenvolvimento 2—Instituições, políticas e sociedade. A. C. Castro, A. Licha, H. Q. P. Jr. and J. Saboia. Rio de Janeiro, Editora Civilização Brasileira. 2, 145–176.

Marques, I. d. C. (2008). O caso da Unitron e condições de inovação tecnológica no Brasil. Empresas, empresários e desenvolvimento econômico no Brasil. A. D. Costa, A. S. Fernandes and T. Szmrecsányi. São Paulo, Editora Hucitec: 156–177.

Marques, I. d. C. (2009). O conhecimento científico como arma política: o caso da Multimistura (1970–2007). Livro de Anais—SCIENTIARUM HISTORIA II— Encontro Luso-Brasileiro de História da Ciência Rio de Janeiro, HCTE/UFRJ.

Marques, I. d. C. (2012). Labordireitórios. Tecnología, Desarrollo y Democracia: nueve estudios sobre dinámicas socio-técnicas de exclusión/inclusión social. H. Thomas, M. Fressoli and G. Santos. Buenos Aires: Ministerio de Ciencia, Tecnología e Innovación Productiva de la Nación. pp. 251–268.

Marques, I. d. C. (2012). Possibilidades de práticas ontológicas situadas. Ciência, Tecnologia e Sociedade noBrasil M. T. M. Kerbauy, T. H. N. d. Andrade and C. R. M. Hayashi. Campinas, SP, Editora Alínea. pp. 67–86.

Marques, I. d. C. (2012). Test de Réalité et limites du relativisme—le cas de programme alimentaire multimixture. *S.A.C. Revue d'anthropologies des connaissances*, 6(2), 165–189.

Marques, I. d. C. (2012). "Teste de realidade" e limites do relativismo: o caso do programa alimentar Multimistura. *REDES—Revista de estudios sociales de la ciencia*, 18(34), 143–170.

Mignolo, W. (2000). *Local histories/global designs : coloniality, subaltern knowledges, and border thinking*. Princeton, N.J.: Princeton University Press.

Mignolo, W. D. (2003/2000). *Histórias locais/Projetos globais: colonialidade, saberes subalternos e pensamento liminar*. Belo Horizonte: MG, Editora UFMG.

Polanco, X. (1985). La ciencia como ficción. Historia y contexto. *Cuadernos de Quipu*, 1(1), 41–56.

Rorty, R. (1982). *Consequences of pragmatism : essays, 1972–1980*. Minneapolis: University of Minnesota Press.

Schwarz, R. (1987). Nacional por subtração. Que horas são? : ensaios. São Paulo. *Companhia das Letras*, 29–48.

Vitebsky, P. (1993). Is death the same everywhere? contexts of knowing and doubting. In M. Hobart *An Anthropological Critique of Development*. London: Routledge. pp. 100–115.

Weber, M. (1987/1904). *A ética protestante e o espírito do capitalismo*. São Paulo, SP: Livraria Pioneira Editora.

Chapter 8:
Decolonising social sciences in remote Australia

Michael Christie

Introduction

"What would happen were we to deny anthropological discourse any epistemological advantage over the native's discourse? This is the same as asking: what happens when we take native thought seriously? When the anthropologist's aim ceases to be to explain, interpret, contextualise and rationalise his thought and becomes one of using it, drawing out its consequences, and ascertaining the effects it may produce on our own?" Eduardo Viveiros de Castro *'Anthropology and Science'*

Unlike many other Australian Aboriginal people, the Yolŋu[1] of north east Arnhem Land in the Northern Territory continue to speak their many ancestral languages, perform ancestral ceremonies, and observe traditional hunting and other cultural practices. They have of course been the subject of much anthropological and ethnographic interest. This paper is about our work resisting the colonial urge to (in de Castro's terms) 'explain, interpret, contextualise and rationalise' Yolŋu discourse, but to 'use it, draw out its consequences, and ascertain the effects it may produce on our own way of thinking'. I use de Castro's three impulses to structure an argument about Yolŋu contributions to the decolonisation of the globalising humanities and social sciences. Beginning with some discussion about how we have been brought to engage it, I try to draw out some consequences of its use in particular contexts, before concluding with some comment on its effects.

---

[1] About 5000 Yolŋu have their ancestral lands along the north east coast and bushlands and islands of the Northern Territory, Australia in the Aboriginal reserve of Arnhem Land.

Coming to Use a 'native discourse'

Learning fluency in Yolŋu languages, and learning how to produce and verify knowledge claims and come to agreement under Yolŋu authority, have been for me long and often difficult processes. Or better put, teaching me speak their languages and to participate properly in their social and political life has been slow and often thankless task for my Yolŋu family,[2] teachers, and elders. This induction into an alternative social science has come about not so much in my slow recognition of the validity of the 'native's discourse', but rather through the recognition of the poverty and impotence of 'globalising' social sciences in the arenas of our work. The problems with which we wrestle (in common with the Aboriginal peoples of all colonised nations) are simply intractable to the enlightenment's progressivist and monologic practices.

I had already been speaking Yolŋu languages for over ten years when the lessons I was learning became public and institutionalised in a remote school curriculum. It was the mid 1980s, and as activist non Aboriginal teachers in an Aboriginal school we were all familiar with the works of radical theorists like Freire (1972) and Illich (1973) which we believed should provide the inspiration and the praxis for our part in the liberation of the oppressed. But the Aboriginal elders who had assumed license to rewrite the school philosophy had no such emancipatory objectives. They saw their task as to institute a distinctively Yolŋu epistemology to engage in good faith a schooling system almost entirely focused upon western knowledge and its goals and practices: English literacy and numeracy, and an orientation towards a progressive future and liberation from a benighted past. The curriculum philosophy the elders introduced was named for a ceremonial site—there are thousands of such sites all through Australia –where people from different (but related) clan groups, different (but related) places, different (but related) ancestral 'dreamings' assemble to sing, dance, celebrate, tell stories, solve problems, and make agreement.

This ceremonial site, in Yolŋu languages called a *garma*, provides a metaphor for a knowledge practice which is situated, performative and negotiated. Its truth criteria are to do with its *right-*

---

[2] Newcomers to Aboriginal communities are generally 'adopted' into the kinship network of the community as a way of inducting and engaging them in appropriate social, political and cultural practices.

ness for the here and now, rather than any representational criteria which sets up an opposition between a truth claim in language, and a reality out there in the natural world. In fact, it is a practice in which, eschewing western dualisms, there is no a priori distinction between nature and culture, language and reality, or in fact Aboriginal and other. In this discourse, the categories through which we understand the world are provisional and must be continually, carefully negotiated as new possible worlds are explored and made as we work together. And we ourselves, as teachers, students, elders, researchers and the knowable world itself are made and remade through this collective action. Each contributes to the negotiation their own history, their own ways of performing, their specialised knowledge and personal convictions. The result is a collective agreement upon who and where we are, right now, and a way of going forward together in good faith.

The *garma* curriculum revolutionised the knowledge work of our small ex-mission school in Arnhem Land. When we came to study mathematics for example, we were led to investigate the ways that numbers work (as a recursive naming system) to place order and value in the things of the modern world. And at the same time we were to investigate how the Yolŋu kinship system (also a recursive naming system) places order and value on the people and things in the Yolŋu world. Instead of seeing the western and Yolŋu worlds as incommensurable, our *garma* curriculum allowed us to see numbers (and kin) in their materiality as they take their place doing order and value in everyday Yolŋu life, and bring with them a moral as well as a technical dimension. It is this process of collectively producing a moral world which came to inform our transdisciplinary academic research (Christie 2006).

Knowledge around everything that is of relevance to Yolŋu children and their futures is amenable to a garma curriculum. For example, land. The everyday experience of remote Aboriginal Australians means they live on a landscape which is inscribed by both ancestral dreaming journeys, and by cadastral practices of the Australian government. It is imperative in an ethical educational practice, for both Aboriginal and anglo-Australian understandings of land to be understood—and produced—alongside each other, coming to agreement while preserving and respecting difference. Or in another example, western understandings of the biomedical body need to be examined and produced in conjunction with Aboriginal understandings of health, sickness, life and death if true informed consent can be attained before medical interventions (see for example Christie and Verran 2014).

Note that the *garma* does not imply a relativist epistemology. There is no presumption that the Aboriginal and the western knowledge traditions are of equal validity (In fact, as already noted, there is no *a priori* presumption of an ontological separation between Aborigines and westerners in this knowledge practice). It is through working the two systems together in good faith that we can agree on how and where each may contribute. Further, this deeply materialist anti-relativist epistemology works precisely because it focuses specifically upon the issues and problems of the moment rather than on building any general theory.[3] The 'problems' may be happy ones like 'How do we celebrate this occasion together?'—but they all have in common the principles that we need to work together on this issue if we are to do the honourable thing by who and where we are and to the people and the things for which we share care and concern. We need, in fact to avoid grand theory if we are to work honestly and collectively going on together in this way.

The *garma* in fact recapitulates the work of the ancestors who, as they travelled the land at the beginning of time, made all the knowable features of the world—hills, clouds, waterways, people, animals and plants, sacred objects etc. through their singing and performing ceremonies, sleeping and crying, talking and dancing. These same creative practices are at work in the everyday *garma* as well as in a properly negotiated episode of knowledge production. There is of course, no room here for the conduit metaphor through which we in the west understand the communication of knowledge from teacher to student as if, unchanged, along a conduit. Such a primitive theory of communication at work in mission schools everywhere (and in fact almost universal in formal education), has the ultimate effect of preserving the unequal power relation between the coloniser and colonised who is always somehow behind trying to catch up. The conduit metaphor has the effect of dehumanising the participants. It assumes that messages have a definitive meaning which can be passed and decoded so long as the encoder and

---

[3] We see a connection here with the pragmatist philosophers John Dewey and Kathryn Pyne Addelson.

decoder share the same logic (Reddy, 1979). The *garma* honours the essential differences between participants—even as the knowledge work may change the participants, remaking them and their worlds in particular ways.

'Drawing out the consequences'

Yolŋu social science is never directed towards the development of a general theory. In fact it is directed against general theory and towards collective action around the problems of the moment. The anti-essentialist metaphysics refuses *a priori* distinctions, but hopes to do the work of making and understanding samenesses and differences collectively. In her discussion of 'Southern Theory', Connell (2007, p200) points out that 'The (Yolŋu) stories about the spirit beings' journeys do not just reflect, they *constitute*, social relations and the groups that practice them. .. The land is *part* of the social order. It is not just infrastructure and is not something that a Levi-Strauss can legitimately abstract away from' (italics in original).

An example: the engagement between academic and Aboriginal (including Yolŋu) knowledge practices looking at the complex problem of housing in remote communities. As part of what could be described as a government policy of Aboriginal 'normalization' (Sullivan, 2011), local community housing associations were disbanded, and Aboriginal housing and its tenants placed under the same regimes as non-Indigenous public housing in urban centres. The role of land owners and elders in decision making about housing disappeared virtually overnight. Our small transdisciplinary research team was invited to evaluate the government negotiations around housing in several Aboriginal communities. The Aboriginal people we talked to all began with stories of the past—of how they came to be where they are, and their connections to land and kin. Those (in very remote places) still able to trace the ceremonial connections of their land to the creation, told of how they continue to name their homes after ancestral resting places. They talked about homes and housing not as passive accommodators of Aboriginal life, but as active participants in contemporary governance. If people make good houses and housing configurations, then houses make good people. Health, education, politics and environmental management are all somehow implicated with housing and with each other. For governments to deal with housing without consulting the whole of community and the whole of government, is to do a violence to holistic ancestral ways of living and making agreement. To this end, Aboriginal participants valued and foregrounded the work of the street-level bureaucrats who had the difficult work of flying or driving to very remote communities and working with Aboriginal people on the difficult issues of overcrowding and the allocation of housing which was now the responsibility of government rather than of community organisations. The Aboriginal theorists identified these people mostly as champions for their cause, flexibly implementing the government rules for reference groups, allowing traditional styles of negotiation and authority to be brought to bear, in ways often invisible, ignored or discounted from above.

The effects on our own engagements

So what were the effects? First of all, there were some positive and surprising changes to government policy and practice, which are to be reported elsewhere (Christie, forthcoming). But in terms of our reflections on our own social science methods, while learning how to represent the needs of Aboriginal housing to government, we were being taught how to engage an Australian Aboriginal metaphysics in which, to borrow Rose's (2004) analysis, we were forced to un-think our assumptions of both time and monologue. The governments[4] were ushering in a new regime where housing would be organised with an eye to a rational enlightened future with particular technocratic introductions (such as removing the authority of the traditional land owners from decisions as to who should be allowed to live where, and the prioritization of bureaucratic decision makers from the department of health and employment). Induced to forget about their miserable past and to look towards a bright redemptive future, the Aboriginal elders however refused this dislocation heard originally through the missionary gospel, but still persisting aggressively alive in the secular vision of progress in the colonizing world. The Aboriginal focus on origins, on ancestral realities, on remembering history, and on the moral agency of the material world of care and concern for the land *as* social order,

---

[4] Australian Federal, Northern Territory, and local shire governments.

grounded them in a time and place which demanded ongoing careful dialogue.

The absence of a meta-narrative of progress, enlightenment and salvation demands attention to an open, morally grounded coeval conversation where the outcomes are not known in advance. Hence the focus on the productive work of the housing officers who *did* listen, who *were* flexible, who bent the rules and went the extra mile. The openness of the housing officers—taking risks and making themselves vulnerable, the very behaviour that could find them in trouble with their bosses—was that which was identified and engaged in the Yolŋu practice. Similarly, our won sometimes fraught involvements refusing the role of judging observer and using our cognitive authority as academic researchers to move towards a certain fragile decolonisation.

Yolŋu cultural authorities are not at all concerned by what could be seen as a western appropriation of their ancestral philosophies, nor with our efforts to find 'redemption in Aboriginal people's culture, as if those we had conquered should now save us' (Rose 2004, p. 2). On the contrary, they take universal participation in their knowledge and agreement production processes to be natural, and in fact essential to anyone of good faith. Coming to this realisation makes the globalizing knowledge practices of the West appear as strange, unconscionable and invasive. We are invited to engage in this ancient 'discourse' together because our Aboriginal teachers know that it is only with the active participation of ourselves in good faith that we can together develop confidence in a just future. We have as researchers, been inducted into the play of coeval dialogue within a world accepted as an active subject, and with all subjects as always situated ethically and physically. We are led to work towards a decolonising politics, and to practical modes of flourishing through ethical engagements, negotiating ways forward, moment by moment. And this requires consistent work against the knowledge practices of the globalising world.

References

Christie, M. (2006). Transdisciplinary Research and Aboriginal Knowledge. *Australian Journal of Indigenous Education*, 35, 78–89.

Christie, M. (2014). Decolonising methodology in an Arnhem Land garden. In B. Neumeier & K. Schaffer (eds.) *Decolonizing the Landscape: Indigenous Cultures in Australia*. Amsterdam: Rodopi pp. 57–70.

Christie, M. and Campbell, M. (2014). Aboriginal contributions to the evaluation of housing (and to postcolonial theory). *Learning Communities: International Journal of Learning in Social Contexts* Special edition: Evaluation (14) Sept 154–65.

Christie, M. and Verran, H. (2014). The Touch Pad Body: A Generative Transcultural Digital Device Interrupting Received Ideas and Practices in Aboriginal Health. *Societies: Special Edition: Beyond Techno-Utopia: Critical Approaches to Digital Health Technologies*, 4, 256–264.

LCJ de Castro Viveiros, E. (2003). (anthropology) AND (science). 5th Decennial Conference of the Association of Social Anthropologists of Great Britain and Commonwealth, http://nansi.abaetenet.net/abaetextos/anthropology-and-science-e-viveiros-de-castro

Freire, P. (1972). *The Pedagogy of the Oppressed*. Harmondsworth, Middlesex: Penguin.

Illich, I. (1973). *Deschooling society*. Harmondsworth: Penguin Education.

Marika-Mununggiritj, Raymattja, Banbapuy Maymuru, Multhara Mununggurr, Badang'thun Munyarryun, Gandalal Ngurruwutthun, Yalmay Yunupingu (1990). The History of the Yirrkala Community School: Yolŋu thinking about education in the Laynha and Yirrkala Area. *Ngoonjook* September, pp. 32–52.

Reddy, M. (1979). The conduit metaphor—A case of frame conflict in our language about language. In A. Ortony (ed.) *Metaphor and Thought*. Cambridge, UK : Cambridge University Press. pp. 284–324.

Rose, D. B. (2004). *Reports from a Wild Country: Ethics for Decolonisation*. Sydney : University of New South Wales Press.

Sullivan P. (2011). The policy goal of normalisation, the national Indigenous reform agreement and Indigenous national partnership agreements. DKCRC Working Paper 76. Alice Springs, NT: Ninti One Limited.

# Chapter 9:
Culturalising Social Knowledges as a Critique of Euro-American Social Sciences:
Learning from Deconstructing Poverty in the Shadow of Gandhian Social Theory

Kumaran Rajagopal

Introduction

The ways in which Euro-American social sciences (henceforth EASSs) grapple with the notion and reality of poverty can be a good window to peep into the the politics of knowledge-making of these EASSs and their hegemonic intentions. It can capture in one sweep the methodological, epistemological and pedagogic one-sidedness and arrogance of the EASSs. The discourses on poverty have helped the EASSs not only to universalise the modern worldview, but also to manufacture a consent for imposing the colonial and neo-colonial domination on the non-Euro-American world. The success of this discourse is so complete that even its victims have been converted into agents, vocally advocating the very idioms and languages by which they are degraded in the first place and through which they imagine their self-images as sick and incomplete persons/nations. The narratives on poverty valorise not just the EASSs but also their entire army of experts, consultants, enterprises and the intrusive institutions such as INGOs, UN, World Bank and IMFs that are located both epistemologically and geographically in the Euro-American world. The seductive power of these discourses on poverty has many converts among the third world leaders and intelligentsia who happened to have been vested with the political mandate to lead their respective nations. Hence, the very construct of what constitutes poverty and poor has filled the very self-definition of the non-Euro-American citizens. Social Sciences in these geographies too have come to share the concerns of the EASSs about poverty so intensely that they have further reified this notion to give it a thick layer of insularity.

Consequently, Social Scientific studies on poverty in all their manifestations have become absolutely immune to the critical inputs from non-Euro-American social knowledges. Intriguingly, non-western knowledge systems are somehow made to become complicit in the indictment that they are essentially inadequate and irrelevant to addressing poverty both epistemologically and programmatically.

Thus, arrogating to themselves the right and privilege to eliminate 'poverty' and pitching their significance only in relation to policy influencing and policy making, the EASSs-inspired poverty studies sacrifice research rigour and critical inquiry for the sake of arriving at spectacularly grand generalizations that are amenable to policy formulations. In the same spirit, they seldom engage in a self-reflexive inquiry into their own ways of constructing the categories that are now taken as 'given', for example 'poverty' as a construct. Since their very existence and relevance rest on postulating a foundational reality called 'poverty', they present it as a well-rounded singular object and as an ever-persisting reality. This applies even to the most self-conscious research works undertaken by third world researchers, who often fail to bring in the insights offered by non-Euro-American Knowledges, worldviews and thoughts.

Only when we rub these entrenched knowledge-making practices and truth claims of EASSs against the touchstone of non-euroamerican knowledges can we bring to light the violence, contradictions and conspiracies of the dominant discourses on poverty. Gandhian Social Theory offers such a possibility. Only when we do so can we realize that poverty studies have never benefited from either a collectivist and moralistic understanding because of its excessive obsession with economism, or from an intense ethnographic research on the poverty experiences of individuals. Even the otherwise sensitive, participatory approaches within Development Studies are short-term engagements with acquiring people's perception on poverty without being foundationally influenced by such non-modern visions as that of Gandhi. The latter not only has a high degree of intellectual value but also political value, since it can unmask the politics of poverty research. The inferences we can make from Gandhian social theory tell us many striking things about what is absent or overly present in poverty studies, Indeed, the problems of poverty studies become more glaring only in the light of the spirit of self-reflexivity (of both the knowledge systems and the knowledge maker) that Gandhian approach as a whole celebrates.

Poverty as Construct

Our understanding of poverty and marginalisation is heavily structured by a divisive logic of modernity. But since this solidified understanding has a strong bearing on policies and practices of governmental and non-governmental organisations, we need to dissect this notion and explore an alternative perspective. Talking about alternative, one can hope to learn a lot from Gandhian understanding of poverty and marginalisation.

Before we embark on the reconceptualization of poverty using the Gandhian framework, it is very important to establish that poverty is not a natural outcome of a society or an individual slipping into a condition of resourcelessness, nor his inherent incapability or failure to manage his affairs properly. Poverty is a social construct in terms of its being a product of an existing structural relationship that favours avaricious accumulation of resources by politically powerful nations or individuals. It is a social construct also because by keeping the quantity of things possessed by a class of people and nations as reference, those who do not posses the same are made to feel that they are poorer. This happens by emptying the notion of poverty of its moral connotations. *Quantity of things* are sneakily equated with the *quality of life*, as if the latter is the necessary outcome of the former. This mode of essentialising poverty as materially embedded, cloaks the very immorality and absolute moral inadequacy of the rich, even as it causes enormous sense of inadequacy in the so called poor. Sadly, the whole world has been converted into unquestioning believers in this construct; hence, debunking this construct requires standing outside the moral universe of those who have a vested interest in expanding the boundaries of that universe. The Gandhian perspective offers that alternative moral universe. This directly offers an intense critique of developmentalism as ideology, into which everyone has become a willing convert. It must be stated in no uncertain terms that developmentalism, is a deeply self-serving ideology propagated by the resource-rich but morally impoverished social minority who vastly benefit out of it.

Once poverty is understood as a 'construct', the deconstruction of it leads to the reinvention of humans as free individuals, who do not define themselves in terms of lack and deficiency. Such is the power of this construct that by successfully amalgamating local conditions of absence of material wealth with the global conception of material wealth as the necessary and sufficient condition of good life, the social majority of humanity has been reduced to the status sub-humans who can recover their full humanity only with external assistance. What is worse, instilling that sense in vast social majority, it has made "seeking assistance" an inevitable trait and the most desirable defence mechanism of the very personality systems of the 'poor' and poor nations. When the non-rich (materially) believe that they are 'poor' and only through external assistance can they overcome their being poor, what gets valorized is the whole army of development experts and their institutional apparatuses—they alone can eradicate poverty!.

What these different avatars (such as Development Studies) of EASSs have done, or what they have failed to question, is absolutisation of 'poverty' as material deficiency. While material deficiency was definitely part of people's experience of distress and destitution in the pre-modern societies they were deeply embedded in their culture and linked to spatial-temporal specialties.

How each culture or even each category of people went about constituting non-materiality, differed from one society to another or even within a society. In a similar manner, a whole host of non-material aspects too were considered as constituting destitution. This non-materiality too was culturally embedded. In some cultures, not having neighbours to live close-by gave them a sense of deficiency, whereas in certain other societies and groups having too many neighbours living in close proximity was distressing. Besides these, other culturally deemed notions, such as abandonment, not having people to love and be loved, neglect, not having respect, domination by others, discrimination, oppression, deprivation, hunger, malnutrition, homelessness, ill-health, exclusion from educational possibilities etc. have been considered as constituting their experience of "distress, destitution and incomplete existence. . .

The mode of deconstruction of poverty will also lead to rescue the human being from a whole gamut of reductionism to which he/she has been subjected to. It may also result in the triumph of local versus global, because, at present, the latter seems to have imposed its abstraction on the lived experience of vernacular societies.

Labour as Human Essence

Both Marxism and Capitalism find a common ground in treating the labour as essence of human beings. Although for Marxism labour is an ontological property, and for capitalism it is an instrumental property, they regard that humans have to necessarily engage with economic/market systems to satisfy their physical and even spiritual needs. Life cannot exist outside these market/economic systems, and if does, it is inadequate and subhuman (read poor). Economic relationship is the only way to realise one's human essence, either under absolute freedom as Marxism fantasised or by deploying pure rationality as Capitalism enjoined.

But this labour-as-essence approach has devalued human beings (who need to be seen as meaning-seeking individuals) and indeed reduced them as saleable commodities, in the same way as the earth has become a saleable product through the notion of land. What it has entailed is that the poor is one who in unable to sell himself/herself to meet his/her requirements by entering into Market and capitalist production processes.

The equation of man with labour and nature with land has its origin in the economization of society, whereby resourcelessness came to be defined as a problem. And resourcefulness acquired extraordinary significance. Therefore, economic resourcefulness largely in the form of material resources became identified with being 'developed' and the lack or absence of which is being 'underdeveloped'. It gets further individualized when such resourcefulness is equated with personal possessions. Those without individual possessions in abundance need to emulate the ones with lots of such individual possessions.

In this scheme of things what is available to the community or group as a whole does not qualify the members of such group or community as 'resourceful' people. For instance, an individual with unusual quantity of wealth even in the midst of the community of people suffering from hunger or malnutrition or oppressions and dominations is still wealthy, whereas the eastern worldview, before being influenced by modernity, saw meaninglessness not at the individual level but at the collective community level. The suffering of one's community or another member thereof is also the suffering of the evaluating individual. The state of existence of any of his/her caste member is also extended upon the evaluating individual of the same caste. Echoing this Gandhi locates the poverty of the community or society not in the poor but in the greedy rich and their thieving nature. Gandhi said, "I suggest that we [the resourceful people] are thieves in a way. If I take anything that I do not need for my own immediate use, and keep it, I steal it from somebody else. I venture to suggest that it is the fundamental law of Nature, without exception, that Nature produces enough for our wants from day to day, and if only everybody took enough for himself and nothing more, there would be no pauperism in this world, there would be no man dying of starvation in this world." In another place Gandhi again emphasizes the collectivist vision thus, "Welfare of the country is certainly included in the welfare of the world, and individual welfare is included in the welfare of the country. On the other hand, individual welfare should include the welfare of the world" (Gandhi, 1934, 22 March).

But what modern/capitalistic logic has done is to subjugate the collective consciousness to quantified individualized global abstractions. In the same way, the cultural understanding of self gets subordinated to the economic understanding of self. This consequently has led to subjugation of local by national and even more dangerously of national by global. What emerged from such series of subjugations is that materiality has triumphed over non-materiality.

The death of diversity in understanding one's existence occurs exactly at the point when the singular global-level abstract definition of poverty is imposed on the psyche of everyone. Thus in contrast to societies that valued detachment over attachment to material possessions, "having more" material wealth rather than "being more humane" has come to be privileged. In place of societies that united the individual with communities when defining their selves, releasing of the individuals from the holds of the communities got prioritized. This reversal of hierarchies ended up privileging a whole host of development experts who can be trained only in western/modern knowledge system. Similarly, the right to judge whether someone is poor has been divested of concerned individuals or their communities and has got vested in global institutional apparatuses located in western world. Curiously these institutions are the creations of the western nations that privilege themselves only on account of possessing more material wealth, though concentrated in the individual hands.

Here one sees a curious paradox: While the western world treats the unusual wealth of one individual/individuals as generalizable to the health of society, it refuses to generalize the wealth/ resourcefulness of the society or communities to the individuals in eastern societies or the impoverished in its own society. This paradox is sustained only because wealth is quantified in the form of GDPs and per-capita incomes, rather than seen as an experience whose quality and necessity is left to the assessment and judgment of individuals/communities. It is true that the so-called rich nations like USA have vast oceans of impoverished people, yet the country remains characterised as a rich nation. If one goes by Mandela's understanding of freedom or Gandhian understanding of liberation, then the so called rich nations will have to lose all their moral authorities to judge other humanities as 'poor'. Mandela in one of the profound statements he has made says "Freedom is indivisible; the chains on any one of my people were the chains on all of them, the chains on all of my people were the chains on me". Gandhi in his own refreshing way says that the dawn of freedom will not occur if the last man in India is not liberated. And it is public knowledge that Gandhi refused to enjoy any luxuries of the world, until such luxuries reached the last man on earth. He advocated the same for all the resourceful people in the world. He said "all people having money or property should hold it in trust for the society" (Gandhi, 1939)."

But such sense of shame and guilt has been made to vapourize with the arrival of experts and expert institutions on the one hand and compartmentalization of individual psyche as conterminous to individual body and experience on the other. The very moment of acceptance of oneself as resourceful is also the very moment at which the moral responsibility and joint humanity with the existence of the other get dispelled from the vision.

In this effort the role of social sciences is decisive. Particularly the science of psychology has contributed immensely to the atomization of individual mind, by inventing such compartmentalized psyche as emerging and dying with the birth and death of such individual. It also psychologises poverty by locating the causes of poverty in the lack of psychological drive for motivation (a la McClelland) or lack of personality resources (as repeatedly shouted by all sort of personality development manuals and self-development handbooks).

On the contrary, in the Gandhian and Buddhist view of poverty one can see the tendency to culturalise and moralise poverty in contrast to the overly secularized and abstract conception of poverty enunciated by western paradigms. In the social science framework, too, such culturalised understanding of poverty was absent until the arrival of Amartya Sen–whose eastern sensibilities aiding that cannot be exaggerated.

The strength of the Gandhian vision is that the cultural context of poverty is called into question rather than a mere condition of poverty. In such a vision one avoids the tragic tendency of locating poverty in the poor—his/her lack of initiative and effort (Rosen, George, 1982, p.437). In the secularized understanding of poverty, not only is the poverty of the individual traced to the individual psyche, but even the poverty of the entire society gets traced to the individual poor. It is through this unfair tracing that the poor gets solidified into a group, though they themselves are a highly variegated people in their own right. But this location of poverty in the poor becomes necessary as it offers a scapegoat in the form of poor, that conveniently erases own culpability of the resource-rich social minority and their variegated apparatuses in the very creation and perpetuation of poverty in the first place and shifts the blame for its prevalence to personal failure of the poor.

But, by locating poverty in the cultural context and seeing it as the product of the prevailing structure of an unequal relationship, the Gandhian vision calls into question the issue of dominance, oppression and inequality in power and conceptual categories organized in favour of the most powerful. Thus, poverty is seen as the outcome of conceptual shifts as well as the result of relationship patterns. This is why Gandhi takes poverty to mean 'impoverishment' in that poverty is an outcome of a range of impoverishing processes. Unlike the term poverty, which imputes the culpability for being poor to the impoverished people, impoverishment locates the problem in the structure of social, economic and political relations into which the impoverished are forced on unequal terms.

Gandhi is also very uncomfortable with the tendency in many poverty studies to describe poverty by describing the poor. Those studies end up constructing a personality of the poor while attempting to understand the phenomenon of poverty. This manner of locating poverty in the personality of the poor tends to posit poverty as the personal problem and failure of the poor. This also imputes an element of passivity to the poor as the essential agents of their own poverty. It is evident form Gandhian understanding that poverty is much more than starvation and the whole panoply of attributes given to it.

Poverty studies also have another tendency, i.e., solidification of poverty as a 'thing' in itself as if it were an objectified reality outside that can be singled out and attacked. As much of the development practice and wisdom aims at constituting a 'thing' called poverty, it tends to hold every experience of the poor as contributing to such constitution. Even the most challenging and against-the-grain experience of the poor, though it may shake the complacency of the existing ideas on poverty, does not fundamentally uproot the edifice on which such existing wisdoms were erected. This objectification of poverty results in treating poverty as a disease to be instantly eliminated whereas it is only a symptom of the prevailing socio-economic political relations in society. This way, the very blame for the perpetuation of poverty is laid at the doorsteps of knowledge producers and dominant groups.

But this uncomfortable vision that is embarrassing for the dominant groups must be laid to rest and put to relegation. As a new scapegoat has to be found so that the 'resourceful' group can exonerate itself, it becomes all the more necessary to locate the scapegoat that has 'frustrated' every well-meaning attempt at development. Excluded *a priori* were those experts that had prepared or advised the general strategies for the eradication of poverty. On the other hand, it was equally embarrassing to accuse the intellectually bankrupt governments of most southern nations for the continued troubled state of affairs. The attack on poverty thus turns out to be an attack on poor, though the latter too credulously connive with this programmatic attack. Hence all sort of poverty eradication projects and programmes target the easiest categories of poor to attack—the low-income groups, the landless labourer, the small farmer, the unemployed craftsman. And since they could be calculated upon not to react or return the attack, experts and government set about the task at will. But what is forgotten and swept under the carpet is the truth that "the principal obstacles set in the path of the emancipation of the poor came not from below but from above—from the ruling groups at the village, regional, national and international levels, who only allowed change on their own terms".

In the Gandhian vision we can note the problematisation of both material and culture of wealth-making as the cause of poverty, rather than the poor. It is immensely significant to remember that when Gandhi talks of trusteeship, he lists out prescriptions for the so called 'resourceful' to revise their wealth-making and their relationship with wealth (Appadorai, 1969, p.326). Throughout his writing/thinking he formulated lessons for the rich and other resourceful groups to change their ways of being. His is a highly ethicised version of poverty. Elaborating further, Jeevan Kumar writes, "Basically, Gandhi suggested this concept as an answer to the economic inequalities of ownership and income, a kind of non-violent way of resolving all social and economic conflicts prevalent in the world. Therefore, man's dignity, and not his material prosperity, is the centre of Gandhian economics. Gandhian economics aims at a distribution of material prosperity, keeping only human dignity in view. Thus it is dominated more by moral values than by economic ideas. According to Gandhi, Trusteeship is the only ground on which one can work out an ideal combination of economics and morality (Kumar 2007, pp 1-3).

In sum Gandhi provides enough scope for the social origins of poverty as it clearly argues that poverty-as-scarcity is socially-produced rather than objectively existing. This vision has immense potential to radically restructure our thought processes and practices concerning poverty elimination, the notion of development and by implication the very nature of social sciences.

References

Appadurai, A. (1986). Introduction: commodities and the politics of value. In A. Appadurai (ed.) *The Social life of things*. Cambridge University Press.

Bauman, Z. (1998). *Globalization: The Human Consequences*. Cambridge: Polity Press.

Bauman, Z. (2005). *Consumption and Global Poor*. Polity Press.

Gandhi, M.K. (1901). *Sarvodaya (Unto this Last)*. Paraphrasing Ruskin's Original Version, Ahmedabad : Navjivan Publishing House.

Gandhi, M.K. (1927). *A Story of My Experiments with Truth*. Ahmedabad : Navjivan Publishing House.

Gandhi, M. K. (1934). *"Talk with Ashram Inmates, Patna"*, 22 March, as in Collected Works (1958–84), Govt. of India, New Delhi, vol.63: 303.

Gandhi, M. K. (1939). *Hind Swaraj or India Home Rule*. Ahmedabad: Navjivan Publishing House.

Gandhi, M. K. (1941). *Constructive Programme: Its Meaning and place*. Ahmedabad: Navajivan Publishing House.

Gandhi, M. K. (1955). *Truth is God*. Ahmedabad : Navjivan Publishing House.

Gandhi, M.K. (1958*). Collected Works*, Govt. of India, vols. III & XIV. New Delhi.

Kumar, J. (2007). Economy and Society—The Gandhian Perspective. *PEKEA Newsletter*, No. 12, October–December 2007

Chapter 10:
Rereading of Metaphysical Foundations of Humanities in the Light of the Qur'an's Teachings

Qodratullah Qorbani

Introduction

Today, humanities and social sciences have multiple roles in explaining many aspects of social life, since they study the reciprocal relations of humans and society, and try to anticipate and control the future events of human societies through getting to universal laws and traditions, in order to resolve and remove human and social problems, and find new horizons. Universal and empirical tendencies of contemporary western humanities and social sciences, however, were/are caused to fail in achieving the mentioned aims. Meanwhile some differences between Islamic and western nations have introduced some different principles, virtues and functions concerning humanities, which may be cleared by investigating into them. Our purpose in this essay is to show that a theistic metaphysics of humanities and social sciences in the Islamic worldview can make it possible to rethink and reread them by referring to Islamic teachings like the Qur'an.

To do this, we try to give a simple and reasonable definition of humanities. There are several definitions of humanities regarding different approaches. Some thinkers say that humanities are sciences whose subject-matter are human activities, that is, those activities involving relations to other people, and in another definition, humanities are sciences that study the human being as an individual and as a collective, free and determined, aware and unaware of his thoughts and deeds (Fround, 2005, P 8–32, 132). It is important to consider that there are four kinds of humanities, including intellectual humanities like philosophical psychology or philosophy of mind, empirical humanities like sociology or anthropology or psychology, transmitted humanities like religious anthropology, and intuitive humanities like mystical anthropology (Khosropanah, 2013, P 20). On the other hand, we should notice that humanities concern the human being by considering his/her thought and behaviour. Therefore, we can say that humanities include empirical and non-empirical sciences that study human thinking and many aspects of his/her individual and collective deeds. This definition covers most of contemporary social sciences like sociology, economics, politics, psychology, ethics, literature, philosophy and religious studies; because all of the mentioned sciences investigate human being's thought and his/her dealings through different approaches, but their main subject-matter is the very human being who is an existing creature having intellect, freedom and the power of choosing and changing.

By considering the centrality of human being in all kinds of humanities, and also social sciences, it is clear that based on humanly changeable virtues and special attributes in humankind, like intellect, freedom and free will, it is possible to speak of different humanities, contrary to the natural sciences, based on different metaphysics and religious teachings of various societies. In western societies, for example, due to modernistic and philosophical metaphysics, like humanism, empiricism, humanly rationality, secularism and materialism, we can speak of empiricist and naturalistic humanities and social sciences, which are under the influences of the mentioned factors of modernity. In Islamic nations, however, due to the extension of Islamic teachings it is possible to rethink and reform contemporary humanities by rereading texts related to the Islamic worldview, which has been explained in the Qur'an.

Contemporary humanities and social sciences in Islamic societies are/were under the influence of secular and western humanities and philosophies. Due to this fact and to the incompatibility between the metaphysics of contemporary humanities and the metaphysical teachings of Islam and Islamic constitutions, such humanities and social sciences were/are unable to remove social and humanistic problems of Muslim nations. Hence, rereading and reconstructing Muslim's contemporary humanities and social sciences based on Islamic metaphysics, is necessary and unavoidable. By reforming the metaphysical foundations of Muslim's contemporary humanities is possible to redefine Islamic Humanities and Social Sciences, which have Qur'anic roots and laws. Therefore, in this paper, we try to indicate that the Qur'an has some significant and essential teachings regarding the metaphysics of humanities and social sciences. Fulfilling this, we study the Qur'anic principles of anthropology and society as well as its universal and general teachings.

Universal Properties of the Qur'anic Teachings

First it should be considered that the Qur'an is the only text immune from alteration and the revealed infallible book, and that the guidance of humans is its main goal. In fact this immortal miracle of the Prophet of Islam, explains all required and universal epistemological, moral and social teachings of humans, as we see this fact in some of its verses, like: *We have sent down to you the book making everything clear, as a guidance, and mercy, and glad tidings to those who submit, and we sent down to you the remembrance so that you can make clear to people what has been sent down to them, in order that they reflect* (Qur'an, 16:89&44). These two verses clarify that the Qur'an, as the comprehensive and divine book, has universal teachings related to humans' real guidance and salvation. Meanwhile immortality, comprehensiveness and universality of the Qur'anic teachings are necessitated so that its teachings can be applied to all times, places and situations for all humans. Hence, it is seen that the Qur'an calls for all people and in some cases all believers without any temporal and spatial limitations. In this verse, the Qur'an, on behalf of the Prophet Muhammad, says: *Say: O' mankind, I am the messenger of Allah to you all* (Qur'an, 7:158), that is, the Prophet of Islam is the saver and mercy messenger for all humans, and then all the Qur'anic teachings are immortal and global ones. So, general consideration of the verses of the Qur'an show that they include epistemological, ontological, moral, political, social, mystical, scientific and theological doctrines. At the same time the Qur'an alone can't be ascribed to any of the mentioned fields: although there are some significant scientific or social teachings in the Qur'an, it does not mean that it is a scientific or social book, but it is the book of divine guidance which has presented whatever is needed for human guidance, as it was mentioned in the verse: *That is the (holy) book, where there is no doubt. It is a guide for the cautious (of evil and hell)* (Qur'an, 2:2).

In short, the mentioned verses show that the Qur'an, due to its divine origin and infallible teachings that explain whatever is needed for human's real salvation, has some essential teachings concerning theology, ethics, anthropology, politics, mysticism, philosophy, natural sciences, humanities and religion. In this case, anthropological and social teachings of the Qur'an can be used as fixed laws and metaphysical foundations of humanities and social sciences. Some of these teachings are called Divine Traditions (Sunnatullah) that are directly related to human thought and to individual or social life that can be applied by social researchers. In fact, the Qur'anic social and divine traditions introduce some universal and comprehensive human and social laws that social researchers try to discover. So, the Qur'an, not only gives information about the totality of the whole system of being, but also introduces us to many levels of the cosmos and kinds of worlds and how we can recognize them.

As was mentioned before, the quality of our conception and understanding of human being, his/her thought and society, form the metaphysical foundations of humanities and social sciences. The Qur'an, however, not only reforms our insight towards the human being, his/her thought and behaviour, and society, but reconstructs his/her thinking of himself/herself, God, death, life, salvation, the hereafter and the whole system of being that can be shaped into a kind theistic worldview in which our humanly and social tendency are reformed and rebuilt. In fact, humanities and social sciences are those sciences that study human thought and acts in the framework of social life, which we can be found in the Qur'an. So, by using the Qur'anic teachings, we can get the real religious worldview in which efficient anthropology and cosmology exist, and it is possible to apply divine traditions for reforming theories and laws of humanities and social sciences.

Theological Teachings of the Qur'an

Theological teachings of the Qur'an constitute the metaphysical foundations of theistic humanities and social sciences. Theology is one of the essential parts of every divine religion. Theology is called to all essential philosophical matters humans are concerned with regarding God, death, the hereafter, justice, salvation etc. In other words, theology or worldview consists of the quality of the human

Chapter 10: Rereading of Metaphysical Foundations 167

being's tendency to the world, himself/herself and the philosophy or meaning of life, and lives according to it (Mutahhari, 2000, Vol. 2, P 392). Such worldview covers the totality of human mundane and spiritual life and also determines the nature of social life and thought that effect humanities and social sciences. In this case in Islam the Qur'an is the first source for drawing religious thought and worldview. The Qur'an introduces many fundamental teachings about God, His existence, theoretical and practical unity, divine attributes, the relation between God and humans and the world, aspects of idolatry, philosophy, necessity and merits of Prophethood, virtues of Prophets, properties of general and special divine guidance, resurrection and its plural virtues. In this case, we can see some verses of the Qur'an. For example, the verse: *Allah, there is no god except He, the living, the everlasting* (Qur'an, 3:2), indicates God's unity and oneness and that only He is the real living existing being. The verse: *He is Allah, there is no god except He. He is the king, the pure, the peace, the confirmer, the watchful, the almighty, the compeller, the sublime. Exalted is Allah, above all that they associate! He is Allah, the creator, the originator, the shaper. To Him belong the most beautiful names. All that is in the heavens and earth exalt Him. He is the almighty, the wise* (Qur'an, 59:23–24), enumerates some of more important attributes of God and teaches that God alone exists in the whole system of being, that all positive and infinite attributes are graceful for Him and humans as His creatures should pay attention to this fact in their theoretical and practical life. There are, also, some verses about eschatology that teach some essential teachings to humans. For example, in the verses: *It was we who decreed death among you. We will not be surpassed* (Qur'an, 56:60), *Wherever you are, death will overtake you, even if you shall be in the fortified, high towers* (Qur'an, 4:78), God says that humans' death is in the hand of God, and there is no means of escape for humans except to accept the reality of death. Hence it can be said according to logic of the Qur'an human is an existent towards death, which must manage his/her mundane life by paying attention to this fundamental fact.

In addition, there are some verses that say death is not human annihilation, but a stage of humans' mundane life so that by dying the human being arrives at the new life in the Hereafter. For example, the Qur'an in these verses says: *Who created death and life that He might examine which of you is best in deeds* (Qur'an, 67:2),

Say: 'the pleasure of this life is little. The everlasting life is better for the cautious (Qur'an, 4: 77), *You must not think that those who were killed in the way of Allah are dead. But rather, they are alive with their lord and have been provided for them* (Qur'an, 3:169). These verses not only emphasize the temporality of mundane life but say that the final goal of mundane life is getting spiritual happiness and salvation in the Hereafter.

There are other verses that explain the relation between human actions and God. These verses: *When He decrees a thing, He only says: 'be, ' and it is* (Qur'an, 2:117), *Everyone is pledged for what he has earned* (Qur'an, 52:21), *Indeed, we have guided him to the path, he is either grateful or ungrateful* (Qur'an, 76:3), *But you shall not, unless Allah wills, the lord of all the worlds* (Qur'an, 81:29), indicate causal and in length relation between God and human actions, and argue that the first real agent and doer of the world is God, and human only by permission of God and His will can do something. Hence the human being is not able to act until God's will is accrued to that act. So, human will is under the sovereignty of divine will, meanwhile humans are responsible for their behaviour since they act freely. In addition, we can consider some verses that indicate a human religious worldview that has many fundamental functions and merits towards other ones. In short, in such worldview some virtues can be identified like the following (Mutahhari, 2000, Vol. 2, P 396–7):

1. The whole system of being has originated from God and will return to Him.

2. The law of causation dominates on all corporeal and incorporeal universes.

3. In spite of generality of divine destiny and providence, a human being can herself/himself determine her/his fate and happiness.

4. The world is constituted and works according to divine justice.

5. The goods and vices of the world depend on humans' thought and actions.

6. Human beings' mundane and spiritual requirements are linked with each other and inseparable, that is, real happiness in the world and the hereafter are jointed and in one line.

7. The world is the cradle and basis of human's real evolution.

8. This world is the best possible, complete and perfect world.

9. The perfect system governs the world and it works according to chains of divine traditions and laws, the necessity over the world is not by efficient cause but by ultimate cause.

Here, it is discussed what role can the Qur'anic worldview have in reforming contemporary Muslim humanities and social sciences. We can say, in response, that our understanding of ourselves and our behaviour give shape to our social life and thought which can effect humanities. In this case, the Qur'anic verses indicate the importance and functional aspects of our approaching to God, His attributes and relation to the whole system of being forms the human theological thinking in order to know his/her real relation to God and recognize his/her correct place and role in the world. In fact, one of the most important metaphysical problems of contemporary humanities is the misunderstanding of humans' relation to God. This is because of modern humanism in which the human being tries to understand and relate to other existing creatures, like God, based on his/her modern rationality and subjectivity that are led to a humanly and caricatured understanding of God. In fact, returning to revealed teachings of the Qur'an helps us to reform our concepts of God and recognize Him as it was introduced in His words. Therefore, the Qur'anic worldview is able to introduce metaphysical insight in which our origin, end and value of life and our place in the whole system of being is defined. So, the Qur'an draws on the totality of human's life, including mundane and spiritual, individual and social aspects of our life, and most of social stable laws which are necessary to reform our social thought and acts.

Anthropological Teachings of the Qur'an

Modern and contemporary sciences like humanities, social sciences and anthropologies have presented a less real and more caricatured picture of human's nature, so far they are not able to exactly study human's thought and deeds. Such modern perspectives, based on their philosophical foundations, sometimes consider human being like an animal, and sometimes as the centre of the whole system of being. Hence there are some anthropological tendencies, such as humanism, secularism, reductionism and materialism which are unable to recognize the real nature and essence of the human being, while the fundamental precondition of reconstructing efficient humanities and social sciences is to have the real conception and understanding of humankind.

It seems, returning to the teachings of revealed religions that they are the best method for understanding humans' real virtues in order to reform modern and contemporary anthropology and humanities. Because in order to pay attention to the human being's epistemological restrictions and complexity of his/her being, the best way is using revealed doctrines. In this case, it seems that the Qur'an is able to redefine our approach to the human being, and bestow us with a theistic anthropology that has many functions in science and human life. Since the Qur'anic teachings teach us the totality of human life with more detail. It is significant to notice that the Qur'anic teachings do not depend on empirical examination or testing, but they are divine, infallible and priory teachings.

The Qur'an provides much information and philosophical, moral, social and political teachings related to anthropology, which can help us in our life and thinking. Some of its very significant teachings are about the human being's creation, his/her ontological and epistemological aspects, his/her the first nature, freedom and determination, his/her divine dignity, caliphate, intellect, heart and internal tendencies.

Human Creation and His/her Existential Aspects

One of fundamental virtues of the human being towards other existing entities is his/her different creation, which takes the prominent place for him/her. In this case, there are many religious and philosophical indications in the holy Qur'an, in which, God by explaining several stages of human creation, emphasizes on blowing of His spirit to the human body. The importance of this kind of creation is that God commanded angels to bow down before human, that this fact indicates the priority and nobility of human towards all other beings, since God has selected him/her as His caliphate on the earth. In this verse, God says: *We created you then we shaped you, then we said to the angels: prostrate yourselves before Adam. They all prostrated themselves* (Qur'an, 7:11). It seems such explanations of human creation can show humans special place in the whole system of the world. So, he/she is the only existing entity who has divine virtues, since God took His spirit in the human body which is one of the great signs of God in human existence. In addition, human being has two body and spirit dimensions, his/her body is made of dust and mud, while his/her spirit is originated from God, as God cited these two dimensions in this verse: *Then He created him and (caused the angel to) breathe into him His (created) spirit. He gave you eyes and ears, and hearts, yet little do you thank* (Qur'an, 32:9). The significant note in this verse is the Qur'an's emphasizing on authenticity of human spirit towards his/her body, that is, the reality of humanity is based on spirit not body. Because of this excellent creation, God says the creation of human being is in the best way, then names it as the best creation and congratulates Himself, in these verses: *Then we clothed the bones with flesh, and then produced it an other creation. Blessed is Allah, the best of creators* (Qur'an, 23:14). *Indeed, we created the human with the fairest stature* (Qur'an, 95:4).

Reason and Heart

Although the nature of the human being's divine spirit is unclear, it is clear that reason and heart are its two important stages, that is, the human being is the only existing creature who has intellect and can think about the world, God and his/her being. This is a fact that is pointed out with many explanations in the holy Qur'an, and it considers human reason as one of his/her fundamental virtues, in such verses, God says: *Say: are the blind and the seeing alike? Will you not think?* (Qur'an, 6:50). *Call to the path of your lord with wisdom and fine admonition. Dispute with them in the best manner* (Qur'an, 16:125), *Say: 'are they equal, those who know and those who do not know? Only those with minds remember*

(Qur'an, 39:9). The conclusion of having reason is the ability of knowing the whole system of existence and getting divine wisdom and supreme knowledge. So, the reason is an epistemic faculty and human distinguished virtues from other existing entities that have arisen from divine spirit (See: Tabatabaei, 1995, Vol. 1, P 179).

Another prominent virtue of the human being toward other existing entities is his/her heart, that is, the human being is an existing creature having love, grace and mercy that are originated from God and has God's signs in his/her heart. In this case, God says: *Those who believe, and whose hearts find comfort in the remembrance of Allah. Is it not with the remembrance of Allah that hearts are satisfied?* (Qur'an, 13:28). This verse shows that there is a close relation between human intellect and heart, it means, intellect is an epistemic aspect and heart is a feeling and faithfulness aspect of human spirit that have some relations with his/her actions. So, intellect and heart are faithfulness and awareness virtues for humans that due to having these virtues are different from other beings and they can be divided into believers and disbelievers (Nasri, 2000, P 131–7). In fact, humans by their intellects and hearts can make sense their life, and control and manage most of social and environmental factors.

Human Nature and *Innate*[1]

The human composition of body and spirit and having intellect and heart bestowed such special nature to him/her different from other existing beings, is called Innate (Fitrah). Here, *innate* consists of all his/her internal abilities and tendencies that are placed by God for his/her creational guidance (Nasri, 2000, P 166). It can be said human nature and innate are applied to most of his/her universal, spiritual and internal abilities and actualities which are prior to all or most of environmental and social effects, and they are not acquired (Vaezi, 2009, P 65–7, & Nasri, 2000, P 167–170). The human being, due to having these abilities, can resist social effects, since these virtues exist in all humans and are constant in most or all of humans. The Holy Qur'an calls this human nature as Divine *Innate* and says: *Therefore set your face to the religion purely, the upright creation upon which He originated people. There is no*

---

[1] *Innate* means "the first nature."

changing of the creation of Allah. This is the valuable religion (Qur'an, 30:30). In addition, we can enumerate some virtues for human's *innate*, for example, he/she is aware of his/her *innate* by intuitive knowledge since this divine innate pertains to his/her spiritual dimension, and also, the human being's *innate* is a potential and not an actual virtue, that is, human being is the one who can actualize his/her divinely *innate* in life in the right or wrong path.

It is necessary to note that there are some roles for social and environmental factors in growing the human being's divine *innate*, that is, some social factors like family, education, economy, political power, culture and so on can effect a human's thought and form his/her innate nature, but it should be said that these influences are not absolute but relative and limited, since the human being, by his/her divine mercies like intellect, heart and innate nature, can control and change the role of those factors. In fact, the human being has two different and opposite properties, including natural and animal instinct, and divine innate. The first one is related to human body and is under the influences of social and environmental circumstances. The second one is originated from God and can react against the mentioned circumstances. So, we may say that although there is some affairs like genetics, inheritance, social forces and environmental effects that can affect human thought, their effects are not universal and essential, since the human being by his/her intellect and divine graces can resist them and control their roles. In other words, by having a divine innate and special nature, the human being has an essence different from other existing beings, since he/she has the godly spirit and sign and has been selected as the caliphate of God that should actualize divine commands on the earth.

Freedom and Free will

Human being is the only being who has the power of selecting and making decisions, and is responsible before his/her acts and his pretence to reward and punishment. The importance of believing in freedom and determination affects the whole of human life, in particular a human being's material living, meaning of happiness, and relation to God and society.

The Qur'an speaks of human freedom in many cases, and mentions that by this divine gift humans can select the right path from the wrong, and salvation from harm. Some verses indicate this fact, for example, *There is no compulsion in religion. righteousness is now distinct from error* (Qur'an, 2:256), *Who created death and life that he might examine which of you is best in deeds* (Qur'an, 67:2), *Say: 'this is the truth from your lord. Let whosoever will, believe, and whosoever will, disbelieve it* (Qur'an, 18:29). Here, the Qur'an links human freedom with its essential results and divine guidance. And there are other verses like: *[we said]: if you do good, it shall be for your own souls; but if you do evil it is likewise* (Qur'an, 17:7), *he who does good does it for himself; and he who does evil does so against himself* (Qur'an, 41:46), which indicate that the result of human freedom and struggling is for herself/himself and there is no reward or punishment without such gifts and examinations (See: Javadi Amoli, 2012, Vol. 14, P 323–327).

In addition, believing in freedom is the most important concern of a human's individual, social, moral and religious life. Hence, the question of freedom and keeping to it or determinism can define our meaning of life. Because, in freedom or determinism can be defined most aspects of human life and how does a human being react before them. For example, believing in absolute determinism, from philosophical and epistemological approaches, means to argue that effects of social factors on human thought is absolute, and rejects any kind of human free will or freedom. On the contrary, keeping to absolute freedom due to referring all things to the human being, negates any power and effectiveness to other existing entities like God. But, believing in relative freedom and determinism, means to accept limited freedom and forces in human life, and a kind of philosophical and social determination of his/her social life, that is, the human being is not determined or free absolutely but has both of them relatively. In this approach it is accepted the effects of social factors on human thought, since it is an objective reality and there is a kind of divine destiny and providence that has some influences on human knowledge, but this approach emphasizes that the forces of cited factors don't reject human freedom and power, because he/she is able to control and manage them, and that divine destination and providence also are applied to a human being's freely acting and are not determined (See: Nasri, Ibid, P 350–370 & Vaezi, Ibid, P 105–120).

So by considering human's relative freedom and determination, we can reject all kinds of absolute philosophical, social and physiologic determinisms. Philosophical determinism is supported by some Islamic and western philosophers and theologians, and is argued that every event, including a human's one, is necessitated and happens based on its determined causes and there is no kind of freedom. We argued that there are, at least, humans who because of their intellect and freedom, act freely, and that there is a kind of causal relation between God's acts and humans ones, which shows human free will in doing actions. Social determinism emphasizes on forces of social and environmental factors on human knowledge and tries to argue that the human being is under influences of the mentioned factors absolutely, and that he/she has no free will before them. This point of view is called socialism and emphasizes that social factors effect on human knowledge extremely and absolutely, and that human personality is formed through social processes, and that his/her morality, thought and behavior are shaped under influences of social factors. Hence the human being is a social existing creature (Vaezi, Ibid, P 124–9).

For criticizing social determinism, we can say, although influences of social factors shape or change human knowledge and morality, they don't deny human's freedom and intellect for controlling and managing their effects. And also, it is necessary to note that philosophical and social determinism in its extreme and absolute form, cause to deny human freedom, identity, responsibility, reward and punishment, while the mentioned virtues are objective and undeniable facts. Thomas Aquinas, about a human being's responsibility before his/her dealings, says that human being has free will; preaches, commands, promotion of the good, prevention of evil, rewards and punishments are otherwise useless (See: Direks, 2001, P 138). So, while the human being is under influences of social factors, he/she is not determined absolutely, but can resist and control their effects.

Human's Divine Dignity and Caliphate

One of the most significant virtues of humans is their divine dignity before God and their high place as the caliphate of God. This fact not only shows the importance of human's divine spirit but indicates that because of this, God has appointed humankind as His vicegerent for actualizing divinely government. In this case, God speaks of human caliphate and says: *When your lord said to the angels: I am placing on the earth a caliph* (Qur'an, 2:30), and when the angels ask God about the reason of such placement, God argues that humans have some divine knowledge which angels are not aware of: *He taught Adam (father of humans) the names all of them and then presented them to the angels, saying: 'tell me the names of these, if you are truthful* (Qur'an, 2:31). In fact, it is clarified that humans are the only existing entities who pretend to receive divine knowledge related to their divine spirit and vicegerent. But it is important to know that human's divine caliphate is not as an actuality in all of them, but this is a potentiality and faculty that can be actualized by using reason, free will and knowledge. It means humans live in an evolutionary process of life and in life their spiritual virtues are increased and they can be appointed as God's caliphate, and also we see the importance of the teachings of all divine prophets, related to this fact, for guiding humans and flourishing their transcendent tendencies (Javadi Amoli, 2012, Vol. 14, P 116, 119). And it is necessary to note that such divine virtues are according and in order to getting immortality which is of the best real desires of every humankinds (Tabatabei, 1995, Vol. 1, P 176, 188). So it can be said that the Qur'an considers two kinds of dignity for humans, the first one is essential dignity for all humans, and the second acquired or spiritual dignity that can be gained by some servants of God. In fact due to acquiring some spiritual virtues, some people, like the Prophets, pretend to get the second kind of divine dignity and related to this, God says: *The noblest of you before Allah is the most righteous of you* (Qur'an, 49:13).

In addition, because of this dignity and divine caliphate, God has placed humans as superior to all other existing beings and has permitted humans to use them in their mundane life and spiritual journey. In fact in the Qur'anic literature, all existing entities are as instruments for humans living and travelling in evolutionary life. In this case, there are some verses, like: *We have honoured the children of Adam and carried them on both land and sea. We have provided them with good things and greatly preferred them above much of our creation* (Qur'an, 17:70), *We established you in the earth and made for you a livelihood* (Qur'an, 7:10), *Do you not* see how Allah has subjected to you all that is in the heavens and the earth, and lavished on you his visible and unseen favors? Yet some people would argue about Allah without knowledge, or guidance, or an illuminating book* (Qur'an, 31:20). Meanwhile, there are some verses of the Qur'an that indicate the right of real servants and believers of God for governing on the earth and actualizing divine commands. For example, we read in the Qur'an: *We have written in the psalms, after the remembrance: 'the righteous among my worshipers shall inherit the earth* (Qur'an, 21:105), *But we wanted to be gracious to those abased in the land, and to make them leaders and inheritors* (Qur'an, 28:5).

In sum, the Qur'anic anthropology helps us to recognize the most hidden aspects of humans, in order to use them in social and individual life and in epistemic, scientific, philosophical, humanistic and social theorizing, while by mere using human sciences it is impossible to get universal knowledge about such hidden and complicated aspects.

Divine Justice and Other Innate Virtues

Seeking divine justice is one of other innate virtues of the human being that maybe he/she in understanding and interpreting it, but this principle itself is not destroyable. Hence it is possible for human to recognize real and divine justice and return to the real path by using of his/her divine *innate*, intellect and reason. Therefore, it can be said that the human being's divine *innate,* justice and intellect help him/her to manage all mundane affairs. Because of the importance of seeking for and living based on justice, God says that the philosophy of sending prophets is establishing justice in all aspects of human life, as it is cleared in this verse: *We have sent our messengers with proofs, and sent them with the book and the scales, so that people might establish the scale (of justice)* (Qur'an, 57:25).

Another essential virtue of the human being is his/her tendency to worshiping transcendent God who is man's creator and to whom he/she obeys. In fact the human spirit as divine sign and grace in his/her existence takes backgrounds for seeking and worshiping God. Hence, it seems that most humans have worshiped God in the past in many ways. This fact and its significance is mentioned in many verses of the Qur'an, for example, we can see such samples*: I* *have not created mankind and jinn except to worship me* (Qur'an, 51:56), *O' you who believe, bow down and prostrate yourselves. Worship your lord and do good in order that you prosper (Qur'an, 22:77)*. In this case, the influence of social and environmental circumstances is only in quality and quantity of this internal tendency, that is maybe human, based on social conditions, worships idols or other humans instead of on real God, but his/her authentic tendency to worship transcendent God never has been removed. Of course human is able to rethink and revive his/her divine innate and to worship unique God or mislead his/her divine innate and go astray (Mutahhari, 1998, Vol. 2, P 94). The final virtue of the human being, which is considered here, is his/her ability and potentiality to seek truth and ask of all things. In fact due to this virtue, man can open new epistemic horizons and discover hidden aspects of existence. This ability can surpass social and environmental forces and conquer them by his/her intellect.

In short, the human being is the only being who is naturally and innately responsible for herself/himself and the people in society, and this property has given him/her the power and ability to resist against social and environmental forces and try to change or manage them.

Society and Social Teachings of the Qur'an

As it was mentioned before, society is one of the two bases of humanities and social sciences so that without having the real recognition of that, it is impossible to have efficient humanities and social sciences. In this case, there are different theories concerning the nature and functions of society. Philosophical approaches emphasize *a priori* definitions, and phenomenological ones pay attention to *a posteriori* definitions. In the Qur'an, it is possible to find some *a priori*, some *a posteriori* and historical definitions of society. In this case, the Qur'an gives information about the nature and essence, kinds and structures, special differences between theistic and atheistic society, social aspects of human's life, authenticity of the individual or society, and some factors about the flourishing or falling of communities. It is necessary to say that some of cited cases are foundations of humanities and social sciences, and some are used as social laws and rules which show social lawfulness of society in the Qur'anic teachings, called Divine Traditions that can

Chapter 10: Rereading of Metaphysical Foundations

be used in social theorizing and extracting social laws by researchers. Here, it is tried to pay more attention to first application, since we try to argue that what virtues the society does have, which consist of some groups of humans, they are used as foundations of social thought.

First it can be said that society includes a complex of humans that are linked by some social systems, traditions, laws, customs and norms, and have a kind of collective living (Mutahhari, 1994, p. 18). This primary definition shows that society is formed based on some requirements, tendencies and thoughts. Then, it is impossible to make a society in a vacuum, and human communities also should, at least, consist of some common needs, aims, tendencies and points of views. The Qur'an pays attention to society by considering human social aspects, and because humans have plural and different requirements, tendencies and viewpoints, the Qur'an uses various terms for describing the meaning of society. There are some expressions like Nation, Tribe, People, Ommah, Village, Branch and Sect that indicate a kind of society in the Qur'an in different approaches. The word Ommah means the people who have common religious leader and thought, and the word Nation means the people who have common traditions and cultures. In this case, the Qur'an says: *Abraham was (equal to) a nation, obedient to Allah, of pure faith and was not among the idolaters* (Qur'an, 16:120), also says: *Follow the creed of Abraham, he was of pure faith, and not an idolater* (Qur'an, 3:95). These verses indicate different appearances of society, namely, it include people who live based on their common thoughts, historical and racial backgrounds and reciprocal requirements, and also have similar aims. Here, therefore, the words Nation and Ommah show that religious commonalities are the base forming societies. There is another verse, in which we find the same meaning of the society by paying attention to the word Tribe (Ta'efeh). In this case, the Qur'an says: *Some of the people of the book say: 'believe in that which is sent down to those who believe at the beginning of the day and disbelieve at the end of it, so that they will return* (Qur'an, 3:72). This verse, also, emphasizes religious beliefs of people in constructing their community, like the people of the book. There are, however, some verses in which, are used words of Village or Tribe and indicate that historical and geographical commonalities are the base of establishing societies. In this case, we read in the

Qur'an: *Before them, the nation of Noah belied* (Qur'an, 50:12); *O' believers, do not let people mock other people who may be better than themselves* (Qur'an, 49:11), *How many a village have we destroyed that were ungrateful in their life* (Qur'an, 28:58). Here, the first meaning of the society is commonality in geographical, cultural, historical or racial virtues, although it is possible to consider some roles for religious thought. In addition, we see the word People (Nas), which has universal indication. We, for example, read: *There are some People who say: 'we believe in Allah and the last day,' yet they are not believers* (Qur'an, 2:8). Mentioned verses of the Qur'an show that although historical, racial and geographical commonalities have a role in establishing communities, and given that the main element of the society is religious and theological thoughts based on that, communities can be divided into good or bad, theistic or atheistic ones. Hence, according to the logic of the Qur'an, society is formed by Nation and Ommah that have common religious beliefs and theistic tendencies. Therefore, it is possible to understand the meaning and significance of the Qur'anic division of societies into theistic and atheistic ones, since the human being's theistic tendency is caused to form a theistic society whose social aspects are contrary to those of an atheistic society, that is, a human being's atheistic and idolatrous thought causes an atheistic society. The Qur'an, in this case, says: *there is nothing but our present life; we die, and we live, and we shall not be resurrected* (Qur'an, 23:37); *They say: 'there is nothing except this life, we die and we live, it is only time that destroys us.' Surely, of this they have no knowledge, they are just guessing* (Qur'an, 45:23). These verses indicate that, the people of some communities live based on their material requirements and atheistic thinking. In theistic society, in contrary, its people believe in their origination and resurrection by the power of God, and consider themselves as God's creatures and the aim of their mundane life for reaching the nearness of God. As the Qur'an remembers this fact in these verses: *Who, in adversity say: 'we belong to Allah and to him we shall return* (Qur'an, 2:156); *O' human, you are working hard towards your lord and you will meet him* (Qur'an, 84:6); *Therefore, race for forgiveness from your lord, and for a garden as wide as heaven and earth, prepared for those who believe in Allah and his messengers. Such is the favor of Allah; he gives it to whom he will. Allah is the owner of great favor* (Qur'an, 57:21). These verses

Chapter 10: Rereading of Metaphysical Foundations 181

specially emphasize on God as human origin and end, and His extensive forgiveness. The importance of dividing societies into theistic and atheistic is to pay attention to criteria that their members select and live based on them. Priority of sense perception and material tendencies and restricting the whole of life to the material world, on the one hand, and paying attention to priority of reason and to everlasting life and salvation, and considering the corporeal world as temporal universe, on the other hand, introduce different pictures of society which help and effect social researchers in humanities and social sciences. In other words, the ways theistic or atheistic thinking of our community form the metaphysical foundations of our thought in humanities and social sciences. Now, if the society that we study is an atheistic community, our social investigation is led to atheistic results. In fact, a human being's religious or secular thought influence his/her tendency to society. Hence, the Qur'an pays more attention to a human being's theistic worldview and its effects on forming religious communities, which is caused to rebuild theistic humanities and social sciences.

Other significant problem, from the Qur'anic point of view, is to understand the relation between individual and the society and the authenticity of each other that this problem depends on how we comprehend the kind of society's composition of individuals. First, it should be noticed that the Qur'an considers society as composed of humans and individuals, that is, society has no meaning without individuals; it does not mean, however, to confirm authenticity of individual and credibility of the society. But it seems the society's composition of individuals is mostly a kind of real composition with unique properties, since, in such composition, society has some structure, identity, functions and sections different from individuals. Martyr Mutahhari and Ayatollah Tabatabaei, two Iranian and Muslim contemporary thinkers, believe that all humans begin to have a social life by their the first innate nature, and that humans spiritually in cooperation with each other make up a new spiritual identity which is called Collective Spirit. This composition is a kind of natural, new and unique compound that has no similar. This kind of composition, as far as its parts have objective reciprocal reactions and change each other and find new identities, is a kind of concrete and natural compound, but as far as the whole or universal does not have a real existence, it is not different from other natural compounds (Mutahhari, 1993, P 28–29; Tabatabaei,

1995, Vol. 4, P 96). It seems these words are compatible with Qur'anic teachings, because some of the Qur'anic verses indicate that this book considers common virtues, fates, ends, understandings, awareness, obedience and rebellions for nations, people, tribes, Ommahs and villages in different societies. As it mentions this fact in these verses: *To every nation a term; when their term comes they shall not delay it by a single hour, nor yet hasten it* (Qur'an, 7:34); *You shall see every nation hobbling on their knees* (Qur'an, 45:28); *We have made the actions of each nation seem pleasing* (Qur'an, 6:108); *And so did the parties after them. Every nation strove against their messenger to seize him, disputing with false arguments to refute the truth. Then I seized them, how was my punishment!* (Qur'an, 40:5). These verses clarify that the functions, fates and the result of nations and people's actions, which have proper tendencies, are related to the whole of society and not to individual. Every society, here, acts as an individual and gets its conclusion. This, however, does not mean denying the authenticity of the individual and his/her independent identity. But it means that society as a constitutional composite of humans who have special worldviews, has virtues different from those of individuals. Consequently, it is possible to take account of independence and authenticity for both the society and individuals. Of course, there are some of the Qur'anic verses that are called Divine Traditions and introduce some fixed social lawfulness. Such laws can be applied to social theorizing and to getting global humanly and social rules. Some of these divine laws and traditions include the tradition of development and fall of civilizations and nations, the tradition of sending the Prophets for guiding people to salvation, the tradition of divine guidance and misguidance, the tradition of victory of right over false, the tradition of punishment and reward, the tradition of sizing, suffering and giving time to sinners.

Conclusion

Philosophical thinking in humanities and social sciences indicates that the Human Being and Society, their metaphysical foundations, have more essential roles, although the role of the human being is more than that of society, since society finally consists of some humans who gather and live based on their common requirements, tendencies, viewpoints, customs and norms. So, the first foundation and essential constitution of humanities and social sciences is very human, so that, he/she is a social being and humanities study his/her thought and acts. The centrality of the human being in humanities and social sciences shows this significant note that the human being is an creature having changeable perspectives, viewpoints and insights and these virtues separate humanities and social sciences from natural sciences. In fact, the human being as the main subject-matter of humanities and social sciences is a complicated entity, it is impossible to anticipate or control him/her previously or empirically, since human and empirical restrictions of the contemporary secular humanities and social sciences are prevented to get universal and comprehensive laws and rules regarding the human being and the society. Meanwhile, the human being with his/her perspective and viewpoint is able to take a kind of worldview in which some of essential metaphysical questions concerning God, himself/herself/ the cosmos, society, etc, find their proper answers. So, due to the human and empirical restrictions of contemporary humanities and social sciences, and also because of the complicated constitution of humankind, there is no choice but to refer to the divine worldview of which we can find its best sample in the Qur'an. Such worldview, by introducing metaphysical and efficient divine teachings, is able to reform and reconstruct the contemporary secular humanities and social sciences that have been introduced to Muslim nations since two centuries ago. This worldview, in short, gives us anthropological, theological and metaphysical teachings that can be used for reforming contemporary humanities and social sciences, and can be called Islamic Humanities and Social Sciences.

References

The Qur'an

Allamah Tabatabei, M. H. (1995). *Almizan Fi Tafsirul Qur'an*, Qom, Almaktaba al Islamyiah, Vol. 1.

Direx, H. (2001). *Philosophical Anthropology*. Trans. to Persian by Muhammad Reza Beheshti. Tehran: Hermes Press.

Fround, J. (2005). *Theories Concerning Humanities*. Trans by Ali Mohammad Kardan. Tehran : Nashr Daneshgahi Press.

Javadi Amoli, A. (2012). *Society in the Qur'an*. Qom: Esra Press.

Khosropanah, A. (2013). *Philosophy of Humanities*. Tehran: Hekmat Novin Islami Press.

Mutahhari, M. (1998). Collections of Works, Vol. 2, Tehran: Sadra Press.

Mutahhari, M. (2000). Notes, Vol. 2, Tehran: Sadra Press.

Nasri, A. (2000). *Principles of Anthropology in the Qur'an*. Tehran: Cultural Institute for Contemporary Knowledge and Thought.

Vaezi, A. (2009). *Human in Islam*. Tehran: Research Institute for Hawzah & University & Samt Press.

Section II: Contributions to the Discourse about Alternative Concepts of Knowledge

Chapter 11:
What is foreign knowledge?

Leandro Rodriguez Medina

Introduction

In the context of globalization, of the so-called knowledge (or information) society, and the rise of information technologies as mediations that have transformed communication, there is a growing literature about new modes of knowledge production. This literature emphasizes the internationalization of academic and scientific disciplines, as well as the encouragement of knowledge circulation in a world transformed by information and communication technologies. While some studies focus on international collaboration (e.g. scholarly mobility programs), other analyses have attempted to think beyond national boundaries, theoretical frameworks rooted in specific societies, and even to think trans-disciplinarily. The main difference, at first glance, seems to be the lack of recognition—or underestimation—of the forces, coming from national configurations (e.g. national systems of researchers), that shape disciplines, theories, and scholarly careers. While some studies recognize and explore forms of local knowledge (although the correct expression would be 'locally-produced knowledge') others maintain that for knowledge to be international it should be 'globally shared knowledge'. In this chapter, I argue for the idea that acknowledging the existence of 'foreign'/'local' knowledge does not prevent us from undertaking transnational projects that contribute to the emergence of 'global knowledge'. I will explore the meaning of 'foreign knowledge' and show that the category is useful, although it may actually appear to be an obstacle for international or global endeavors. On the one hand, the category allows us to understand different practices in knowledge production and how networks of people, objects and institutions assemble differently. Practices involve not only institutionalized habits that constitute the daily life of academic activities (e.g., writing a paper or delivering a lecture) but also the non-institutionalized ones (e.g. academic clientelism) that also shape the field. On the other hand, however, the idea of 'foreign knowledge' might obscure the fact that knowledge may be critically appropriated beyond the context of production, giving rise to an original process of reception. Finally I discuss what we should do with foreign knowledge, highlighting the fact that foreignness brings about certain decisions and practices that deserve our attention.

Further clarification is still necessary. Knowledge can be a very vague concept, since it may refer, at the same time, to the process and the product of such a process. Scientific knowledge, for example, is the outcome of several intertwined processes ranging from data collection and analysis to presentations in conferences, and articles written and published in journals. It is also a set of specific propositions (ideas) materialized in articles, chapters, and books. There are at least three important differences between these conceptualizations that have consequences for the understanding of knowledge production and circulation. First, while it makes sense to say that practices are situated (i.e. they happen in specific places and times, under certain material conditions), it is less clear what it means to say that an idea (e.g. a hypothesis or a theory) is situated, because the focus in this case is the structural, textual, linguistic form of the idea. Second, since the late 1970s, science and technology studies (STS) have shifted their interest from knowledge as product to knowledge as process. This change can be observed in the growing attention to actors (be they human or non-human), their interests, their practices, and the entanglements they enact. This epistemic shift also implies a move from more philosophical approaches (focused on the logic of research) to more empirical studies (focused on scientists, laboratories, devices, and institutions), which have relied frequently on ethnographies and other qualitative methods. Third, concerned as they are for the process of knowledge production, STS have recently witnessed a geographical turn, that is, literature that deals with the importance of place (from regions to offices) for the production of knowledge. As Livingstone puts it,

> While monumental efforts have gone into constructing "placeless places" for the pursuit of science, spaces that aspire to ubiquity, I believe that there are questions of fundamental importance to be asked about *all* the spaces of scientific inquiry. What excites my interest, therefore, is the attempt to determine the significance for science of the sites where experiments are conducted, the places where knowledge is generated, the localities where investigation is carried out (Livingstone, 2003: 3; emphasis in the original).

The criticism implied in this passage is that the idea that universal knowledge is a modern, European construction based on the notion of placeless places, which implies that knowledge can actually circulate because it is the same in different settings and because specificities related to space do not affect the content of knowledge. Objectivity itself might be seen as the outcome of successfully leaving the local behind (Livingstone 2003: 1), because it needs consensus beyond localities. However, this consensus—strongly linked to the idea of truth and, in empirical research, to matters of facts—has been reconceptualized by the history of science, according to which, in order for knowledge to move to a different place, there are some conventions (social, material, epistemic) that must also be mobilized. In their classic study on Leviathan and the air-pump, Shapin and Schaffer, for example, have shown that 'the dissemination of air-pumps was a key aspect of the development of Boyle's pneumatic experiments' (1985: 235), which, in turn, were key aspects to sustain his theory of vacuum. Replication of experiments (one of the main issues of scientific knowledge objectivity) is thus a practical matter and 'knowledge production depends not just on the abstract exchange of paper and ideas but on the practical social regulation of men and machines' (1985: 281).

Although I understand knowledge as a process which translates into many materialized forms (from a PowerPoint presentation to a textbook), in this chapter I mostly focus on theories because they have been seen as the quintessential delocalized knowledge product and, as such, represent a tougher test for my argument. Traditionally, theories, by definition, attempt to transcend their context of production and explain phenomena beyond the data that informed them. They, as abstract entities, condense a whole system of ideas but are usually thought as disconnected from the specificities of places and sites. At the same time, they are only circumstantially related to the person(s) who puts them forward: since they seem to concretize ideas coming out from someone's mind, theories can be seen as a decontextualized intellectual product.[1] Yet, as I hope to show in the next paragraphs, they can (or should?) be analyzed through the lens of space and under the same assumptions that have shaped most of the current research in STS.

In this chapter, I present my argument in four parts. First, I deal with the notion of foreignness and the foreign in order to see whether it can be used to describe knowledge (be it as product or process). Then, I review current literature that has relied on the notion of 'foreign knowledge', which will allow me to show that this idea has been particularly fruitful for business/management scholarship. The third part revolves around the relevance of space by considering the nation-state in the process of knowledge production. In this section I provide reasons to believe that, even in the age of globalization, the national level of analysis is still relevant and probably the most significant through which to understand present trends in knowledge production and circulation. Finally, after showing how space matters, I raise the question of what we should do with foreign knowledge. While at a phenomenal level, the Western tradition has made us think of theories as delocalized knowledge (i.e. a text to be read, criticized, and used to write new pieces), at a sociological level we do *more* with theories (i.e. we position ourselves within academic fields, we try to be published by international publishing houses, we attempt to obtain funds from philanthropic organizations), which obliges us to (re) connect them with their context of production and/or reception.

---

[1] For example, in Bunge's terms, 'a scientific theory is a system of propositions deductively and thematically linked. In a well-organized theory, an axiomatic theory, every proposition is either a premise or a consequence from some premises taken together' (1999: 144). Accordingly, Nastasia and Rakow, focusing on this traditional approach to theory, refer to 'theory as puzzle-solving' (because) the object of study or problem (is) given and taken-for-granted, as exterior to the theorist, overcoming individual theorists, or as more venerable and more important than studying subjectivities' (2010:2). There are also opposite views. Abend, for example, has argued that theory, 'rather than an abstract philosophical problem, (...) is a practical problem, which—insofar as agreed-upon logical and semantic bases are a prerequisite for any sort of epistemic progress—sociology cannot neglect' (2008: 174). Consequently, he has found at least seven different meanings of theory (2008: 177–181).

Foreignness and foreigner, categories to enact boundaries

According to the Oxford English Dictionary, foreign has two different meanings, one connected to spatiality and the other to strangeness. As an adjective, 'foreign' is 'of, from, in, or characteristic of a country's language other than one's own', which can be used in at least three different ways: (a) dealing with or relating to other countries, (b) of or belonging to another district or area, and (c) coming or introduced from outside. At the same time, the connection with something/someone strange, or with which/whom we are not familiar, makes clear the idea of foreign (and foreignness) as an 'other' which/who is, at least partially, unknown. The relationship between foreign and the country and language (barbarians were those who cannot speak Greek, which can be considered the origin of the word and its use) also speaks of the central role of states (which, for example, have devoted substantial resources throughout history to enforce identity through cultural and education policies) and their defining features in our understanding of the concept.[2]

Scholarly debates have also transcended these common-sense ideas, but also explored the implications for other relevant aspects of our social and political lives, such as democracy, citizenship, family and the rule of law. In his classic study *On Hospitality*, Derrida connects foreignness with justice and rhetorically he asks,

> What is a foreigner? (...) It is not only the man or woman who keeps abroad, on the outside of society, the family, the city. It is not the other, the completely other who is relegated to an absolute outside, savage, barbaric, precultural, and prejuridical, outside and prior to the family, the community, the city, the nation, or the State. The relationship to the foreigner is regulated by law, by the becoming-law of justice (Derrida, 2000: 73).

In the passage, Derrida brings to the fore the fact that the notion of foreigners requires not only outsiders, not only the other who is

---

[2] Although the concept has been employed in different ways since its first uses, its origins show a clear connection between politics and language. The Ancient Greek word βάρβαρος (*barbaros*), "barbarian", was an antonym for πολίτης (*politēs*), "citizen" (from πόλις - *polis*, "city-state"). Onomatopoetically, the sound of *barbaros* seems to come from the act of babbling—i.e. the image of a person speaking a non-Greek language (Pagden 1986).

disconnected from society, but the act of being regulated by law, that is, the ethical and political instance of recognizing outsiders as such from the point of view of a society to which they are, from that moment on, linked. But this judicial aspect has a different substratum: language, and in particular the language of the power(ful).

> In [Plato]'s "The Apology of Socrates" (17d), Socrates addresses his fellow citizens and Athenian judges. He defends himself against the accusation of being a kind of sophist or skillful speaker. He announces that he is going to say what is right and true, certainly, against the liars who are accusing him, but without rhetorical elegance, without flowery use of language. He declares that he is 'foreign' to the language of the courts, to the tribune of the tribunals: he does not know how to speak this courtroom language, this legal rhetoric of accusation, defence, and pleading; he does not have the skill, he is like a foreigner. (...) the foreigner is first of all foreign to the legal language in which the duty of hospitality is formulated, the right to asylum, its limits, norms, policing, etc. He has to ask for hospitality in a language which by definition is not his own, the one imposed on him by the master of the house, the host, the king, the lord, the authorities, the nation, the State (...) and that's the first act of violence (Derrida, 2000: 15).

Seen from the perspective of the language of the state, the concept of foreigners leads us to the very core topics of political and social theory: democracy, citizenship, rule of law. At the same time, it allows us to understand many of the current problems of the state in the age of globalization, from migration to the reconfiguration of sovereignty. Honig, for example, has pointed out that:

> In classical political thought, foreignness is generally taken to signify a threat of corruption that must be kept out or contained for the sake of the stability and identity of the regime. This somehow xenophobic way of thinking about foreignness endures in the contemporary world, though other options—from assimilation to the many varieties of multiculturalism—are now also considered viable. All these options persist in treating foreignness as a problem in need of solution, however. Even many of the most multiculturally minded contributors to diversity debates treat foreignness as a necessary evil and assume that we would be better off if only there were enough land for every group to have its own nation-state (Honig, 2001: 1–2).

In a previous work, Honig (1998) had already connected the problem of foreignness with those of migration and the mythical foundations of the United States as a multicultural nation-state. In this regard, she argues that 'the myth of an immigrant America depicts the foreigner as a supplement to the nation, an agent of national reenchantment that might rescue the regime from corruption and return it to its first principles, whether capitalist, communal/familial, or consensual' (1998: 1). From both passages, it seems that foreigners (and foreignness) are a theoretical and practical problem, that is, something that should be addressed in order to find a way to include them and to give rise to a harmonious community.

If Honig is right about the relevance (and implications) of the scholarly definitions of foreignness, empirical studies show that this theoretical argument has permeated into the practicalities of the exercise of power in contemporary societies. Mescher (2012), in her study of Islamophobia in Germany, argues that, when asked about 'What is a foreigner to you?' police officers replied: (a) a person I do not know personally, 78.7%, (b) those who do not speak German, 59.9%, (c) those who have different values, 36,7%, and (d) those who were not born in Germany, 23.9%. From the most common answers we can infer that foreignness appears as a category to deal with what is not familiar and, consequently, with which we can barely communicate. Language becomes the barrier that enacts the state's boundaries.[3]

Another way of looking at foreigners is through the historical development of the document that has become vital for people who wish to travel: the passport. Torpey (1999) has argued that one defining feature of modern states (and the system of states) is that they have monopolized control over the circulation of people, especially, but not exclusively, at the international level.

> The result of this process has been to deprive people of the freedom to move across certain spaces and to render them dependent on states and the state system for the authorization to do so—an authority widely held in private hands theretofore. (...) People have also become dependent on states for the possession of an'identity' from which they can escape only with difficulty and which may significantly shape their access to various spaces. (...) In the course of each of these transformations, workers, aggressors and travelers, respectively, have each been subjected to a form of dependency they had not previously known (Torpey, 1999: 4).

---

[3] On the other hand, when several states share a common language (such as the Commonwealth area or the Ibero-American states), the idea of international communication emerges and might bring about an expanded community more or less integrated by this common cultural feature. This situation, however, cannot prevent us from appreciating differences between countries, usually associated to the colonial past in its entanglement with ethnicity issues (Alesina et al. 2003).

It is so widely accepted that people should have an identity, backed by documents issued by states, that official websites to apply for visas or to request passports barely explain why citizens need to do so. These websites point to the 'obvious' fact that if you want to visit a country (for tourist, business or whatever reason you might have) you have to obtain some kind of visa. In fact, strange as it sounds today, the increasing circulation of people, facilitated by the new transport system in Europe, forced governments to suspend such requirements in the 19th century.

> The rising popularity of rail travel in the mid-19th century led to an explosion of tourism throughout Europe and caused a complete breakdown in the European passport and visa system. In answer to the crisis, France abolished passports and visas in 1861. Other European countries followed suit, and by 1914, passport requirements had been eliminated practically everywhere in Europe.[4]

More recently, the growing concern of countries with security and terrorism has strengthened the control over the circulation of people, especially in border areas and specific settings, such as airports and seaports. These new forms of control, from biometrical information to new e-passports, also show the connection of countries with private companies (some of them actually in charge of border control) as well as the reliance upon modern technology. Interestingly, and paradoxically if one accepts the surveillance discourse of the state, the more strategies that are implemented to keep borders safe, the more mechanisms of control should be in operation. Thus, as pointed out by Torpey, (the possibility of an) aggression is suddenly transformed into a catch-all explanation that justifies stricter scrutiny and multiplies regulations on circulation.

While 'foreigner', as a noun, has been used to refer to a person who does not belong to a territory from the perspective of such a territory's authorities or society, foreign, as an adjective, has also been used to refer to goods. In fact, countries have invested heavily not only in the border control of people, but also in the supervision of goods that travel across borders. At the very heart of international trade, export/import controls appear to be a key element to facilitate/constrain the circulation of commodities worldwide. This regulation is based on—and reinforces—the idea of local/foreign

---

[4] http://www.cic.gc.ca/english/games/teachers-corner/history-passports.asp, accessed June 2014.

products, since it establishes distinctions around which 'us' and 'them' can be identified. One case will illustrate my point. In a recent symposium, the U.S. Trade Representative Michael Froman, argued that:

> *Our* ability to grow *our* economy, to create more jobs *here*, to promote growth is critically dependent on *our* ability to increase exports. *We* need to make sure that the message that trade is good for jobs, good for growth, good for *the country* is shared and understood across the country (emphasis added).[5]

Through 'we', 'our' and 'country' it is not difficult to infer 'they', 'their' and 'the rest of the world'. Recognizing the relevance of trade for the health of the local (U.S.) economy, the representative is pointing to the need to distinguish, which sustains the idea of foreignness. What is produced here should be exported (implicitly, should have the quality to be bought by people in other countries) in order to keep our jobs and our growth. Only if 'they' consume what 'we' produce, will the United States benefit from international trade. From that specific political goal, the institutional decision of the United States in 2003 to concentrate the entire supervision of the borders in only one organization is clearly understood. The entanglement of business, security and politics cannot be clearer.

> U.S. Customs and Border Protection (CBP) has direct responsibility for enhancing U.S. economic competitiveness. By reducing costs for industry and enforcing trade laws against counterfeit, unsafe, and fraudulently entered goods, CBP is working to enable legitimate trade, contribute to American economic prosperity, and protect against risks to public health and safety.[6]

The relationship between trade and local/foreign distinction is at the heart of the debate between free trade and protectionism. Schematically, while the former argues in favor of a free circulation of products and of states (and polities) which do not distort the general laws of the market, the latter aims to emphasize the need for (some kind of) regulations that protect local products (or producers?) from its foreign counterparts. This long debate has opened up opportunities to acknowledge the shortcomings of both sides and the increasing relevance of introducing people and ideas into the picture of free trade and/or protectionism (Driskill 2012).

---

5 http://www.cbp.gov/newsroom/spotlights/2014-03-20-000000/facing-future-east-coast-trade-symposium-emphasizes-looking, accessed June 2014.
6 http://www.cbp.gov/trade, accessed June 2014.

There are good reasons to establish in small successive steps the free movement of people throughout the world. There are, however, no good reasons to limit, even temporarily, the free movement of ideas. The movement of things should be judged beneficial to humanity to the extent that it is based on arrangements inviting the movement of ideas and of people. The movement of ideas and of people, overpowers in material and moral significance, the movement of things; the single most important consideration in assessing the organization of the latter is its relation to the organization of the former (Mangabeira Unger 2010).[7]

If people and goods have been framed in the local/foreign dichotomy, however, how can we avoid doing the same with ideas and knowledge? Put differently, does it make any sense to refer to knowledge or ideas as local/foreign intellectual products? In the next two sections I aim to answer these questions. First, I will review the academic literature in order to see how the concept of foreign knowledge has been used,[8] then I will focus on the importance of space for knowledge production and circulation, illustrating theoretical claims with empirical findings from social science research.

Literature on foreign knowledge: a managerial perspective

Based on what I argued in the previous section, foreign knowledge is knowledge which, from the perspective of those who are going to use it, has not been produced in their own context and carries with it characteristics of its context of enunciation, be they specific fragments of texts or implicit assumptions, which in either way constitute premises of the argument. Thus, foreign knowledge includes a procedural dimension (where and how knowledge has been produced) and a textual dimension (knowledge whose logically-interconnected propositions have, explicitly or implicitly, references to its context of production). The foreignness of knowledge

---

[7] The free trade vs protectionism debate has had an impact on the circulation of knowledge through the regulation of the commerce of books and of property rights. See Eisenstein (1982), Johns (2000, 2010), and Sherman (2009) for historic analyses on this topic.

[8] For broad studies on indigenous, local and/or traditional knowledge, see Ramos and Yannakakis (2014), Sefa Dei et al. (2000), Semale and Kincheloe (1999), Brush and Stabinsky (1996).

may reside in its content (ideas) or its format (materialization, manufacturing), but in both cases it affects, in one way or another, what the user can do with it. Insofar as a piece of knowledge is the outcome of, and seeks to contribute to, the intellectual advance of a field which is not ours, we can consider that piece to be foreign knowledge. It could be argued that, for any scholar, knowledge is foreign if it is directly imbricated into the dynamics of academic, intellectual, scientific or technological fields which are not the ones in which s/he is engaged. Although this definition does not exhaust the subtleties and intricacies of this notion of foreign knowledge, to which I will return in the next sections, it is enough to review scholarly literature on the topic.

Three important observations must be made in relation to the literature on foreign knowledge. First, foreign knowledge has not been a widely used category in scholarly studies of knowledge production and circulation. Second, while its relevance transcends disciplines, management and business have been the two areas that have produced the most knowledge on this topic.[9] Third, although disciplinarily focused, this literature can give us important

---

[9] An interesting exception is van Sant (2012), in which foreign knowledge is used to refer to Western medical ideas during Japan's Tokugawa Era. In this article, the foreignness of these ideas is not explored because foreign knowledge is simply something produced in Europe and carried to Japan at the end of 18th century as a book. However, as the analysis progresses, it can be seen that local entanglements of people, practices, institutions and objects had to be enacted in order for foreign knowledge to be appropriated. Indirectly, it points to the (in)abilities of local knowledge producers and users to engage themselves with ideas coming from abroad. Another, more complex exception is Webb (2012), who analyzes foreign books in Arabic literature in the writings of al-Jahiz. In this text, Webb shows how the ideas of foreign, foreignness, and foreigners intersect each other and allows al-Jahiz to reflect on the suitability of books for knowledge circulation, rivalries between Arabs and non-Arabs, and the relevance of having translations of writings from pre-Islamic civilizations. But these are precisely the kinds of things that are explored by the literature that criticizes the westernization and universal knowledge model. They are not "exceptions"... Thematically, these things might be part of a tradition in specialized literature critical to the westernization of knowledge. However, most authors in this tradition rarely use the notion of foreign knowledge as part of their criticisms. Van Sant and Webb, in that regard, are indeed an exception. As I try to do in this chapter, they use the idea of foreign knowledge to criticize Western knowledge (and, implicitly, any form of imperialistic knowledge). In other words, for me, the problem with Western knowledge is not its western-ness but its foreign-ness in relation to the context where it has been attempted to be implemented/used.

insights not only into the nature of foreignness but also into social and organizational aspects of knowledge use and circulation. In the remaining part of this short section, I want to expand these three findings and provide empirical evidence to contextualize scholarly debates on the topic.

Unlike notions such as 'local', 'traditional' or 'indigenous' knowledge, which have been growing in use in recent years and refer to the geographical, social, economic, and cultural roots of knowledge, the expression 'foreign knowledge' has been far less often used in scholarly reflection. If we look for works on this topic in Google Scholar, we obtain 5,750 hits ('local knowledge' = 442,000 hits), which indicates the rather residual position of the concept in the landscape of categories. According to the Library of Congress Online Catalog, the largest library in the world, it has 161 books with the expression "foreign knowledge" in the title, and if we use it as a keyword, the number is 595.[10] The largest online bookstore these days, Amazon.com, lists only 3 books in which 'foreign knowledge' can be found in the title and only 63 if it is used as keyword in the search. An examination of databases focused on scientific and academic articles does not change the picture. In JSTOR there are only 4 articles with 'foreign knowledge' in the title and 400 if we track this category in full-text. Finally, ISI Web of Science, one of the most important academic databases, returns only 58 articles in which the expression is in the title.[11]

Although recognizing the marginal place of 'foreign knowledge' as a category, it has been used in some articles on which I will now focus. The majority of these articles, as Table 1 shows, have been published in business journals (71%) and the concept has only occasionally appeared in journals of other research areas such as engineering, ecology, and public administration. Among other reasons for this disciplinary concentration, we can note the increasing role of knowledge in business, in the context of a globalized economy in which talented people and innovative ideas seem to be the key to commercial success. At the same time, knowledge is usually seen in business literature as patents, which should be registered in national or regional organizations, such as the United States Patent

---

[10] Accessed July 2014; criterion used: Title/KTIL= "foreign knowledge" and Keyword/GKEY= "foreign knowledge".

[11] Accessed June 2014; Database: ISI Web of Science Core Collection, criterion used: TI="foreign knowledge".

and Trademark Office and the European Patent Office. In this context, multinational corporations are frequently responsible for the circulation of knowledge, and that is why direct foreign investment (DFI) often appears as an indicator of knowledge reception (Sofka 2007). Knowledge is easily made material (through patents) and moved (through DFI) and, consequently, its epistemic value is only rarely discussed. Moreover, knowledge is usually technological knowledge, although the adjective is not always clearly stated. Knowledge is therefore considered useful because it translates into products, services or processes, and organizations can profit from this transformative progression (Miesing et al. 2007).

Field: Research Areas	Record Count	% of 58	Bar Chart
BUSINESS ECONOMICS	41	70.690 %	
ENGINEERING	5	8.621 %	
ENVIRONMENTAL SCIENCES ECOLOGY	4	6.897 %	
PUBLIC ADMINISTRATION	4	6.897 %	
AGRICULTURE	2	3.448 %	
COMPUTER SCIENCE	2	3.448 %	
EDUCATION EDUCATIONAL RESEARCH	2	3.448 %	
ENERGY FUELS	2	3.448 %	
GEOGRAPHY	2	3.448 %	
INFORMATION SCIENCE LIBRARY SCIENCE	2	3.448 %	
INTERNATIONAL RELATIONS	2	3.448 %	
LITERATURE	2	3.448 %	
OPERATIONS RESEARCH MANAGEMENT SCIENCE	2	3.448 %	
URBAN STUDIES	2	3.448 %	

Table 1: Articles devoted to foreign knowledge by research area
Source: ISI Web of Science, accessed June 2014

In her analysis of the use of research and development by firms to augment their technological capabilities, Berry (2004) summarized how business literature conceptualizes foreign knowledge and its circulation. In accordance to previous research, she recognizes that foreign knowledge is structurally linked to a gap between countries, which is the foundation of the center-periphery model.

Over the past decade, a number of studies have focused on firms seeking new knowledge and capabilities through their foreign direct investments (FDI). Many of these studies emphasize the relative technological position of the firm's home country (to the position of the host country of the foreign investment). The results from many of these studies suggest that 'technologically lagging' firms invest in foreign countries to source foreign knowledge (Berry, 2004: 3).

In other papers, however, this need for foreign knowledge is analyzed in some detail and important findings can be pointed out, in particular those that have significance beyond the context of business literature. Boeing et al. (2012) have argued that for Chinese firms cooperation between national partners has an impact on productivity, and long-term collaboration requires institutional structures that support it.

> With regard to foreign knowledge sources, we find that only joint ventures with foreign partners and acquisition of foreign firms increase firm productivity. Thus, we argue that it is the deep and enduring organizational integration of a foreign knowledge source that enables knowledge transfer in comparison to a rather short term and project-based international research collaboration (Boeing et al., 2012: 4).

What has been more striking in Boeing et al.'s study is probably the finding that the participation of foreign inventors (people who patented their idea, are not Chinese and do not live in China) does not contribute to the productivity of firms. Put differently, the place where the investor works, where they are physically located, has a correlation with the productivity of their ideas for firms.

> The country of inventors' residence appears to be of high importance when making knowledge useful for an organization. Foreigners living in China may be exceptionally well positioned to translate foreign knowledge in a way that makes it accessible for Chinese firms. Conversely, inventors living abroad do not add to Chinese firms' productivity. Here it does not matter whether they are of Chinese or of foreign origins. We argue that firms cannot absorb external knowledge if researchers are too distant from the own organization (Boeing et al, 2012: 20–21).

Why is place so important for knowledge circulation? Can we find an answer in the business literature? My answer is yes, and we should move our attention to the concept of 'absorptive capacity'

(Sulanski 1996).[12] According to Zahra and George, it is 'a set of organizational routines and processes by which firms acquire, assimilate, transform, and exploit knowledge to produce a dynamic organizational capability (2002: 186). González Duarte et al. explain these steps by arguing that:

> The first means acquisition (identification and acquisition) of knowledge and assimilation of capacities (interpretation of information). The second means transformation (combination of existing knowledge and new knowledge) and exploitation (application). Absorptive capacity is normally analyzed at the organizational level (González Duarte, 2014: 17).

The notion of absorptive capacity brings to the fore the idea that the use of foreign knowledge depends on the ability of organizations to have available: (a) related knowledge previously produced or acquired, and (b) professionals with backgrounds that allow for the creative use of imported knowledge (Cohen and Levinthal 1990; González Duarte et al. 2014). For Chinese firms, for example, Boeing et al. found that:

> The absorptive capacity is sufficiently developed when a higher degree of integration is achieved by means of joint ventures and acquisitions. (However) in research collaboration between Chinese and foreign research partners, the latter have developed effective strategies to protect their intellectual properties. Therefore, they seek to prevent knowledge transfer and only contribute marginally to the knowledge sourcing of Chinese partners (Boeing et al, 2012: 5).

The relevance of the capacities of organizations or countries that receive foreign knowledge has been widely agreed upon in the literature. Li et al. (2010) emphasize the internal efforts of Chinese firms to strengthen their absorptive capacity in order to capitalize on innovation clusters. Fu et al. have argued that to enhance the circulation of knowledge 'the explicit and well-focused encouragement of indigenous innovation and acquisitions of foreign knowledge must work in parallel' (2010: 18). In similar fashion, Szogs and Wilson have argued that:

---

[12] The notion of absorptive capacity has also been used in developing country contexts with many sub-categorizations besides the one I have described. Concepts such as "institutional learning", "individual learning", "collective learning", "learning processes", among others, deserve to be mentioned. I thank Hebe Vessuri for calling my attention to this way of referring to the same phenomenon with a multiplicity of theoretically-informed, disciplinary-shaped expressions.

> The domestic knowledge base is further developed by the technology and knowledge transferred from the foreign source. However, the domestic system needs to be in a position to internalize the input of the foreign knowledge sources. This ability to develop adequate capabilities to absorb the knowledge output of the collaboration with MNE (multi-national enterprises) is one important challenge (Szogs and Wilson, 2006: 95).

Some scholars have focused on the impact of technology and knowledge transfer on the receiving countries, whose absorptive capacities can be hindered by such transfer. Xie and Li (2013), studying emerging economies and their efforts to develop technological competitiveness and to invest in research, have found that the predisposition of receivers and the availability of knowledge from elsewhere obstruct the likelihood of building and strengthening local capacities to absorb foreign knowledge.

> Exporting tends to stimulate less indigenous technological efforts when 1) the knowledge receivers (i.e. emerging economies' exporters) are better prepared and motivated to acquire foreign knowledge and 2) the knowledge sender (i.e. foreign customers and investors) make foreign knowledge more available (Xie and Li, 2013: 248).

Scholars who have studied the relationship between foreign direct investment and intellectual property regimes have also described this tension. Packniat and Rezazadeh, analyzing Iran, have argued that the search for foreign knowledge can be favored by strengthening intellectual property regimes that guarantee beneficial conditions for patent holders (usually, multi-national corporations). However, at the same time, protection of intellectual property affects the real chances of accessing cutting-edge knowledge that might trigger a catch-up process in the developing country. As they put it,

> While knowledge-based development requires using foreign knowledge (so that appropriability of foreign knowledge should be decreased); increasing FDI requires protecting foreign innovators rights to ensure them that their technology would not be used freely in the nation (2005: 8).

The paradoxical effect of foreign knowledge and technology on the receiving country can explain why, as Table 2 shows, China brings together much of the literature of the topic. Concerned as it is with the gap between its economy and that of the developed countries, China seems more interested than other countries not only in exploring the causes and consequences of knowledge transfer, but also in understanding that its role in the 21st century depends, largely, on its ability to produce knowledge locally.

Field: Countries/Territories	Record Count	% of 58	Bar Chart
PEOPLES R CHINA	12	20.690 %	
USA	8	13.793 %	
SPAIN	4	6.897 %	
CANADA	3	5.172 %	
ENGLAND	3	5.172 %	
ITALY	3	5.172 %	
NETHERLANDS	3	5.172 %	
SOUTH KOREA	3	5.172 %	
AUSTRALIA	2	3.448 %	
CZECH REPUBLIC	2	3.448 %	
DENMARK	2	3.448 %	
FINLAND	2	3.448 %	
FRANCE	2	3.448 %	
GERMANY	2	3.448 %	
JAPAN	2	3.448 %	
SINGAPORE	2	3.448 %	
SWITZERLAND	2	3.448 %	

Table 2: Articles devoted to foreign knowledge by country/territory
Source: ISI Web of Science, accessed June 2014

Absorptive capacity does not refer exclusively to technical knowledge and skills. Buckley et al. (2005) pointed out that 'the transfer of knowledge across national boundaries within multinational enterprises depends both on a common language necessary for communication and on the shared social knowledge necessary to understand and predict the behavior of those engaged in the knowledge-transfer process' (2005: 47). Accordingly, Todo and Miyamoto have pointed out that 'workers with advanced foreign knowledge should be distinguished from those who only know operational skills of foreign machinery. By employing (the former), the domestic firm is likely to be able to introduce new capital goods and hence improve its productivity' (2002: 7). Neither should absorptive capacities be analyzed exclusively at the level of the organizations. For González Duarte et al. (2014) the notion can be used to deal with the country level. More interestingly, they argue that the materialization of these capacities through organizations should not prevent us from understanding that it is people who are responsible for foreign knowledge acquisition, transformation and use. 'This means that the education, qualifications, training and professional experience of individuals ultimately determine an organization's (or country's) absorptive capacities' (2014: 18).

If we extrapolate this finding to the social science realm, we could argue that the reception of social science foreign knowledge requires a set of conditions (from up-to-date libraries to proper working conditions) that make it possible for local scholars to critically appropriate foreign knowledge. More than contributions to the depiction of the international division of academic labor (Alatas 2003), my previous works have pointed precisely to the peripheral practices and actors in the process of reproducing the center-periphery model (Rodriguez Medina 2013, 2014). Attention to the conditions that are necessary to deal with foreign knowledge, exemplified in the idea of absorptive capacity, is something still missing in some empirical analyses that rely on the structure of centers and peripheries. However, I do think that scholars who have described science in peripheral regions (see, for example, Kreimer 2010; Díaz et al. 1983) have attempted to show that processes taking place there have specificities that affect not only the conditions of knowledge production, but also the capacity to absorb knowledge produced elsewhere. These scholars have brought to light power relations in science and technology studies that, although critically engaged by many, are normally underrated by much of the scholarship on this topic. The way that power relations connects with space and location is explored in the next section.

A geographical turn in knowledge production and circulation: does space really matter?

Space (be it regional, national, or sub-national) and knowledge are intertwined in ways that have epistemic consequences, because they contribute to organizing the process of research and, by so doing, they shape the outcomes (e.g. theories, methodologies, philosophical assumptions). In the following paragraphs, I will focus on some entanglements of space and knowledge and provide empirical evidence and examples to illustrate my argument. In particular, this section will revolve around: (a) the role of the state in shaping scientific and technological research, (b) the increasing interest in specific settings of knowledge production, such as libraries or laboratories, (c) the existence of geographies of reading, and (d) the idea of space as a label to organize knowledge.

a) The state (and systems of states)

Every state has a set of institutions to promote scientific and technological research, and they are usually responsible for funding, supporting professional and academic organizations, supporting journals and other means of communication, awarding prizes, and contributing to curriculum development by guiding the disciplines in specific directions. If we take, for example, the sources of funding (Table 3) we can observe that the participation of industry is bigger in the developed world but the state is, by far, the main source of resources for Latin American countries. In general, investment in science and technology throughout the region comes fundamentally from states (63%).

	Business	Other Sources
Japan	77	23
Korea	75	25
China	69	26
Finland	68	32
USA	66	34
OECD	64	33
Ireland	59	41
Spain	47	53
EU27	45	55
LAC	37	63
Brazil	45	55
Mexico	42	58
Uruguay	38	62
Argentina	29	71
Colombia	27	73
Ecuador	23	77
El Salvador	2	98
Paraguay	0	100
Panama	0	100
Guatemala	0	100

Table 3: Sources of funding for science and technology by country
Source: Inter-American Development Bank Database, available at http://www.iadb.org/en/topics/competitiveness-technology-and-innovation/moving-data/data-for-science-technology-and-innovation-in-latin-america-and-the-caribbean-a-statistical-compendium-of-indicators,3293.html, accessed July 2014.

National institutions tend to define research questions whose answer is considered by the state as a priority or as strategic for specific reasons. In fact, it could be argued that priorities might be useful to identify which interest groups are behind certain policies or even behind the state as the set of institutions and power resources that mobilize social, economic, cultural, and political actors in order to achieve specific goals, locally and internationally. Reprehensible as they were and are, Project Camelot and the Minerva Initiative, for example, show clearly how the state's interests and policies influence the research agenda of social and natural scientists. In connection with this, Parmar (2012) has maintained that the intermediary role of philanthropic organization has been crucial to understanding how these national interests translate into social science research.[13] Relying on internal communication, and in particular a report written by Reynold Carlson, former Associate Director of Latin American Programs at the Ford Foundation, Parmar studied Project Camelot and has argued that:

> Given the focus of Project Camelot on Chile, Carlson's report shows how closely aligned was Ford's thinking with official U.S. state thinking—first, a state-private shared approach to social science as an aid to preserving and advancing American 'national' interests, and second, the conversion of social scientists into sources of intelligence ahead of possible future military or other interventions to ensure that societal problems were resolved within the 'existing political and legal' order, in which the United States had strong and well-established vested interests (Parmar, 2012: 188–189).

Almost fifty years later, the interests of some states (usually, great powers) remain as guidelines for social research. The Minerva Initiative, funded by Congress with 17.8 millions of dollars only in 2014, is a new attempt by the U.S. Department of Defense to engage social scientists in projects that aim to understand and eventually control massive protests. According to its website:

> The Minerva Initiative is a Department of Defense (DoD)-sponsored, university-based social science research initiative launched by the Secretary of Defense in 2008 focusing on areas of strategic importance to U.S. national security policy. The goal of the Minerva Initiative is to improve DoD's basic understanding of the social, cultural, behavioral, and political forces that shape regions of the world of strategic importance to the U.S.[14]

---

[13] It is interesting to note that Parmar (2012) has not defined 'national interest' in his book, perhaps due to his view of philanthropic organization as entangled with other political, economic and cultural organizations. He points out that '(foundations) are intensely political and ideological and are steeped in market, corporate, and state institutions—(...) they are a part of the power elite of the United States' (2012: 2). In a way, Parmar recognizes that the state as an abstract, neutral, impartial entity somehow detached from daily politics (and protected from the interests of powerful groups) does not apply, at least during the 20th Century hegemony of the United States. It is important to highlight that Parmar contributes with his analysis to a long tradition of studies on the interplay between the United States, philanthropic organizations and the social sciences (see Fisher 1980, 1983; Bulmer and Bulmer 1981; Grossman 1982; Bulmer 1984; Geiger 1988; and Ahmad 1991, amongst many others).

[14] http://minerva.dtic.mil/overview.html, accessed July 2014.

Although this passage seems to present the initiative as a strategic joint venture between the state and universities, some of the priority research topics depict the goals more clearly. Within the section "Belief Propagation and Movements for Change", for example, there is a sub-section titled "(1-A) Belief formation and influence" and its description is:

> Research on belief formation and emotional contagion may help analysts, policy makers, advisors, and trainers better understand the impact of operations on seemingly disparate populations. *This research may also inform the development of countermeasures to help reduce the likelihood of militant behaviors* (emphasis added).[15]

Less ambitious (and less dangerous), the scholarship programs offered by national and some international organizations contribute to shaping scientific and technological research by directing the flow of scholars and students. In this regard, we can speak of national or regional strategies to encourage knowledge circulation.[16] For example, at the Organization of American States there is a program created by this body and Mexican counterparts (CONACYT—OAS—AMEXCID Scholarship Program) which 'reflects the great interest of these institutions in contributing to the improvement of scientific and technological capacities, as well as to the mobility of graduate students in the Americas.'[17] The postgraduate programs actually included in this accord are, however, only in engineering and natural sciences, 'categorized in the following areas: Biology and Chemistry, Physics (only for master's programs) and Mathematics, Geosciences, Engineering, and Biotechnology.'[18] Similarly, the Eiffel Program, instituted by the French Ministry of Foreign Affairs in 1999, aims to support French higher education institutions to internationalize their studentship as part of a long tradition in international cooperation. The objective of the program, which seems to reflect a center-periphery structure, is 'to help to train future foreign policy makers, from the private and public sec-

---

15 http://minerva.dtic.mil/topics.html, accessed July 2014.
16 This is why a comparative history of agencies of international academic cooperation is much needed. The trajectory of DAAD, Fulbright, the British Council and the Confucius Institute, to mention only a few, could shed light on connections between the nation-state (and supranational organizations) and the path of knowledge production and circulation worldwide.
17 http://www.oas.org/en/scholarships/conacyt.asp, accessed July 2014.
18 http://www.oas.org/en/scholarships/conacyt.asp; accessed July 2014.

tors, in education priority areas, and encourage applications from students from developing countries to obtain a master's level and from emerging and industrialized countries to obtain a doctoral level'.[19] Like the Mexican case, France also specifies which areas are top priorities: engineering sciences, mathematics, physics, chemistry, life sciences, nano- and bio-technology, earth and environmental sciences, information and communication sciences and technology, economics and management, and political science.[20] It could be argued, in summary, that every nation-state has its own set of priorities, and the higher education sector and the institutions that promote scientific and technological research are its intellectual arm (Anderson and Steneck 2011; Kapur and McHale 2005; Luchilo 2011; Tejada and Bolay 2010).

There is another way in which the nation-state plays a role in dis/encouraging knowledge production and circulation and is related to countries' perception beyond their borders. In other words, the influence of the states (and societies) on knowledge may be indirect, through the influence of some thinkers, schools of thought, institutions and culture. Two examples will illustrate this point. In the context of anti-positivism that prevailed in Argentina at the beginning of the 20th century, two editorial projects became fundamental to introducing German thought to the country: *Revista de Occidente* and *Biblioteca de Ideas del Siglo XX*, both directed by José Ortega y Gasset. According to Blanco, 'a derivative effect of that opening to German culture was the implantation (...) of German sociology in Argentina, (and that situation) affected how sociology was taught and understood' (2007: 14–15). Unlike other dimensions of the state's influence on knowledge, this cultural perspective revolves around representations, ideals, and even prejudices that transcend boundaries and facilitate (or inhibit) the circulation of certain ideas. The second example comes from Michael Polanyi's time in Berlin, before moving to the United Kingdom in 1933. His years in Germany provided him with first-hand experience of the conditions required to produce knowledge and, by idealizing them, he carried with him a particular perception of Germany's scientific and academic culture that influenced his theo-

---

[19] http://www.campusfrance.org/sites/default/files/vademecum_eiffel_20 14-2015-uk.pdf, accessed July 2014.
[20] http://www.campusfrance.org/sites/default/files/vademecum_eiffel_20 14-2015-uk.pdf, accessed July 2014.

ry of science. In her analysis of the origins of the social construction of science and the role of Polanyi in it, Nye argues that:

> Michael Polanyi's thirteen years in Berlin gave him the experience of what he later transformed into an idealized vision of scientific research community. Polanyi's late reflection on the world he had lost propelled him into an intellectual exposition and defense of the social and institutional preconditions that are necessary for the flourishing of modern science. The freedom of research that he had experienced in a tightly networked community of world-class colleagues within the tree-lined precincts of Dahlem became an induplicable but idealized memory that formed the foundation of his later writings on the nature of scientific life and scientific achievement (Nye, 2011: 83).

German sociology (Blanco 2007) and German research community (Nye 2011) might be an illusion, an idealized notion of a set of heterogeneous actors and not-always-harmonious relationships between them. However, this does not prevent other actors (e.g. Argentinian sociologists or Polanyi's colleagues in the UK) from using them as a way of identifying some products and conditions of knowledge linked to a specific country (Germany) in a specific period (beginning of the 20th century). One important consequence of this is that the connection between knowledge and place can be suggested (or even invented) by those who are not directly involved in the process of knowledge production but by others who can use such a connection to advance their intellectual (or economic and political) agendas.

b) The site

In the last decades, science and technology studies have paid special attention to sites of knowledge production. As Livingstone has argued,

> The enterprise we casually refer to as 'science' embraces a huge range of activities carried out in many venues. In these miscellaneous spaces, nature has been differently experienced, objects have been differently regarded, claims to knowledge have been adjudicated in different ways. It is only when the practices and procedures that are mobilized to generate knowledge are located—sited—that scientific inquiry can be made intelligible as a human undertaking (Livingstone, 2003: 86).

Livingstone (2003: 17–86) analyzes the house of experiment (a pre-laboratory), cabinets of accumulation, field operations, gardens of display, spaces of diagnosis, ships for scientific voyages, the court, the coffeehouse, and public houses, and even the body as a site of knowledge production. His main point is that the materiality of space (e.g. instruments, spaces, furniture) affects the way scientists think and consequently the knowledge they can produce.

Probably the quintessential place of knowledge production is the laboratory, because laboratories were thought of as the sites from which pure knowledge emanates. For many historians and philosophers of science, 'knowledge from the lab was apolitically, asocially, transtemporally, translocally true' (Doing 2008: 279). However, since the late 1970s, ethnographies of laboratory life have confronted this view. As Knorr Cetina puts it, students of science can, 'through direct observation and discourse analysis at the root of where knowledge is produced, (understand) the process of knowledge production as "constructive" rather than descriptive' (1995: 140–141). These approaches to laboratories were made under the assumption (or trying to prove that) 'science that exists in practice is not at all like the science we read about in textbooks' (Lynch 1985: xiv), which implied a challenge to studying science by focusing on its intellectual outcomes (e.g. theories). Under these assumptions, empirical studies have shown that laboratories are historically and spatially embedded, with relevant epistemic consequences. Analyzing the case of Venezuela, for example, Vessuri (1997) has described how the instruments available in local university labs prevented at one point Venezuelan immunology researchers from publishing in competitive journals that would not accept their papers because the data had been obtained from a previous generation of scientific instruments. This is a very frequent condition of science practice in the South and clearly identifies the features of the locality.

While previous examples come from natural sciences, social sciences have also provided illustrative instances of this concern with sites because, as some scholars have shown, the assemblage of objects, practices and humans is a precondition for the production of knowledge (Latour 2005). One famous case is Niklas Luhmann's slip box. According to Krajewski, 'the arrangement consists of wooden boxes with drawers that pull out in the front, and cards in octavo format' (2003: 105) with which the German sociologist organized the material that he used to work. The consequence of this is that:

The materiality of systems theory (...) draws its productive power, persistent for three decades, from the generative pairing of man and machine. When Niklas Luhmann decided in 1951 (...) to no longer gather loose sheets into portfolios, as Goethe once did, but rather to take up work on a slip box, just like his implicit benchmark Hegel, the position of the Other became occupied by a paper machine. Instead, both systems (man and machine) partaking in the communication (...), the 'psychological' and the 'systems of notes', form a constellation that is shaped by the term 'partnership' (Krajewski 2013: 105).

The assemblage of objects might also refer to the identity of scholars, because, as Becher and Trowler have pointed out, an individual's sense of belonging to academic disciplines:

>...also involves artifacts—a chemist's desk is prone to display three-dimensional models of complex molecular structures, an anthropologist's walls are commonly adorned with colorful tapestries and enlarged photographic prints of beautiful black people, while a mathematician may boast no more than a chalkboard scribbled with algebraic symbols (Becher and Trowler, 2001: 45).

Recently, interest in sites of social knowledge production has been highlighted by Camic et al. (2011). In this study, the authors recognize that the traditional sociology of the social sciences has neglected 'the day-to-day actions and processes through which the producers of social knowledge actually go about the on-the-ground work of making, evaluating, and disseminating the kinds of social knowledge that they are involved in producing' (2011: 6–7). Contrary to this tradition, they suggest turning to science and technology studies and concentrating on practices, defined as 'the ensembles of patterned activities (...) by which human beings confront and structure the situated tasks with which they are engaged' (2011: 7). Since practices take place in specific contexts, this new approach attempts to bring to the fore their situatedness, and put into question the idea (l) of social scientists as delocalized minds whose main goal is to read/think/write. Thus, the traditional sociology of social science:

...has fostered an enclosed vision of the locational sites where the activities of knowledge making occur. Reading, thinking, writing—these are not actions that ordinarily have strong spatial associations. To the extent that sociologists of knowledge have situated these activities at all, this has generally been within an imagined nexus that the sociologist constructs by overlaying the particular macrosocial forces that he or she wishes to emphasize onto the bounded space of the intellectual tradition, school, field, or academic unit to which the social thinker under study belongs. The circumscribed nexus that results is, by implication, the location of the thinker's cogitating, reading, and writing, as traditional sociology of social science overlooks other, more concrete sites of knowledge practices (Camic et al., 2011: 9).

The main consequence of this new approach—to which this chapter wants to contribute—is that attention is paid to phenomena such as library research infrastructure and humanistic and social science scholarship (Abbott 2011), archives and filing (Lemov 2011), academic conferences (Vessuri and Canino 2002, Gross and Fleming 2011), evaluative practices of peer review panels (Lamont and Huutoniemi 2011), documents (Stark 2011), and polls and surveys (Igo 2011). These practices shape—and are shaped by—the specific configurations of sites of social knowledge production, which is another way to say that space actually matters.

c) Geography/ies of speech and reading

The relationship between space and knowledge can be studied from a different perspective, one in which place appears as a constitutive part not of the text itself but of the practices around its production and reception. Following Livingstone's (2003, 2005, 2007) pincer movement, I will deal in this subsection with place as situated filters for interpretation and as geographical locus of enunciation. Regarding the former, Livingstone shows that 'where scientific texts are read has an important bearing on how they are read' (2005: 391). In his text, he proposes a geography of reading, a theoretically rich concept that aims to grasp four dimensions of the interplay between knowledge and space: (a) spaces of textual circulation, (b) sites of textual hybridity, (c) cartographies of textual reception, and (d) cultural geographies of reading. The first refers to an ontological position according to which, and following Said (1991), Livingstone argues that theories (and knowledge) change when they travel. The first implication of this position is that there are different processes of representation and institutionalization, where knowledge is produced and where it is read, interpreted or used. The second is that there are no misreadings or incorrect interpretations, but rather re-localizations of knowledge. Third, as Said has put it, 'no reading is neutral or innocent, and by the same token every text and every reader is to some extent the product of a theoretical standpoint' (1991: 241). Textual hybridity is a useful concept because it points to the (inner) process of interpretation that any reader undertakes when dealing with a text. Livingstone puts it nicely: 'the meaning that any new work has for an individual reader is shaped by the other texts and theories and practices they have engaged' (2005: 393). Furthermore, reading is hybridizing because it locates the new text within a tradition, a set of previously read texts that enable and constrain the number and quality of possible interpretations. Through cartographies of textual reception, Livingstone moves away from Gadamer's (1997) and Said's (1991) individual approaches to interpretation (i.e. a focus on notable interpreters who contribute to expanding or challenging textual traditions) and proposes a holistic alternative. In this regard, he argues that there are shared elements, strongly linked to culture, that play a role in the way texts are read in specific contexts; these elements constitute what can be called 'reviewing culture'. Consequently, it would be possible to find place-specific interpretations of texts, such as a British reading of Humboldt texts (Livingstone 2005: 394). Finally, the cultural geography of reading refers to the need to transcend scholarly interpretations and to include spaces and audiences underrated as objects of study by academics. In Livingstone's words, 'this account moves the analysis of reading from the public reviewing culture (...) into private sites and conversational spaces' (2005: 395).

On the other hand, in his work on science, site and speech, Livingstone (2007) tries to show the connection between places and enunciation, showing that 'sites enable and constrain what may be said, and heard, about particular scientific claims' (2007: 71). Given the power to constrain, places become 'spaces of speech', which are usually circumscribed to specific settings (from cities to professional associations to university departments) and play a fundamental role because they determine what may count as a logically interconnected argument, and what is not permitted to be articulated. In this way, places (and the practices, people and devices entangled with them) act as a de facto Gadamerian horizon of interpretation, setting subtle boundaries of what can be thought. For example, the reception and application of Darwin's evolutionary theory presents sharp differences between Ireland and the southern states of the United States.

> What could be said about Darwin in 1870s Dublin to one religious denomination could not be said in Belfast to their co-religionists for the simple reason that the public spectacle of John Tyndall's speech at the British Association marked out the rhetorical radius within which the debate there was conducted. At the same time, in Londonderry, the local investment in the Irish culture wars over higher education conditioned how another Presbyterian spokesman engaged evolution. In the American South, the politics of sectionalism and racial ideology shaped in one way or another talk about evolution. The failure to say what particular communities wanted to hear about Darwin resulted in professors losing their positions; long-standing presumptions about racial differences dominated conversational networks and shaped how Darwin's theories were talked about. Darwinism's fortunes in both Ireland and the southern states of America, I contend, were crucially dependent on the microgeographies of speech spaces in both places (Livingstone 2007: 92).

It is worth highlighting that Livingstone recognizes the role of materiality in the process of interpretation. Although focused on texts and the ideas embedded in them, he illustrates some of his theoretical reflections with historical examples about the history of book and print culture. Thus he continues a tradition opened up by the classic study on Boyle and Hobbes regarding the existence of vacuum (Shapin and Schaffer 1985). Here it is clearly shown that the replication of the experiments undertaken by Boyle in Oxford and London in other settings (for example, The Netherlands), which was the foundation of similar interpretations of nature beyond the United Kingdom, required the circulation of people (who transmitted know-how) and instruments (which always needed calibration). Livingstone (2005)'s four-step analysis of interpretation can therefore be complemented by what Don Ihde (2009) has called 'material hermeneutics', which refers to the interpretation of non-textual objects in humanities and social sciences, and to giving voice to things by acting upon them. If successful, a materially sensitive interpretation will be based on a different kind of observation (i.e. beyond reading) that would move the social scientific and humanistic disciplines closer to the natural sciences. 'To observe (would) be to enact the questions asked through material, instrumental means. Materiality, in a double sense, would pervade (...) sciences, both in the form of what is investigated and in the instrumental modes by which the investigation proceeds' (Ihde 2009: 68).

At this point, Livingstone (2005, 2007) and Ihde (2009) have provided us with a historical and philosophical framework through which to understand the relationship between place and knowledge, in particular for scientific theories. Place enables and puts constraints on what can be said and what can be thought. Place is where specific practices occur, where specific scholars work, where specific instruments are found, where specific ideas emerge. Place is connected to culture, institutional arrangements and societal organization in an entangled way. A materially sensitive geography of speech and reading therefore has to be thought to complement other perspectives on knowledge production (e.g. sociological, anthropological or historical analyses).

d) The label

The last part of my argument in this section is devoted to space as a label, that is, as a symbolic reference to non-explicit connections between knowledge and place. In this case, 'foreign' is too vague a category (although useful in some situations) and is often replaced by others that denote specific locations (e.g. German idealism or French Theory). Labeling is the process through which a classifying name is applied to something or someone, and has, at least, two levels. At the level of information, labels contribute to creating categories whose 'material force (...) appears always and instantly' (Bowker and Star 2000: 3) to produce specific socio-material orders based on more or less explicit classifications. Put differently, we use labels to classify because we want to (re)produce a certain order of things and people (see also Busch [2011] for the pragmatics of classifications through standardization). At the level of practices, especially in the sociology of knowledge, labeling is what Baert (2012) has called an intellectual intervention.

> Intellectuals can use labels to flag their own position (e.g. Marcus and Fischer's 'reflexive turn' in anthropology) but they can also use labels to incriminate others (e.g. Said's 'orientalism'). The introduction of labels can facilitate the dissemination of ideas, but once many others adopt the same label (sometimes expressing different ideas), they may undermine the clarity of its meaning or the distinctiveness of those associate to it (Baert, 2012: 311).

At both levels, labels refer to the textual/material product with which classifications are produced and to the pragmatics that focus our attention on the effects of such classifications and the interests of actors (individual or institutional) in raising them. The process of the appropriation of French Theory by American cultural analysts is a good example. According to Cusset (2008) the success of French Theory in the United States lies in the ability of U.S. scholars to disconnect the theory from the other philosophical traditions that, in France (its context of production), had played a fundamental role.

> All 'travelling theories' (...) carry with them such a risk (of turning real social critics into trendy conservatives), for they have always involved disconnection from a specific context and reconnection with a new one—in this case, disconnection from a certain Continental notion of writing, from the horizon of Marxism and revolution, and from a timely critique of semiology and the linguistic turn. And reconnection with many American traditions and particularities, to which any import has to connect if it wants to become an integral part of the receiving culture (Cusset 2008: xvi-xvii).

The passage shows that the label 'French' indicates not only the nationality of thinkers who shared the intellectual field in France during the second part of the 20th century, but also, and more fundamentally, the group of theories and thinkers that, as a reviewing culture (Livingstone 2005), enabled and constrained the horizon of interpretation by those theorists. According to Cousset, what makes Derrida or Guattari French theorists is their (sometimes-antagonistic) relationship with Marx(ism), Continental philosophy, and semiology. In a way, they constitute what Fish (1989) has called an interpretive community and they share common readings, not a similar approach to contemporary philosophical problems. Cousset (2008) goes on to suggest that the Frenchness of some theorists' production lies, from the perspective of their American counterparts, in the re-connections established with some American intellectual traditions, in particular pragmatism. Thus, French theory is knowledge that originated in a specific setting (Paris in the second half of the 20th century), as a reaction to certain intellectual European contributions (e.g. Marx's analysis of capitalist societies) and travelled elsewhere (e.g. United States) to be hybridized by a different intellectual tradition (e.g. Pierce and Emerson). The crucial point here is that Foucault, Derrida, Deleuze, Guattari and the other theorists who, according to Cousset, transformed American intellectual life did not see themselves as French theorists. In fact, "French theory" is a label created in the United States.

> One wonders if there is anything left to expect from this weird textual American object known as *theory*, born between the two world wars or in the crazy 1970s, depending on historical accounts, but definable today as a strange breed of academic market rules, French (and more generally Continental) detachable concepts, campus-based identity politics, and trendy pop culture (Cousset 2008: xi; emphasis in original).

Interestingly, Holub (1992) depicted the conflictive relationship between theoretical reflection produced in France and Germany with the expression 'French Theory' and 'German Thought'. Surprised by the strong influence of French thinkers in the American intellectual realm, Holub wonders why such inspiration did not cross the Rhine, especially because of the place of German thinkers (such as Marx and Nietzsche) in French intellectual circles. In Holub's words,

> Few would doubt that *German thought* has dominated *French theory* for the past two and a half decades. Nor can one cite a lack of exposure or opportunity as the reason for the scarcity of German interest in poststructuralism either. By the early eighties most of the major writers usually associated with poststructuralism had seen their works translated into German at major publishing houses. (...) Reasons for these missing receptions (are) in the first place, poststructuralism has found no influential advocate or advocates in intellectual and theoretical circles in Germany; a second (...) factor has to do with the scarcity of positions at German universities (and) a final reason (...) has to do with *the tradition into which it had to be absorbed. The German philosophers that were so important for the French poststructuralists were often viewed quite differently on the other side of the Rhine* (1992: 41–42; emphasis added).

Once again, the community of readers/interpreters plays a crucial role since the authors labeled as 'German' by the French theorists were read differently in Germany, in the same way that Derrida, Foucault and Deleuze were read differently in France than in the United States. Reading, let me repeat again, seems to be the door to the connection between space and knowledge, because in the act of reading we include space/place/setting as a kind of implicit premise that needs to be taken into account for interpretation.

Before moving on to the concluding section, I would like to argue that there are at least two ways in which I do not see space and knowledge connected. In my view, there is no location from which someone might have a vantage perspective. For some scholars (e.g. postcolonial theorists) the former colonies, which are still trapped in the network of colonial power, are seen as a privileged standpoint from where innovative, non-Eurocentric, non-Westernized, local knowledge can be produced. Highlighting the epistemic consequences of oppression in these regions, scholars attempt to raise them as loci of enunciation where real border thinking emerges (Mignolo 2000). Although I share their concern about recovering (and respecting) long traditions of knowledge production predating colonial endeavors, they usually pay little attention to circulation of knowledge and the difficulties for peripheral scholars and intellectuals to engage, in better conditions, in the international division of academic (and excessively Western) social sciences. Put differently, by focusing on the originality and relevance of knowledge produced in the peripheries they tend to underestimate the consequences of the mobility of knowledge itself and of transculturation as a phenomenon with epistemic implications. On the other hand, the idea of blurring regional, national, sub-national, and site-specific boundaries and replacing them with a notion of global knowledge (as a new kind of space in the scenario of knowledge production) is not very fruitful.[21] I do believe that something such as global, transnational, or international science is necessary, especially when analyzing the social sciences, because they have been attached to the building of nation-states for a long time. However, I do not think that global knowledge means the eradication of local differences, but rather their recognition and articulation through difficult negotiations (which are always situated). Neither do I think that reducing social science production to reading/thinking/writing is useful because, as Camic et al. (2011) have shown, this perspective idealizes the knowledge producer, removes power from academic/scientific relations, and forgets to problematize the very 'activities of reading, thinking, and writing, each understood as joined to the others in a seamless bloc—and to characterize the production of social knowledge in this manner is, in effect, to depict it as a monolith (in miniature)' (Camic et al. 2011: 9). Insofar as reading needs libraries, thinking necessitates software,

---

[21] Interestingly, the phrase "global knowledge" returns 83,100 hits on Google Scholar, clearly between the numbers for 'foreign knowledge' and 'local knowledge'.

and writing demands computers—among other requirements—these activities must be seen as geographically and culturally situated.

Conclusions: what should we do with foreign knowledge?

In this last section, I will return briefly to some of my points, I will connect them, and suggest their practical implications. Perhaps the fundamental point of this chapter is whether space plays a role in knowledge production and circulation. While it is rather obvious that spatial considerations are not always present in texts of the social sciences, I will argue, in this last part of the chapter, that they still are premises of the argument, although invisible in the written text.[22] This idea is precisely that for which the notion of enthymeme accounts. According to Scenters-Zapico, an enthymeme is:

> A discursive structure that inscribes consensus, for the elided assumptions of an enthymeme are supplied by the intertextual network of experiences and associations shared by readers, writers, speakers, and hearers. The deleted premises of an enthymeme must be supplied by the audience for its argument to achieve closure. In a very real way, the missing premise of an enthymeme must be occupied by the reader, and this makes the enthymeme intertextual by its very nature (1994: 71).

This notion allows me to retrieve some ideas developed in previous sections. First, since ideas related to the space of knowledge production are not explicitly stated in the arguments (usually, in sci-

---

[22] The absence of spatial references in a text should not be confused with the universalistic scope of the knowledge produced. As Baber has put it, 'More often than not, the title of the body of work in question constitutes a good indicator of its claim for universalistic, general status. Thus an article or book produced by a scholar situated in a non-metropolitan society and reporting on research conducted on a non-metropolitan site will almost invariably disclose the identity of the location in its title. (...) Conversely, it is much harder to find titles of papers and books ending with 'in the United States', 'in Britain' or 'in France', signalling the claim that when it comes to the results of research in these societies, location and context do not matter. The unstated assumption is that when it comes to the sociological study of metropolitan societies, the disclosure of the location of the study is largely irrelevant since the results are presumably of universal not provincial significance' (2003: 617).

ence, focused on facts), then they constitute an enthymeme. They are part of the logical argument but not visible in the text; they remain unwritten. Second, only the reader can fill the gap, which means, following Livingstone's (2005) idea of the geography of reading, that the reader will bring to the front the texts previously read in order to make new, innovative, original connections/interpretations. In this sense, the argument is completed only when it is read and introduced into a new logical argument, proposed by the reader/user, and this tends to produce consensus between the original, written idea and the one enacted by the community of interpreters. Third, readers actually fill the gap when they have the intention to produce effects, beyond the traditional trilogy of reading/thinking/writing. When you want to see your article published in a journal, you have to cite works that previously appeared in that journal. When you want to see your book proposal approved by an international publishing house, you have to show that you have mastered the textual and para-textual dimensions of academic writing and of your discipline (Canagarajah 2002). When you want to see your research grant awarded, you must comply with the fashionable literature of the moment. When you want to see your piece published in a national newspaper you need to understand the political climate of the time. Briefly, we habitually want to do more things with our words than simply and exclusively contribute to the growth of knowledge. Due to these intentions, scholars must fill the gaps in the arguments with other premises (coming from their previous readings) that increase the likelihood of achieving such goals.

I will focus now on two of the multiple implications of the ideas outlined in this chapter. First, although foreign knowledge—and perhaps any knowledge—calls for interpretation, one role of peripheral scholars has been to profusely introduce premises to foreign ideas in order to adapt them to local realities. It seems that scholarly life in peripheral regions is reduced to this adaptive process, according to which originality comes in the form of ability to make connections with research questions embedded in local(ized) problems. This does not need to be the case. If foreign knowledge can be applied to/used to understand local contexts in a more or less straightforward manner, it should be appropriated.[23] If not, maybe it should be ignored altogether, that is, it should be considered irrelevant (Alatas 2001), even if not acknowledging it diminishes the chances of getting published in international journals (Canagarajah 2002). It is neither necessary nor fruitful to devote scarce resources (such as time and funds) to profound exercises of the transformation of foreign knowledge mainly because we are expected to cite cutting-edge foreign research.[24] Accordingly, the institutions created to promote (local) scientific and technological research should develop peer-review mechanisms to discourage this scholarly strategy of imitation.[25]

---

[23] Possible uses of foreign knowledge are as a case study, as data, and as evidence. Focus should be placed on the local situation that needs to be explained. One way of provincializing Anglo-European knowledge is to take it merely as information.

[24] I do not imply that the use of foreign knowledge to cite cutting-edge research in order to get published in international journals is the only reason for academics in the periphery. In fact, if we asked scholars why they cited the work of some other scholars published in the most prestigious journals they would probably answer that they wanted to acknowledge the latest developments in their disciplines or they needed some ideas to contrast their own, or they wanted to have access to new data, or... However, from my point of view, the angle is different. Cutting-edge research, by definition, is precisely the works that reviewers of important journals suggest submitters to read in order to improve or update the text submitted. When a scholar is asked to review some article or book, s/he is being requested to pay tribute to major contributions of the field and s/he is well aware of the possible consequences of not citing those works. Will s/he learn something from the recommended literature? Probably yes. Is such literature a mandatory reading in the sense of being essential for the argument? Not necessarily. Will the article be published if s/he decides not to cite those works? Probably not. Therefore, my point is that scholars and scholarly institutions in the periphery must rethink their reward system in order to encourage original knowledge–in multiple formats–instead of strengthening strategies that prioritize foreign knowledge recognition/use over other criteria (e.g. applicability to local circumstances or entanglement with locally-produced theories).

[25] CONACYT, the Mexican agency to encourage research, prefers members of its National System of Researchers to publish in international journals (i.e. journals based in U.S. or Western Europe, published by internationally-known publishers, and in English) instead of its local or regional counterparts, usually not indexed in international databases (e.g. ISI Web of Science). See Foro Consultivo Científico y Tecnológico and Academia Nacional de Ciencias (2005) 'Una reflexión sobre el Sistema Nacional de Investigadores a 20 años de su creación', available at http://www.coniunctus.amc.edu.mx/libros/20_sni_final.pdf, accessed February, 2015.

Second, our labels should be problematized, in particular those we use to organize knowledge. Due to our peripheral position in the international division of academic labor, we need to create new classificatory systems that connect foreign knowledge with local production (see Springer and Turpin 2015). Putting local knowledge before foreign knowledge is not a fanatic nationalist exaltation of hidden virtues. Instead, it is a practical, situated, viable strategy to reconnect knowledge from different parts in order to permit and encourage different dialogues and interpretations. For example, why do we not classify Comte's *Introduction to Positive Philosophy* or Spencer's *First Principles* as *responses* to local debates about civilization and barbarism (in Sarmiento's *Life in the Argentine Republic in the Days of the Tyrants; or, Civilization and Barbarism*) or the ordered city (in Rama's *The Lettered City*)? This would break, of course, a chronological order, but nothing forces us to accept the chronological sequences of intellectual products as the only structuring principle we can use to store and organize knowledge. This will help in challenging the canonization of Anglo-European authors and schools of thought, bringing about important consequences for the structuring of curriculum (from primary school to higher education) in peripheral regions. At the end of the day, it is all about creating new possibilities for the scholars of the next generations.

References

Abbott, A. (2011). Library Infrastructure for Humanistic and Social Scientific Scholarship in the Twentieth Century. In C. Camic, N. Gross and M. Lamont (eds.) *Social Knowledge in the Making*. Chicago: The University of Chicago Press.

Ahmad, S. (1991). American foundations and the development of the social sciences between the wars: comments on the debate between Martin Bulmer and Donald Fisher. *Sociology*, 25(3): 511–520.

Alatas, S.F. (2001). The Study of the Social Sciences in Developing Countries: Towards and Adequate Conceptualization of Relevance. *Current Sociology*, 49(2): 1–19.

Alatas, S.F. (2003). Academic dependency and the global division of labour in the social sciences. *Current Sociology*, 51(6): 599–613.

Alesina, A., Devleeschauwer, A., Easterly, W., Kurlat, S. and Wacziarg, R. (2003). Fractionalization. *Journal of Economic Growth*, 8(2): 155–194.

Abend, G. (2008). The Meaning of "Theory". *Sociological Theory*, 26(2): 173–199.

Anderson, M.S. and Steneck, N.H. (eds.) (2011). *International Research Collaborations. Much to be Gained, Many Ways to Get in Trouble*. New York: Routledge.

Baert, P. (2012). Positioning Theory and Intellectual Interventions. *Journal for the Theory of Social Behavior*, 42(3): 304–324.

Barber, Z. (2003). Provincial Universalism: The Landscape of Knowledge Production in an Era of Globalization. *Current Sociology*, 51(6): 615–623.

Becher, T. and Trowler, P. (2001). *Academic Tribes and Territories: Intellectual Enquiry and the Culture of Disciplines*, Buckingham: Society for Research into Higher Education and Open University Press.

Berry, H. (2004). *Leaders, Laggards, and the Pursuit of Foreign knowledge*, Working paper 2004–06, Reginald H. Jones Center, The Wharton School, The University of Pennsylvania.

Blanco, A. (2007). La temprana recepción de Max Weber en la sociología argentina (1930–1950). *Perfiles Latinoamericanos*, 30 (July-December): 9–38.

Boeing, P. Mueller, E. and Sandner, P. (2012). What makes Chinese firms productive? Learning from indigenous and foreign sources of knowledge. Working Paper 196, Frankfurt: Frankfurt School of Finance and Management.

Bowker, G.C. and Star, S.L. (2000). *Sorting Things Out: Classification and its Consequences*. Cambridge MA: MIT Press.

Brush, S.B. and Stabinsky, D. (eds.) (1996). *Valuing Local Knowledge: Indigenous People and Intellectual Property Rights*. Washington DC: Island Press.

Buckley, P.J. Carter, M.J., Clegg, J. and Tan, H. (2005). Language and Social Knowledge in Foreign-Knowledge Transfer to China. *International Studies of Management & Organization*, 35 (1): 47–65.

Bulmer, M. (1984). Philanthropic foundations and the development of the social sciences in the early twentieth century: a reply to Donald Fisher. *Sociology*, 18(4): 572–579.

Bulmer, M. and Bulmer J. (1981). Philanthropy and social science in the 1920s: Beardsley Ruml and the Laura Spelman Rockefeller memorial, 1922–29. *Minerva* 19(3): 347–407.

Busch, L. (2011). *Standards. Recipes for Reality*. Cambridge MA: MIT Press.

Camic, C., Gross, N. and Lamont, M. (eds.) (2011). *Social Knowledge in the Making*. Chicago: The University of Chicago Press.

Canagarajah, A.S. (2002). *A Geopolitics of Academic Writing*. Pittsburgh: The University of Pittsburgh Press.

Cohen, W.M. and Levinthal, D.A. (1990). Absorption capacity: a new perspective on learning and innovation. *Administrative Science Quarterly*, 35: 128–151.

Cousset, F. (2008). French Theory: How Foucault, Derrida, Deleuze, & Co. Transformed the Intellectual Life of the United States. Minneapolis: University of Minnesota Press.

Derrida, J. (2000). On Hospitality. Anne Dufourmantelle invites Jacques Derrida to Respond. Stanford CA: Stanford University Press.

Díaz, E., Texera, Y. and Vessuri, H. (1983). *La Ciencia Periférica*. Caracas: Monte Ávila Editores.

Doing, P. (2008). Give Me a Laboratory and I Will Rise a Discipline : The Past, Present, and Future Politics of Laboratory Studies in STS. In E. Hacket, O. Amsterdamska, M. Lynch, and J. Wajcman (eds.) *The Handbook of Science and Technology Studies*. 3rd Edition, Cambridge MA: MIT Press.

Driskill, R. (2012). Deconstructing the Argument for Free Trade: A Case Study of the Role of Economists in Policy Debates. *Economics and Philosophy*, 28(1): 1–30.

González Duarte, R., Márcio de Castro, J., Miura, I.K., Almeida de Moraes, R., Feijó, J., and Zaara de Carvalho, J. (2014) FDI inflows, transfer of knowledge, and absorptive capacity: the case of Mozambique. *African Journal of Business Management*, 8(1): 14–24.

Eisenstein, E. (1982). *The Printing Press as an Agent of Change*. Volume 1 and 2, Cambridge: Cambridge University Press.

Fisher, D. (1980). American Philanthropy and the social sciences in Britain:, 1919–1939; The Reproduction of a Conservative Ideology. *The Sociological Review*, 28(2): 277–315.

Fisher, D. (1983). The Role of Philanthropic Foundations in the Reproduction and Production of Hegemony: Rockefeller Foundations and the Social Sciences. *Sociology* 17(2): 206–233.

Gadamer, H.G. (1997). *Verdad y Método I*. Salamanca: Sígueme.

Geiger, R.L. (1988). American Foundations and Academic Social Science, 1945–1960. *Minerva* 26(3): 315–341.

Gross, N. and Fleming, C. (2011). Academic conferences and the making of philosophical knowledge. In C. Camic, N. Gross and M. Lamont (eds.) *Social Knowledge in the Making*. Chicago: The University of Chicago Press.

Grossman, D.M. (1982). American foundations and the support of economic research, 1913–29. *Minerva*, 20(1–2): 59–82.

Holub, R.C. (1992). *Crossing Borders: Reception Theory, Poststructuralism, Deconstruction*. Madison: The University of Wisconsin Press.

Honig, B. (1998). Immigrant America? How Foreignness "Solves" Democracy's Problems. *Social Text 56*, 16(3): 1–27.

Honig, B. (2001). *Democracy and the foreigner*. Princeton: Princeton University Press.

Igo, S.E. (2011). Subjects of Persuasion: Survey Research as a Solicitous Science; or, The Public Relations of the Polls. In C. Camic, N. Gross and M. Lamont (eds.) *Social Knowledge in the Making*. Chicago: The University of Chicago Press.

Ihde, D. (2009). *Postphenomenology and Technoscience. The Peking University Lectures*, Albany: SUNY Press.

Johns, A. (2000). *The Nature of the Book: Print and Knowledge in the Making*. Chicago: The University of Chicago Press.

Johns, A. (2010). *Piracy: The Intellectual Property Wars from Gutenberg to Gates*. Chicago: The University of Chicago Press.

Kapur, D. and McHale, J. (2005). *Give Us Your Best and Brightest. The Global Hunt for Talent and Its Impact on the Developing World*. Washington DC: Center for Global Development.

Knorr Cetina, K. (1995). Laboratory Studies: The Cultural Approach to the Study of Science. In S. Jasanoff, G. Merkle, J. Petersen and T. Pinch (eds.) *Handbook of Science and Technology Studies*. Thousand Oaks CA: Sage.

Krajewski, M. (2013). Paper as Passion: Niklas Luhmann and his Card Index. In L. Gitelman (ed.) *"Raw Data" is an Oxymoron*. Cambridge MA: MIT Press.

Kreimer, P. (2010). *Ciencia y periferia. Nacimiento, muerte y resurrección de la biología molecular en la Argentina*. Buenos Aires: Eudeba.

Kuhn, M. (2013). "Academic Dependence": The World Social Science Arena—a Battlefield among Parochial Thought? In M. Kuhn and K. Okamoto (eds.) *Spatial Social Thought: Local Knowledge in Global Science Encounters*. Stuttgart: Ibidem Verlag.

Lamont, M. and Huutoniemi, K. (2011). Comparing customary rules of fairness: evaluative practices in various types of peer review panels. In C. Camic, N. Gross and M. Lamont (eds.) *Social Knowledge in the Making*. Chicago: The University of Chicago Press.

Latour, B. (2005). *Reassembling the Social. An Introduction to Actor-Network Theory*. Oxford: Oxford University Press.

Lemov, R. (2011). Filing the Total Human: Anthropological Archives from 1928 to 1963. In C. Camic, N. Gross and M. Lamont (eds.) *Social Knowledge in the Making*. Chicago: The University of Chicago Press.

Li, J., Chen, D., Shapiro, D. M. (2010). Product Innovation in Emerging Economies: The Role of Foreign Knowledge Access Channels and Internal Efforts in Chinese Firms. *Management and Organization Review*, 6(2): 243–266.

Livingstone, D.N. (2003). *Putting Science in its Place: Geographies of Scientific Knowledge*. Chicago: The University of Chicago Press.

Livingstone, D.N. (2005). Science, text and space: thoughts on the geography of reading. *Transactions of the Institute of British Geographers*, 30: 391–401.

Livingstone, D.N. (2007). Science, site and speech: scientific knowledge and the spaces of rhetoric. *History of the Human Sciences*, 20(2): 71–98.

Luchilo, L. (coord) (2011). *Más allá de la fuga de cerebros. Movilidad, migración y diásporas de argentinos calificados.* Buenos Aires: Eudeba.

Lynch, M. (1985). *Art and Artifact in Laboratory Science: A Study of Shop Work and Shop Talk in a Research Laboratory.* London: Routledge & Kegan Paul.

Mangabeira Unger, R. (2010). *Free Trade Reimagined: The World Division of Labor and the Methods of Economics.* Princeton: Princeton University Press.

Mescher, H. (2012). Policing and Muslim Communities in Germany. Structures, Workplace Cultures and the Threat of Islamophobia. In C. Husband (ed.) *Social Cohesion, Securitization and Counter-Terrorism.* Helsinki: Helsinki Collegium for Advanced Studies.

Miesing, P., Kriger, M.P., and Slough, N. (2007). Toward a Model of Effective Knowledge Transfer within Transnationals: The Case of Chinese Foreign Invested Enterprises. *Journal of Technology Transfer*, 32(1–2): 109–122.

Mignolo, W. (2000). *Local Histories / Global Designs. Coloniality, Subaltern Knowledges, and Border Thinking.* Princeton: Princeton University Press.

Nastasia, D.I., and Rakow, L.F. (2010). What is theory? Puzzles and Maps as Metaphors in Communication Theory. *triple C Cognition, Communication, Co-operation*, 8(1): 1–17.

Nye, M.J. (2011). *Michael Polanyi and his Generation: The Origins of the Social Construction of Science.* Chicago and London: The University of Chicago Press.

Pagden, A. (1986). *The fall of the natural man. The American Indian and the origins of comparative ethnology.* Cambridge: Cambridge University Press.

Parmar, I. (2012). *Foundations of the American Century. The Ford, Carnegie, and Rockefeller Foundations in the Rise of American Power.* New York: Columbia University Press.

Peckniat, M. and Rezazadeh, M.H. (2005). Appropriability of Foreign Knowledge in Developing Countries: Implications for Developing Sectoral Innovation Policies. paper presented at Globelics Africa 2005, South Africa, October 31-November 4; available at http://www.globelics2005africa.org.za/papers/p0041/Globelics2005_Packniat_Rezazadeh.pdf, accessed July, 2014.

Ramos, G. and Yannakakis, Y. (eds.) (2014). *Indigenous Intellectuals: Knowledge, Power, and Colonial Culture in Mexico and the Andes.* Durham: Duke University Press.

Rodriguez Medina, L. (2013). Objetos subordinantes: la tecnología epistémica para producir centros y periferias. *Revista Mexicana de Sociología*, 75(1): 7–28.

Rodriguez Medina, L. (2014a). *Centers and Peripheries in Knowledge Production.* London and New York: Routledge.

Rodriguez Medina, L. (2014b). *The Circulation of European Knowledge: Niklas Luhmann in the Hispanic Americas.* New York: Palgrave Macmillan.

Said, E. (1991). *The World, the Text, and the Critic.* London: Vintage.

Scenters-Zapico, J. (1994). The Social Construct of Enthymematic Understanding. *Rhetoric Society Quarterly*, 24(3–4): 71–87.

Sefa Dei, G.J., Goldin Rosenberg, D. and Hall, B.L. (eds.) (2000). *Indigenous Knowledges in Global Contexts: Multiple Readings of Our Worlds*. Toronto: University of Toronto Press.

Semali, L.M. and Kincheloe, J.L. (eds.) (1999). *What is Indigenous Knowledge? Voices from the Academy*. New York: Routledge.

Shapin, S. and Schaffer, S. (1985). *Leviathan and the Air-Pump. Hobbes, Boyle and the Experimental Life*. Princeton: Princeton University Press.

Sherman, W.H. (2009). *Used Books: Marking Readers in Renaissance England*. Philadelphia: University of Pennsylvania Press.

Sofka, W. (2007). What Makes Foreign Knowledge Attractive to Domestic Innovation Managers? ZEW Discussion Paper 07–055, available at http://hdl.handle.net/10419/24629, accessed July 2014.

Springer, A-S. and Turpin, E. (eds.) (2015). *Fantasies of the Library*, Berlin: K Verlag and HKW, open access, available at http://monoskop.org/log/?p=13616, accessed February 2015.

Stark, L. (2011). Meeting by the minute(s): how documents create decisions for institutional review board. In C. Camic, N. Gross and M. Lamont (eds.) *Social Knowledge in the Making*. Chicago: The University of Chicago Press.

Sulanski, G. (1996). Exploring internal stickiness: impediments to the transfer of best practice within the firm. *Strategic Management Journal*, 17: 27–44.

Szogs, A. and Wilson, L. (2006). Effective Knowledge Sharing: the Tanzanian Industrial Research and Development Organization as Mediator between the Foreign and Local Sector. *KM4D Journal*, 2(1): 92–104.

Tejada, G. and Bolay, J-C (eds.) (2010). *Scientific Diasporas as Development Partners. Skilled Migrants from Colombia, India and South Africa in Switzerland: Empirical Evidence and Policy Responses*. Bern: Peter Lang.

Todo, Y. and Miyamoto, K. (2002). *Knowledge Diffusion from Multinational Enterprises: the Role of Domestic and Foreign Knowledge-Enhancing Activities*. OECD Development Centre Working Paper No. 196, OECD Publishing, available at http://home.hiroshima-u.ac.jp/jea2002/yastodo.pdf, accessed July 2014.

Torpey, J. (1999). *The Invention of the Passport: Surveillance, Citizenship and the State*. Cambridge: Cambridge University Press.

Van Sant, J.E. (2012). Rangaku Medicine and "Foreign" Knowledge in Late Tokugawa Japan. *Southeast Review of Asian Studies*, 34: 207–214.

Vessuri, H. (1997). Science for the South in the South. Exploring the Role of Local Leadership as a Catalyst of Scientific Development. In T. Shinn, J. Spaapen and V. Krishna (eds.) *Science and Technology in a Developing World*. Dordrecht: Kluwer Academic Publisher.

Vessuri, H. and Canino M.V. (2002). Latin American catalysis as seen through the Iberoamerican Catalyst Symposia. *Science, Technology & Society*, 7(2):339–363.

Webb, P. (2012). "Foreign Books" in Arabic Literature: discourses on books, knowledge, and ethnicity in the writings of al-Jahiz. *Journal of Arabic and Islamic Studies*, 12(2): 16–55.

Xie, Z. and Li, J. (2013). Internationalization and Indigenous Technological Efforts of Emerging Economy Firms: The Effect of Multiple Knowledge Sources. *Journal of International Management*, 19: 247–259.

Zahra, S. and George, G. (2002). Absorptive capacity: a review, reconceptualization, and extension. *Academy of Management Review*, 27(2): 185–203.

Chapter 12:
Alternatives to the Globalising Humanities and Social Sciences:
Comments to the ideas presented at the Mexico WSSHNetwork workshop

Michael Christie

1 Introduction

Globalisation is often taken implicitly as an opportunity for ushering in global political stability and equality of political and economic opportunity. Globalisation is also understood as a threat. One of the ways in which we may begin to develop some critical analyses of the nature and potentials of the Globalising Humanities and Social Sciences (GHASS) is to look carefully at its alternatives which are characterised by both their politics and their epistemologies.

2 Key concepts framing our discussion

In order to bring some coherence to this analysis without totalising the alternatives we have found, we begin with some fundamental assumptions which I suggest guide our thinking.

2.1 All Knowledge is Local.

Even the Grand Theories of the now globalising European tradition have been developed, assessed and implemented in thousands of local contexts around the world. Papers in libraries, and even the ones and zeros on computers in cyberspace are always situated somewhere materially, and accessed by knowledge workers in very material setting and practices. The always local and situated nature of knowledge work is primary. Globalisation is subsequent and epiphenomenal.

2.2 Alternatives to the globalising HASS are manifold.

Reacting against the totalising impetus of globalisation, I suggest we resist totalising the alternatives we examine. They are alternative in very different ways, they have different spatialities, different objectives, different traditions, different politics, and different epistemologies. We should also resist the tendency to mobilise a dualism between the globalising HASS on the one hand, and their alternatives on the other. The boundaries are always contingent, political and labile.

2.3 Knowledge is a cultural, social and political process.

To take seriously alternative knowledge practices, we must resist an automatic embrace of western positivist epistemology. Our *performative* epistemology should understand the material phenomena of books, databases, archives etc, not to *contain knowledge*, but rather *traces of knowledge work* which may or may not be mobilised in ongoing culturally, socially and politically embedded knowledge work.

2.4 The new globalising knowledge practices exist in dynamic tension with their alternatives.

Increasingly, in many arenas of engagement, alternative knowledge practices are marginalised, repudiated or ignored by the globalising HASS. Each contains and generates the other. Those working on grand theory in the great institutions of learning do their work in located piecemeal practices. Those working with and through alternative knowledge practices increasingly access the instruments of globalisation—numbers, taxonomies and disciplinary thinking for example. In each site of knowledge production, the localised and individual knowledge histories and practices work in a dynamic tension with others.

3. The *politics* of alternatives to the Globalising Humanities and Social Sciences

Alternatives to the globalising HASS exhibit very different histories and traditions, and different politics and positioning. Politically, I suggest to discern four tropes:

3.1 Deliberate marginalisation by the governmentalities of globalisation.

Over recent years, some parts of government within the People's Republic of China have worked to marginalise and undermine the theory and practices of Traditional Chinese Medicine (TCM). Here we see China's move towards a modern, enlightened industrial state, reflected in a political imperative to value rational and empirical sciences. While TCM remains popular with all levels of society on the streets of China and in fact around the world, it is often marginalised in the universities and medical schools of China. The utilitarianism of the increasingly globalised biomedical models of the body, pathology, treatment and health, the pressure to invest in biochemical research on a competitive global level, and the drive for empirical evidence of the effectiveness of biomedicine, evidence-based medicine and health policy, have meant a vibrant alternative knowledge practice is marginalised and mostly unrecognised. A political strategy to marginalise alternative medical practices within the academy is to label them 'ethnomedicine', 'ethnopharmacology' etc.

3.2. Deliberate dissociation from institutional forms

Some knowledge practices, like those that give rise to the 'little magazine movement' in Tamil Nadu, maintain their vibrancy, partly through their active opposition to the globalising social sciences, and in fact, to a large extent, to each other. These alternative practices still actively engage with some of the theoretical currents of the majority but also tap into deeply cultural root. Traditional Chinese medicine described as marginalised above, and other traditional practices, like the continuing folk use of medicinal herbs in northern Europe, are also finding a significant role in the diagnosis, prevention and treatment of disease in settings quite outside of, and often in opposition to the biomedical and the pharmaceutical industries. Unacknowledged by biomedicine, there coexist entirely alternative theories and practices of health, pathology and treatment as people around the world deliberately maintain their knowledge traditions separated from the mainstream.

3.3 Persistent pre-globalised (including Indigenous) practices

The persistence of particular alternative knowledge traditions can be attributed in some cases to a holistic (sometimes referred to as 'spiritual') connection between a people, their history, their knowledge practices and their place, which resists disentanglement and categorisation by the globalising HASS. Their resistance to dismemberment and their embeddedness and embodiment in local places and people enable their persistence. In other cases (eg orthodox Hinduism or Judaism) commitment to an ancient cosmology entails metaphysical and ontological commitments which also resist colonisation by the globalising HASS (see section 4 below). In other cases, knowledge practices may persist uncoopted where they are geographically or economically remote, where they are deemed irrelevant to the globalising political arena or where in fact, they may be quite invisible to them.

3.4 Alternative practices created and sourced by globalising capital

At the same time, the globalisation of capitalism itself has in various settings embraced and in fact created alternative knowledge practices outside of the governance and ethical constraints of the institutionalised HASS. 'Crowd sourcing' for example, is a knowledge practice where large numbers of people voluntarily give small amounts of their time to researchers undertaking brand-focussed research to improve competitiveness within the capitalist system. Regional variations in taste and style, historical preferences, and willingness to change are all factored into a knowledge practice where the emerging consumer classes throughout the world are mobilised to create a particular form of globalising knowledge hand in hand with global capital, but outside the institutional forms of HASS found within academic knowledge work.

4 Some *epistemological* features of alternatives to globalising HASS.

Alternatives to the globalising HASS are not just political. The following analysis suggests some epistemological dimensions through which alternatives are manifest, in different practices, to different degrees, and may be identified and analysed as we work towards a clearer view of the political and historical contingency of their globalising alternatives.

4.1. Alternative foundations: Categories and dualisms.

All knowledge practices begin with metaphysical commitments. A primary characteristic of the globalising HASS is its commitment to various dualisms. Some of the most profound and influential dualisms, often characterised as continuing effects of the European enlightenment, are hidden in knowledge work, or taken for granted in ways that disregard and devalue alternative knowledge practices. For example, the split between *nature and culture* allows for the persistence of discourses within which nature is something 'out there', to be controlled. The nature/culture dualism obscures the important insight that all nature is cultural (as it is produced as knowable), and all culture is natural, (consistent with the other workings of the universe). In another example, the dualism of *mind versus matter*, often foreign to some alternative knowledge practices, gives rise to an understanding of the human condition as some split between the mental and the physical, a split which allows for specialisation and disciplinarity (psychology, biology), but which undermines alternative and holistic approaches. Here we explore three examples.

4.1.1. Subject—object, and representation.

In this received metaphysics, the work of science is to generate and test claims about an already given world 'out there'. Truth claims are produced in language, and assessed in terms of the accuracy of those representations. The viability of this 'positivist' knowledge practice depends upon an *a priori* split between mind and matter (and subject and object). When there is admitted no *a priori* dualism, the work of representation as providing a truth claim is rendered powerless. We must seek an alternative. Some alternative truth claims are discussed below, but first we expand on some alternative, hidden dualisms, and their effects.

4.1.2 Time—space, determinism and emergence

Some alternative knowledge practices resist the received western metaphysical figure of *matter set in time and space*, where time and space, are ontologically prior to human action, including knowledge production. In this knowledge work, time and space *emerge* from human action (rather then precede it), and categories, boundaries and hierarchies are understood as created rather than discovered. The interactions between a Western colonial and an Indigenous knowledge practice often entail the domination of the latter through notions of determinism and linear time, where the past is unenlightened, the present troublesome, but the future a vision of plenitude and salvation through progress brought by western science and technology.

4.1.3 Categorical starting points and foundations.

Disciplinary forms of the Social Sciences and Humanities generally proceed from fundamental categories—the individual as ontologically prior in psychology for example, the group as ontologically prior in sociology, historical materialism as the foundational substrate in Marxist analyses. Knowledge practices which resist foundationalism have trouble finding a place within the disciplinarities of academic institutions.

4.2 Alternative foundations: Emergence and performativity.

Non-foundational knowledge work, which eschews a priori categories and dualisms emphasises the creative work which it entails. In this epistemology, knowledge is not *discovered* so much as it is *created* within a particular tradition, as all categories are ultimately revisable (including subject/object), and as categories change, new possible worlds emerge. This very creative process is the antithesis of representation which depends upon assessment of the accuracy of models of the world. Where there are no valid representations to be made, or where representation is seen as just another sort of performativity, other evidential practices are required. These must entail some sort of generativity, where the knowledge work actually generates changed worlds or changed practices (rather than reflects or predicts them). Examples include Australian Aboriginal knowledge. Yolŋu (north east Arnhem land) Aboriginal epistemology uses the model of ceremonial practice which continues the creative work of the ancestors, singing, painting, dancing, crying, talking and forming the unfolding world into its ongoing existence (Christie, forthcoming). Another example would be the anarcho-syndicalists whose ways of working together over political action involve the radical provisionality of all categories and rules—which must be discussed and agreed upon moment by moment in the context of the ongoing struggle for a just world (Addelson, 1994).

4.3 Alternative foundations: Partiality and Investment.

An essential part of the process of GHASS is to rid knowledge work of its subjective attachments. Objectivity has a positive value as it leads towards generalizable theories through divesting itself of particular local agendas and investments. Alternative knowledge practices on the other hand, depend upon and in fact celebrate particular investments and partialities. They are partial in both senses of the English word: partial in the sense that they are not complete, not total. They only prosecute one particular version of the world. They are also partial in the sense that they are politically invested. They are not *im*partial (as GHASS claim to be). They are mobilised in order to address a particular problem, about which the knowledge community is concerned. Bringing theory (and even aspects of the GHASS) to bear upon the problems of the moment are strategic decisions. The careful deployment of theory and other action in solving public problems is a difficult and skilled political process. It cannot escape moral questions. In this world, knowledge has its definite limits. As an utterly human product, it has no way of exhausting the world.

4.4 Evidential practices.

What counts as evidence for a truth claim? Who decides? Where representations (statistics for example) are deemed insufficient or unreliable in an alternative knowledge practice, where knowledge is seen as performative rather than positivist, what epistemic resources are available? What are alternatives to representationalism? Even in the globalising knowledge practices (mathematics for example) other scientists make assessments of truth claims on the basis of their 'elegance', not simply their positivist truth value. The notion of rightness carries within it the idea of correct, but also of probity—of integrity, justness, and honour. In highly performative knowledge practices, like those of many Indigenous groups, aesthetic criteria are brought to bear on assessments as to how a performer has acquitted a particular performance of a negotiated truth—often linking the ancestral imperatives with the here and now, through songs, dance, painting, or oration. Again the GHASS are not immune to the engagement of stylistic criteria in their assessment of truth claims.

5 Responses of the GHASS to its alternatives

The GHASS have in various ways attempted to embrace and engage alternative knowledge practices, or use these practices to examine their own practices. Here we present an example of each.

5.1 The 'ethnosciences.'

Ethno-botanists, ethno-musicologists, ethno-epistemologists etc all attempt to reconstitute what serve as particular scientific practices of others, excluding all observations, interpretations or personal notions and categories of their own. This work may arise out of a concern for the preservation of a particular local knowledge tradition, or a desire to benefit from the traditional knowledge of others—pharmacology for example. Ethnoscience can also be brought to bear as a critique of the underlying assumptions of GHASS and its various disciplines, how some work is counted in science and other discounted, but this work which understands *all* science as 'ethnoscience', is seldom seriously undertaken. Enthosciences are seen to be beset by primitive and magical thinking, in contrast to the objective institutionalised sciences. Ethnoscience has a tendency to filter out all those aspects of a knowledge practice which don't quite fit the categories of institutionalised science, whether they be the 'none of the above' in a classification system, or the appeal to some mechanism of process which, incomprehensible to the scientist, is deemed mystical or magical and resistant to analysis.

5.2 Science Studies

The academic discipline called, in the past, the History and Philosophy of Science has branched more recently towards what is known as Science Studies. In the context of our present work, Science Studies can be seen as often undertaking the task of interpreting western science as an Indigenous knowledge system. Bruno Latour and others make observations of technoscience which reveal it as remarkably similar to say, an Indigenous knowledge practice. They demonstrate that truth is not entirely to be found through experiments or precise calculations, but rather through a negotiated process—often hidden, where the theories are underdetermined by the facts. There is always some leeway or provisionality as to what kind of knowledge is produced. This is where for example aesthetic criteria play quite a central part in most of the physical sciences including mathematics. Complicated solutions are discarded in favour of simpler more elegant solutions, and some people have more authority than others to make and assess truth claims, a right which, as in an Indigenous practice, is ultimately determined through political means.

5.3 The Knowledge of everyday life.

Similarities have also been found between the way scientists do their work, and the knowledge practise of everyday life. Sociologists of knowledge have compared the ways in which the decisions of everyday life, in the garden for example, mirror the work of scientists—or vice versa. The gardener makes hypotheses as she examines the health of her vegetables. She makes assumptions about how the world works, cause and effect, trial and error. People who try to fight plant pests with their traditional knowledge, have come to collective agreement over the years that this or that is the best way of doing it and they continue to test it out making slight changes here and there, and passing these new ideas on to their neighbours. A key difference between the knowledge of gardeners and of scientists, according to science studies, is that scientists try to create time-stable generalizable, universal facts that are consolidated, fixed and have withstood attempts at deconstruction, whereas this is not the aim of every day knowledge. We have many ways of going about the various practices of knowledge production, and fluidity is in some cultures a virtue, and hidden and denied in others.

5.4 Transdiciplinarity

What does it take for the GHASS and its localized alternatives to work productively together? Fruitful collaborations can be found where knowledge communities come together to address particular 'public problems' (Dewey, 1927). Where various academic disciplines work together on particular programs, we find *multidisciplinary* approaches to be celebrated for their productivity. Where knowledge practices outside the academy (eg Indigenous knowledge) are enlisted alongside scientific practices, the *transdisciplinary* collaborations are often highly productive. Even if each practice can not fully recognise the other, (they have different metaphysical commitments, different evidential practices etc), they often can agree just enough, just here and now, on a productive and honourable way of going on together. Examples include the development of sustainable environmental management regimes (for example traditional and scientific practices of fire ecology working together and the working together of biomedical and traditional understandings of health, sickness, care and the body (Christie & Verran, 2014). It is through these productive interactions that we gain further understandings of the limits and possibilities of globalizing scientific practices and their alternatives.

References

Addelson, K. P. (1994). *Moral Passages: Toward a Collectivist Moral Theory.* New York: Routledge.

Christie, M. (forthcoming) Decolonising social sciences in remote Australia. In M. Kuhn and H. Vessuri (eds.) *Contributions to Alternative concepts of knowledge.* Stuttgart: ibidem.

Christie, M. and Verran, H. (2014). The Touch Pad Body: A Generative Transcultural Digital Device Interrupting Received Ideas and Practices in Aboriginal Health. *Societies* (4), 256–264.

Dewey, J. (1927). *The Public and its Problems.* New York: Henry Holt and Company

Chapter 13:
Some comments about spatiological thinking—the final universalisation of the "European" social sciences

Michael Kuhn

Space, a cognitive resource in spatiological theorizing

Southern, northern, local, global, glocal, the more politically phrased western and "foreign" knowledge or "indigenous knowledge", the cultural variation of spatial knowledge: Stating that any knowledge is created by a thinker some*where* and that any object of thinking is some*where* would be more than banal. In spatiological thinking it is not banal, but the epistemological essential of thinking.

If the *where* of theorizing was not one of *the contemporary epistemological* concerns in the discourses about social science theorizing, it would be a childish banality to mention this: There are phenomena which are here but not there. Any thinker from here or there reflects about the phenomenon, presents the theory the thinker created and shares this with other thinkers from here and there. This is it—not in spatiological thinking.

In the modern globalised version of the social sciences, may be more precisely the post-world-war II social sciences discourses, the *where* of thinking is not considered at all to be banal, but what is rather one aspect of the object of social thought, becomes the resource of theorizing and even the cognitive driving force of thinking, I therefore call spatiological theorizing.

"..the proposition that thought is related to places is central to my project provincializing Europe"[1]

---

[1] D. Chakrabarty, *Postcolonial Thought and Historical Difference,* 2000, Princeton University Press, p xiii

According the modern, postcolonial globalised social science approach to social thought, *where* one thinks decides about *what* one thinks and therefore global thought under the regime of social sciences knows above all a distinction between spaces of knowledge, namely the one between inter-national and national and many other dichotomic couples of knowledge spaces, such as local and global, may it be their combination in glocal, or southern and northern theories, foreign or the culturally inspired variation of indigenous knowledge, they all share that the whereabouts of thinking are an essential cognitive power in social science theorizing.

Southern, northern, local, global, glocal,: In postcolonial social science thinking, the banality, the where, is not just the spatial aspect of the object of any thinking as it is time, but is considered as a an attribute crafting the thinking, describing the how of theorizing, a cognitive force creating thought that affects the contents of thought, and, thus, decides what we think about any phenomenon. Space, the where of things and the where of the thinker, politically constructed spaces of the social, the locality of theorizing in nation states, has been transformed into a cognitive actor through which social thought voices the thought of politically defined places, the thought of nationally constructed social entities.

In contemporary global social thought under the approach of postcolonial social science thinking the "where" of the objects of thinking and the where of the thinking subject craft thought[2] and constitute the uniqueness of spatially constructed objects of thinking, a theoretical perspective, and a spatially constructed way of thinking, through which a spatially distinguished multiplicity of unique thought about a spatially unique social is created.

> "To 'provincialize' Europe was precisely to find out how and in what sense European ideas that were universal were also, at one and the same time, drawn from very particular intellectual and historical traditions that could not claim any universal validity. It was to ask the question about how thought was related to place. Can thought transcend places of their origin? Or do places leave their imprint on thought in such ways as to call into question the idea of purely abstract categories.?"[3]

Discussing the most abstract category such as "*to ask the question about how thought was related to place*", a question that, though

---

[3] D. Chakrabaty, *Pronvincialising... p xiii*

it may not claim any universal validity, one might feel invited to ask the question, to which place, raising such an abstract question, if *"places leave their imprint on thought"*, to which place this question is "related" to, a question that obviously is not only a rhetoric question, but a determined answer, and this answer is: Yes. While it is *the* cognitive challenge in scientific thinking to eliminate factors that mislead thinking towards any given biased thought, the postcolonial social science approach to thinking considers any thinking as the necessarily "biased" creation of thought, "biased" by the "places" where thought is created and does not only not terminate a scientific nuisance of explicitly "biased" thinking, but insists on such spatiologically constructed thought, making scientific thought voicing what the politically constructed space wishes to say and insists on this, on social thought as articulating what I therefore call patriotic messages, and presents this, scientific thinking as articulating the voices of patriotisms, as being the nature of any scientific thought.

It must be an irony of social science thinking, that people working throughout their life to create thought about the social reality, feel appealed by the idea, that social thought must be a mere impact of the reality on humans mind, "transcending" their thought to the thinkers. Since thinking "transcends" nothing but non-knowing by gaining insights, the reality does not disclose, and even *where* anything is must be found out by thinking, constituting a whole branch of scientific thinking, geography, and since it might be therefore wiser to not trust that the mystic cognitive forces of the place where the thinkers about "place" found their theories about place and to just visit to these places, but to better trust the cognitive forces of human mind and to think about what these thinkers say, they were told from their "where" about how this "where" left its "imprints" on thought, it might be better to visit their thought and to see what space told them about space as a cognitive force. .

What space knows

So, what are the insights places disclose to thinkers advocating place as a source of thought?

"Until I arrived in Australia, I had never seriously entertained the implications of the fact that an abstract and universal idea characteristic of political modernity everywhere—the idea of equality, say, or of democracy or even of the dignity of human being—could look utterly different in different historical contexts. Australia, like India, is a thriving electoral democracy, but Election Day there does not have anything of the atmosphere of festivity that I was used to it in India."[4]

It is always the same one and only argumentative game social science thinking is playing, presenting their theories about the world as a theory voiced to them by the reality, here named place, an argumentative game, for which social science thinking created the very telling notion of "evidence", just as if the reality was telling them, what they see. The place is saying nothing—and the observations about let's say, as in this case, "democracy", is what this social science thinker *observes* about democracy in India and Australia, while he is interpreting democracy practices in these two places.

Strictly speaking, stating that "*Election Day there does not have anything of the atmosphere of festivity that I was used to it in India*", does not even say anything what a scientific thinker thinks about the difference of the enthusiasm or the routine to practice elections, a difference only a thinker observes and feels worth mentioning, who is keen on this difference- and who obviously wants to let us know what his personal preferences is the "*atmosphere of festivity*". Why this is the case, that Indian people like elections and why he likes it that Indian people like elections he does not reveal, since pointing on this difference aims at arguing about why the this observation that people in India appreciate elections must have an impact on what scientific thinkers think about them and it is not demanding to sense, that he wants to argue, that because people like elections in India, a theory about elections in India must be different from a theory about elections in Australia. Distinguishing between the ways people in India and Australia see and practice elections in the first place wants to post the message, that without any argument, neither about elections and nor about the relations electing people have to elections, that what elections categorically *are* must be different between India and Australia, just because the observer of the electing people in different nation states *sees* them practicing elections differently.

---

4   (Chakrabati,p xii)

Chapter 13: Some comments about spatiological thinking 247

Hence, so the conclusion of the spatiological theorist, theories about elections in India *and* Australia, like any "*abstract and universal ideas*", must fail, because the electing people practice elections with a different view on elections. If this was the case, that is how people see or practice elections decides about what elections are, how then does spatiologically thinking know, that both things are though the same abstract thing, elections, and not something entirely different? Spatiological thinking only plays with pointing on the reality as a point of reference to prove that their *theories* about the cognitive power of the reality are not what they think about the reality, but to present their theories about the reality as being voiced by the reality to the thinker, and thus, a theory as being voiced by the thinker making what they think about the reality an undisputable insight proved as a fact. Since people in India appreciate elections a theory created in India about elections must articulate how people see them, is a remarkable concept of theorizing, since it says that what scientific thinking finds out via thinking is to voice what the people of a country think about anything. Social thought about elections is the loudspeaker of how the public opinion appreciates elections or not? What if the public opinion changes its view on elections and who represents the public opinion, the very opinion the thinkers shares? Scientific thought is articulating the appreciations of the thinkers, or more precisely, spatiological thinking is articulation the appreciations of the where, the appreciations of a nation state, like in our case India: According to spatiological thinking scientific thought about election in India is that in India Indian people like elections. Spatiolological think as predecessor of the most modern way of face-book theorizing: Like it/Don't like it?

However, thinking about election is only an example to argue about how spatiological theorizing works. It is the very selective view on the reality, the appreciation the thinkers shares spatiological thinking cites as a witness for the objectivity of what only they think about the objects of thought and their impact on thinking, it is the proof for the indisputably spatiolologically dependent knowledge, voiced to the thinker by the reality, in this case by different appreciations of elections, ironically in this case while proving the necessity of a spatial relativism of thought dependent on the space where thought are created, to prove with the relativism of thought dependent on the where of thinking, here about elections, nothing else but the objectivity of the theory about space as the resource of thinking. A theory that argues that theories are an effect of the where, the where they are created, cannot avoid the obvious contradiction to advocate scientific thought about a phenomenon as the subjective appreciation of it and proves this theory about thinking, thought as the subjective appreciation of what it thinks about, as an objective necessity of theorizing. There must be an objective space, indistinguishable from any other place, the place as such, that voices the epistemologically correct categories about how theorizing works as an impact of space to the mind of the thinker, advocating the relativism of spatiological thinking as the impact of any particular local. The where of this everywhere is not revealed.

There is no way out; arguing against categories to prove the relativism of thinking as a category founding theorizing remains an argumentative nuisance. What is indisputably proved for spatiological thinkers such as Chakrabarty with his example about elections, is that the particularity of any place disproves the theory of "*an abstract and universal idea characteristic of political modernity everywhere*", *of* an abstract idea, here elections, an abstract idea he though argues with by saying that they, these very abstract ideas, "*look utterly different in different historical contexts*".

Arguing with categories against categories is a theoretical endeavour, spatiological thinking must master, since arguing against categories is what spatiological thinking is all about.

Yes, they may look different, but an observation of a difference in the way something is looking *argues* with something that is essentially the same and has different ways of practising an abstract same thing in different ways in different places, otherwise he could not compare them as elections, thus using the very abstract ideas for proving that they are not existing and that it is the specific space the critiqued "Western" theories ignore as imprinting thought any thinker anywhere thinks due to his "where".

Accusing the "Western" social sciences for ignoring space as a dimension of theorizing is, however, a very pretentious misinterpretation of the theories created in the West and a very false, though very consequent, critique of spatiological thinking opposing the scientific forms of knowledge the European social sciences insist on beyond what their knowledge is saying.

Chapter 13: Some comments about spatiological thinking 249

The fact that, despite of the proclaimed spatiological relativism of theories, these theories do insist on being—however relativated—scientific knowledge, the advocators of spatiological thinking critique the for this very purpose spatiologically coinded "Western" theories for insisting on being scientific knowledge, when they oppose their claim of being universal knowledge. Just as Chakrabaty claims for his theory about space and knowledge that it is universal knowledge, the theories created in the West, insist on being universal knowledge, which is nothing more and less but saying that their theories are—what else—universally valid theories, just as the advocators of spatiological thinking do, what any scientific theory does, when they argue for spatiological thinking as an epistemological necessity of any thinking anywhere,—what else, as we will see—not only in India.

The European social sciences and space

Accusing the "Western" social sciences for ignoring space as a dimension of theorizing is a very pretentious misunderstanding of the theories created in the West.

The fact that, despite of the proclaimed scepticism of social science theories, these theories insist on being—however relativated—scientific knowledge, the advocators of spatiological thinking critique them for insisting being scientific knowledge, when opposing their claim being universal knowledge. Just as Chakrabaty claims for his theory about space and knowledge that it is universal knowledge, the theories created in the West, insist on being universal knowledge, which is nothing more and less but saying that their theories are universal valid theories, just as the advocators of spatiological thinking do, of course, when they argue (sic) for spatiological thinking as an epistemological necessity.

And this knowledge created in the "West" is indeed as very spatiologically constructed as the opposition from the spatilological theories claims it should be, if they suggest to provincialise European theories.

Just to illustrate this, briefly a few spatiological features of social science theories, created in the accused "West" for their claim of universal knowledge:

Social science thinking is thinking about confined nation state socials

Social sciences thinking presupposes that any social phenomenon could be understood as a nationally confined phenomenon and theorize about the social as national constructs. To do this, social sciences above all off-think the world, that is off-think how any social phenomena are made by the world of nation states.

Certainly, thinking in nationally confined units of analysis could be better shown but in how social sciences think internationally, when the compare the country studies, never knowing against which tertium comparationis this could be compared.

> "This item response theory methodology is first applied to assess the differences in happiness across selected European states."[5]

Admittedly, theorizing about the happiness of people is certainly also a quite odd topic for social sciences and has the strong taste of EU-propaganda, comparing happiness across European nation states, nation states, which day by day boast with their policies to deteriorate the life quality of Europeans with ever creative policy agendas making Europe an attractive global business location.

However, it is not the odd topic and the obvious propaganda of this study, but its most typical way of thinking, may this be about the happiness of European humans. It is in fact very typical for social science thinking that the *"happiness across selected European states"* must be a matter of comparing nationally constructed humans and the differences of their happiness a matter of nationally constructed data, "indicating" how they feel as nationals, as citizens of each country. Thinking about national socials by off-thinking any other national socials while theorizing about a group of national social strongly politically and economically bound to each other, is a masterpiece of social science thinking, a masterpiece of ignorance, off-thinking the relations between nation state socials while comparing them, as a method of theorizing.

---

[5] Rynko, Maja, On the Measurement of Welfare, Happiness and Inequality, European University Institut, http://cadmus.eui.eu/handle/1814/20694

Social sciences think about the secluded nation socials through the idealized rationale of nation states

Adornos reflections about what he circumscribes as "Auschwitz" might be an example for a discrete way to theoretically appropriate the individual state science rationales in social science thinking, presented as an issue of a nationally social, secluded from the world's social, and most critically opposing nation state practices with an ideal mission of a nation state:

> "Die Forderung, daß Auschwitz nicht noch einmal sei, ist die allererste an Erziehung. Sie geht so sehr jeglicher anderen voran, daß ich weder glaube, sie begründen zu müssen noch zu sollen." [6]
>
> (Postulating, that there may be no other Auschwitz again, is in the first place one towards Education. This is so much a primary postulation, that I believe, I neither need nor should I motivate why.") (own translation MK)

Making Auschwitz a matter of education, and making this so determined a matter of education, that any reasoning, why Auschwitz must be seen as a matter of education, would violate the high moral mission education is attributed by this thinker; making Auschwitz a matter of education, does, however, only not need to be "motivated" only for a mind, that considers Ausschwitz as a matter of the—failed—morality of people, the moral responsibility and the moral failure of badly educated Germans, and thus discloses the very critical and very German moral mission, this philosopher considers as the mission the nation state he reflects on as a social science thinker should aim at.

And this is a most critical mission of a most critical social science thinker, that, thanks to his interpretation of Auschwitz as a moral issue, though somewhere matches with *the very real* post war rationale of German imperial politics until today. By making Auschwitz as matter of moral education, rather than a matter of the cynical rationale of wars—this critique dissolves the cynical rationale of a war not only of the German political elite into a mission of moral education, the German nation state as the German failed—and thus. off-thinks, what only the most violent imperial actions of nation state can do by transforming the rational of war

---

[6] T. W. Adorno, Erziehung zur Mündigkeit. Frankfurt a.M.:Suhrkamp, 1. Auflage 1971, p 88

into a failure of his responsibility for educating the values of humans morality. Shifting the debate about Ausschwitz from the debate about the political rationale of the German political elite towards a moral failure of the German nation state and from there of the Germans as such, is to make this issue, firstly a matter of morality and via doing this, secondly a matter of *the* German as a member of this nation state, a subject that is attributed the policy rationale of the nation state as if war was the committed rationale of their citizens, those citizens nation states use for this rationale of an imperial war.

Thus, creating with the confession of being a moral failure, creating *the post war national "we"*, a morally shared guiltiness of *the* German, unifying all Germans in sharing a national cleaned German, by committing the German to a moral failure, is the post war concept of the German nation state, which very much helped to build a new German "we", a new German national identity, after the old one, the image of the higher race, was destroyed by losing the war. Very soon after, swearing "Never again war", this new self-incriminating "we" re-established the new German military forces—for the next war. Confessing a national moral guiltiness of the German, nobody is allowed to question, if he does not want to be suspected to still share the old one, is until today the foundation of the German nation state rationale that opened and opens the world for the post world war global German imperial policy agenda.

Idealizing the mission of the German nation state after world war II as a moral imperative and accusing it of being a moral failure, compared to what the very mission of the nation state supposedly is, is an idea that ennobles this nation state via accusing it failing to match with its genuine mission.

To summarize: Social sciences, not only those is the incriminated "West" are very spatiologically constructed theories, which raises the question, why they are though made a matter of the project to "provincialize" them and what this notion is then really opposing?

Anti-scientism for patriotic thinking

It is the insistence on a the last remains of scientificy, preserved in the epistemological auspices of a scientific universalism, that disturbs the project to create theories constructed to contribute ex-

Chapter 13: Some comments about spatiological thinking 253

plicitly nationally constructed knowledge, patriotic theories to global social science thought, explicitly nationally constructed theories representing a particular nation state view, here a view about and through India, the advocates of spatiological thinking present—oddly enough -, not as the political desire for an authentic patriotic view in a global concert of patriotic theories, but—since they are no politicians but scientists—as an epistemological necessity.

> "No concrete example of an abstract can claim to be an embodiment of the abstract alone."[7]

Since the advocates of spatiological thinking are no politicians, but very social scientists—they present the need to create nationally constructed theories as an epistemological must of scientific theorizing as such, and present, thus, ironically, a very "*abstract and universal idea*" about space, they so much oppose as long as it helps them to argue for space as a cognitive instance in theorizing in order to justify patriotic theories as a need of thinking.

What Chakrabarty and all the social science thinkers, advocating the cognitive power of place, want to say is that it is a theoretical mistake to create abstracts ideas that tell us something about the same thing in different places, may this be with different interpretations of the same. They argue against what abstract categories say as what they denounce as "tabula rasa", discrediting the contents of these abstract ideas they know very well as meaningless, with the false argument, that a category is not the same as observed things. With their observation that elections are seen and practiced in different ways in India and Australia, they want to say that the category "election" is meaningless, because it abstracts from what makes a category a category, from their differences, allowing them to insist on their view on elections as different things as an objective observation voiced by place.

A cat, is a category, and these social scientists want to persuade us, that due to the fact that there are white and black cats, they very well know to distinguish from white and black horses, that the category "cat", they very well use for their distinction in two kind of cats, is meaningless, because they falsely interpret the abstraction any category makes as extinguishing what both animals essentially

---

[7]   (Chakrabarty, ...xii)

share, because they do not share the same color, just as if they want to say that, since anything white was a cat and anything black was a cat, cat is no category. In other words, spatiological thinkers argue to backdrop scientific thinking behind a status of thinking already our language and its categories achieved and, thus, to oppose thinking and to prove their very category of a place "imprinting" knowledge to the thinker, in order to advocate their theory that thinking must be articulating patriotic views, patriotic views voicing the view of their home land.

The advocates of the place as a cognitive instance argue against what constitutes scientific thinking, if not already the abstractions already languages make, creating abstract judgments, saying something about what different things, may this be in different places, share, such as elections, and advocate that theories must vary dependent on the place where they are produced, thus, opposing what scientific knowledge essentially is, that knows to distinguish between, let's say, what elections are and how they are perceived and practiced in different locations. It is what makes thinking scientific thinking and even what already language does, abstractions from the differences realized as variations of the same, such as elections in India and Australia, the advocators of the place as a cognitive instance want to oppose and overcome, because it is this essential of scientific thinking, they detect as an obstacle for theorizing they must deconstruct, to arrive at theories representing the particularity of a place, not coincidentally identified with nation states, such as India and Australia in our example.

Needless to say, also a spatiologically arguing scientist is also a thinker who creates categories by abstracting from non-essential differences, and thus also insists that his theory about thinking as voicing the view of the "where" is not only a plea for spatiological thinking in a single "where", let's say in India, and not only any category spatiological thinking was voiced by any particular local patriotism, but a theory advocating the plea that patriotic knowledge is an epistemological must that applies to thinking everywhere independent from any space:

> "If this argument is true for India, then it is true of any other place as well, including, of course, Europe or, broadly, the West."[8]

---

[8] (Chakrabarty,... xii)

Categories, once they articulate what postcolonial thinkers were "transcended" by one place, India, postcolonial thinkers know and enjoy what categories are, an abstract *"that can claim to be an embodiment of the abstract alone"*, they just denied to say anything, that categories are meaningless abstractions, "tabula rasa". Unless a category is saying that theorizing is voicing patriotic views about nation states, then categories are not only meaningful, but the advocates of patriotism, passionate fighters against categories and even more against universal categories, detect essentials of scientific thinking in categories, and are bold enough, to claim that interpreting science as voicing patriotism is a universal truth about social science thinking, independent from anywhere, the where they so much argue for as the instance crafting thought dependent on any particularities of the many "wheres".

This, postcolonial theorizing about global social thought, advocating that global social science thinking must be patriotic thinking across the whole world, is not considered as being imperial thought, because this imperial thought is only an epistemological necessity, obeying the nature of thinking beyond the disturbing abstract categories of scientific thinking and—more importantly phrased as an opposition against the colonial imposition of the "European" social sciences. It is in fact an opposition, but an opposition against what?

The critical self-purification from critique to arrive a patriotic thinking

It is certainly not any opposition against what these opposed theories are saying and it is the therefore the discrete charm spatiological thinking appreciates among the opposed "Western" theories that spatiolological thinking not only uncritically accepts the discredited "Western" theories as theories about the "West", but by doubting their universal validity ennobles these theories towards the world's references theories compared to which the other spatiallogically constructed theories have to prove their particular localness.

It is a very particular double irony in the history of the world sciences that it is an opposition of academics from or better—considering that spatiological thinking was the creature of academics educated in the European science traditions—arguing in the names of the developing countries against both the Marxism of the Soviet Union, the theory that did—rightly or not is again no issue for spatiological thinking—oppose the European social sciences and against the European sciences, more precisely the monopole on scientific knowledge they held across the world, therefore, not critiquing but downplaying these thus excepted theories as only one local way of seeing the world.

It is their critique of the "Historical Materialism", the ideology the Soviet Union had established against the Western ideology production and spread across the world as an opposing world view, mainly adopted by the intellectual oppositions in the colonised world against colonialism supporting their fights for independence.—It is this—ironically—correct *critique* of the Soviet Union ideologies, namely their determinism, that has helped to establish the false theory about space as crafting knowledge, a false theory at the same time was presented as an opposition against the "European" social sciences, both preparing the ways to establish these opposed "European" way of social thought as completing the universalization of their way of theorizing, completing this across the world—and this is the second historical irony—more than the universalisation of the "European" social science concept of theorizing itself ever could during colonialism.

The critique of the Soviet Union Marxism was only the first step towards the final universalisation of the "Western" way of social thought thanks to theory of spatiological thinking and its successful implementation across the world as an opposition against the "European" social sciences and their "Eurocentrism"..

Chakrabaty's arguments against the "Historical Materialism" stands for an essential and historical theoretical error of an opposition against "Historical Materialism" and the proposition for spatiological thinking —a historically twofold purposeful epistemologically phrased accident:

Chapter 13: Some comments about spatiological thinking 257

"No historical form of capital, however, global its reach, can ever be a universal. No global (or even local, for that matter,) capital can ever represent the universal logic of capital, for any historically available form of capital is a provisional compromise made up by History 1 modified by somebodies's History 2....Grasping the category "capital" entails grasping its universal constitution. My reading of Marx does not in any way obviate that need for engagement with the universal. What I have attempted to do is to produce a reading in which the very caterory "capital" becomes a site where both the universal history of capital and the politics of human belonging are allowed to interrupt each other's narrative:"[9]

Firstly, the wrong self-critique of a false theory of the Historical Materialism, the ideology of the Soviet Union, an interpretation of Marx as a type of scientific religion that critiques a caricature like Marx interpretation, that could not more contradict Marx's theories. It was already Engels, who was often critiqued by Marx, when Engels used the term "Marxism," for Marx' theory about capitalism, thus interpreting Marx' theory about capitalism as an *approach* to science, a transformation of Marx's theory about capitalism towards a method thinking about the world, the Soviet Union Marxism further developed towards the caricature like notion of the "Historical Materialism", a way to think about the world as the historical automatism, a most radical example of deterministic thinking.[10]

Uncritically adopting the "Historical Materialism", the social movements against colonialism used the very deterministic thinking, because it was promising the inevitability of victory as the law of history for their fight for the independence of colonial countries, which then, once the former colonies became independent, was

---

[9] (ibid, p 70)
[10] Deterministic thinking, as opposed by Chakrabarty and at the same time practiced with his notion of thought as an impact of the reality, is, of course, not the privilege of the Historical Materialism. The social sciences are rich of examples presenting humans will and actions as the impact of the social reality, the whole idea of Behaviourism constructs will and humans actions as a reaction on being. However, advocating a pluralism of relative knowledges that allows the former colonies to create their own nationally driven social sciences theories, sounds more convincing while advocating the implementation of the very model of nation state, that was responsible for what the colonies were, since it needs to transform the opposition against the colonisers into congenial partners as a new member in the global family of nation states—especially if one aims at getting the sympathies for the project building a nation state and their sciences from the new imperial and scientific supervisors over the world of nation states and the social sciences.

now critiqued by the same academics in the new decolonized states as an obstacle to reign the new nation states and to create their *local* national identity-building process with an own theories, in the above quotation discussed as a self- critique of the un-historical readings of Marx theories about capital, just as if theorizing about the social was the same as creating any arbitrary, politically inspired scientificized opinion—a concept of relative knowledge, they perfectly learned from the discriminated "Western" social sciences. Thus, the "historical materialism" was now critiqued by the same theorists from the "periphery" as a theory, needless to say, not as a theory that provided false explanations about the world, but as a theory that did not know any particular "where" or those "historical interruptions" in the world's narratives, those "interruptions" of the historical automatisms, they still believe in as an overarching "global", however not a "universal" narrative, since the complementation of the historical automatism with "interruptions" is the very eclectically constructed view that allows the creation of their own political narratives and the according *local patriotic* worldviews, once they became independent nation states.

Then secondly, it is the second historical irony of these post colonial discourses, that it is this, the critique of the "Historical Materialism", the correct critique of its indeed false determinism, a critique of the Soviet ideology which subsumes the whole world under its odd dogma of an *historical automatism*—in which, by the way, the political authorities in the Soviet Union did themselves not believe—the fighters for independence once found appealing to support their opposition against colonialism and then opposed once the transformation of the colonies into independent states was achieved, since this dogma made them to supernumeraries of history and imprisoned their thought into repeating believes that did not allow the new nation states to create "independent" theories—they appreciate to present as being voiced by the national space of the new home countries.

Confronted with their own dogmatic reading of Marx, coinciding with the ideas of the Historical Materialism stating that the world follows the same economic laws theories in the developing world, they rightly opposed this dogma and did it, though, with a wrong conclusion for the very purpose to develop their dogma of spatialogical thinking, justifying the creation of patriotic theories as an epistemological necessity, a critique which—again most iron-

Chapter 13: Some comments about spatiological thinking

ically—not only repeats the deterministic logic of the Historical Materialism, but radicalizes this deterministic logic towards interpreting even the creation of thought as an impact of space on thinking. However, the fact, that their critique of the Historical Materialism rightly detected in the false logic of this deterministic way of theorizing the very logic they apply to their theory about place, inducing knowledge to thinking, does not bother this critique, since it helps to justify the need for a particular patriotic nation state view of the new nation states and to arrive a what they were aiming at, advocating social science theorizing as spatiological thinking.

It is therefore another only consequent irony, accompanying social thought that advocates the need for nationally constructed theory bodies in the former colonies, to advocate spatiological thinking and to "provincialize Europe" with the support of all of those European philosophers which are the most nationalistic European of all nationalistic European thinkers, such as with the German "Blut und Boden" philosopher Heidegger.

> "PE (Provincialising Europe, M.K.) mobilizes argument and evidence that are in tension with analyses that point to paths of salvation inevitably proceeding through the lure of the non-place. Working through Hedegger and the hermeneutic tradition of thinking Gadamer belongs, PE attempts to bring into a productive gestures of thinking from nowhere and particular ways of being in the world."[11]

If one wants to justify that ones national patriotism needs a scientific voice in the global concert of nationally constructed social science theories, and if a thinker has the temerity to present his patriotism as the natural effect, as a necessity of a where, a voice voiced by his home land, yes, then Heidegger and his mystification of national thinking is, no doubt, the best philosophical advocate for theorizing as celebrating ones mystic attachment to a home country.[12]

---

[11] (Ibid, xviii)
[12] Distancing himself from his religious-like Marxist deterministic world view obviously for Chakrabarty has seemingly achieved the status of struggling with a psychological trauma, he still feels to reject as if it was a nightmare, he obviously still believes in: "Difference is not always a trick of capital. My sense of loss that ensues from my globalisation is not always an effect of somebody else's marketing strategy. I am not always being duped into 'mourning' by capital, for mourning does not always make a consumer of

Spatiological thinking—the final completion of the global reign of the "Western" social sciences

The idea of spatiological thinking though encountered next to the opposition against the scientificy incorporated in categories, the determinism of the Historical Materialism a final enemy, that is the idea of universal knowledge, an idea that insisted on the truth of theories independent from where it has been created, spatiological thinking needed to be opposed to advocate spatiological thinking as the final way of social science theorizing across the world as the means of thinking in a world of nation states.

And it is this idea of a scientific universalism that is again both another odd idea of the European social sciences that is as oddly critiqued by spatiological thinking, again ironically to help completing the global reign of an approach to social thought they opposed via a spatial notion, the "Western" social sciences.

Concluding form the mere fact, that there are certainly many things that only exist at a certain place, that knowledge and sharing this knowledge about them must be bound to a being in this location is the final end of a debate in the social sciences that began in post-colonial discourses about the idea of a scientific universalism.

The notion of a universalism of science is an odd idea, only a way of thinking can create, that struggles with a multiplicity of admittedly spatiolologically constructed social thought, not with the question which thought is a correct theory about any social phenomenon anywhere in the world, but with the question, which theory about which where is a worldwide acknowledged theory across all the nationally constructed theories. The idea to stress the universalism of theories is not the most simply fact, that any theory about anything in the world is a theory and that this theory is a theory, false or not, that can be shared or not independent from where the theory originates and where the recipient of these theories receives them.

Only an approach to social thought that decides about the question if knowledge is knowledge or not, that this does not depend on the coherence of its reasoning, but on the extent to which it is knowledge shared by others, and, only an approach that considers

---

> me...Not every aspect of our sense of the local can be commodified (I wish it could)." Ibid. p xviii

knowledge as a reflex of the object of thinking voiced through the thinkers by the where of thinking, is confronted with a multiplicity of patriotic theories and the fact that all those theories can rightly claim to be true theories, and only therefore, confronted with the contradiction of many true scientific knowledges (a contradiction that was, by the way, the finally omitted by wild thinkers like Foucault), creates the idea that what knowledge is must be a matter of its spatial spread, to arrive from there at claiming that true knowledge is the same as universally shared knowledge, thus insisting on the objectivity of scientific knowledge as knowledge that is shared across the universe. Consequently, defining knowledge via the extent to which it is shared, provokes the debate, that essentially founds the false opposition against the idea of a universal theories as the plea to consider all theories equally as spatially constructed theories and thus to acknowledge a multiplicity of the many spatial truth theories. It is this critique of universal knowledge that founds the opposition against the "Western" theories, a critique which—again ironically—established the opposed theories as the reference theories for the many spatial true theories.

Only this—false—critique of the concept of a scientific universalism that shares this equalisation of true knowledge as universally shared knowledge, opposes the claim of universal knowledge, creates alternative spatial knowledge and does not ever think about critiquing the faults of any of the theories it opposes, thus, after all does not only not critiques any of the opposed theories other but as insisting that this opposed knowledge must be knowledge that also only represents any other provincial "where". Only an opposition against social thought that shares the view that knowledge depends on the extent to which it is shared can be trapped by the idea of universal knowledge, interprets the notion of a scientific universalism as a claim for knowledge that exceeds the "where" of its origin and rejects the spatial claim of universal knowledge by advocating a multiplicity of spatially, that is nationally constructed prejudiced theories. Hence, it is the odd nature of this opposition that it opposes this knowledge *and* accepts it and compliments it with other knowledge of the same kind, insisting that both are spatially confined, because they are bound to space, no matter what this knowledge is about, no matter what the knowledge is saying—thus paving the ways for spreading the opposed theories as global reference theories and abolishing an historical anachronism.

Clearing a historical anachronism

With the post war II globalisation of the US model of nation state and the transformation of the colonised world into nation states, making the whole world a world of nation states, social science theorizing was confronted with a paradox, a historical anachronism. Social sciences thinking that is thinking about and through the view of nation state constructs on the social, knowledge created from theorizing about the particular nation state socials in the imperial nation states was the knowledge about the world' social, across also those nation state socials of the former colonies.

Theorizing through space, the de-politicized phrase of nation state socials, is the epistemological notion and the topic of a discourse, under which social science theorizing, theorizing about nation state socials through the view of the nation state constructs, was completed as the global way of theorizing including social thought in the new nation states.

It was this global completion of social science as social thought across the universe of nation states that abolished the anachronism of nation state knowledge that represented the nationally constructed knowledge from the imperial nations as knowledge across the whole world's .nation state socials—and it did this universalisation of nationally constructed social thought with and thanks to the nationally constructed social sciences theories in the imperial world that rules the world's social thought, from there on also social thought in the new nation states.

That of all things, the application of the nation state society model to the colonies, the model constructing a society that was responsible for making the colonies what they were, a means of the imperial nation states, would make them political entities on the globe, "independent" from the reign of the imperial nation states, is one of the odd tragic ironies, world history orchestrates. One must have witnessed how this tragedy was made a reality after world war II and the new reign of the US concept of a post-colonial globe of nation states, to believe that perceiving the creation of the new nation states from the former colonies was the same as liberating them and their people from being the material of the imperial world, that this illusion was not meant to be bad historical joke. It was what really happened and happens until today: Thinking about how to organizes human life beyond the concept of nation states is no option even for the most critical thinkers. The wars, gaining this kind "independency", an independency that made them more dependent than before, are telling everything, what this project creating independent states was about: Making the US empire the ruling empire about a world of nation states constructed along their model of nation states and thus disempowering the for colonizes from their reign over the colonized world, the US did not have.[13] Consequently, this historic tragedy making the colonies nation states, was repeated in the world of social thought: Once the new states were founded, the new nation states also applied the concept of social sciences to social thought, theorizing about nation states through the idealized rationales of nation states, a view that already guided the very illusion of a nation state serving its people, articulated in the paradoxical appendix of an "independent" nation state, including the institutional settings of Higher Education—and detected a historical anachronism.

As anywhere else in the history of nation states, it was the opposition against the nation state that helped to abolish the anachronism of thinking in nation state views and making the view of the imperial nation states the view of the whole of nation states and thus to finalize the global reign of the system of social sciences and to make this system of social sciences the global system of social thought.

Not coincidentally, it needs scholars from former colonies such as Chakrabarty, educated in social sciences theorizing in the imperial world, to articulate and to orchestrate this historical scientific opera, advocating the need, to complete global social thought as a

---

[13] Unlike the concept of nation state before world war II, the main new feature of nation state was, that the nation states were constructed to compete among each other about gaining their power means by benefitting from serving the global capital. The clearest measure putting this concept into practice is and was, that nation states had and have to finance the economic means for their political power via lending money from the global financial market they supervise. Subordinating their national currencies under the judgment of the global financial capital, was, oddly enough, interpreted as a loss of sovereignty, just as if it was not these nation states that sets these rules for the world's nation states and for the global capital as the global rules for their competition about political and economic power.

multiplicity of nationally constructed social science thought, abolishing the paradox of the new nation states, scientifically participating in a world of a multiplicity of nationally constructed knowledges with knowledge about the imperial national socials. Epistemologically, completing social science thought as a multiplicity of nationally constructed knowledges, implied to replace the claim for truth of theories in the social sciences by a multiplicity of "contextual" theorizing resulting in the many spatiological truths, the pluralism of relative local knowledges the very "Westerns" social science epistemologies advocated and violated thanks to the political power of the colonial part of the world.

Hence, the global reign of social thought under social sciences was completed by the erosion of what constitutes them as scientific knowledge, the erosion of their concept of objective *and* relative knowledge, replaced by a global relativism of spatiologically constructed theories.

Accusing social science to ignore that theorizing is a matter of space is an odd and most pretentious misunderstanding about the social sciences and can only be articulated by very social science thinkers who learned their lesson to think from the social sciences that thinking is thinking about and through national constructs. To misread the universal claim of the validity of scientific knowledge of the "European" knowledge as knowledge that is lacking a spatial dimension, is the pretentious intervention, that aims at claiming under the epistemological notion that knowledge must be dependent on the space in which it is created, the creation of the very nation state way of theorizing and theories in the new "spaces" of the new nation states.

By opposing the notion of "universal" knowledge the opposition against the European science under the notion of "eurocentrism" and alike, social scientists advocate a multiplicity of spatiologically constructed knowledge, a debate also after all led by thinkers from the very "European" social sciences, and opposed the last rationale element of social science theorizing, their insistence on a at least a form of objectivity in the notion of universal knowledge, and finally abolished what makes social science a form of scientific, objective knowledge.

Just as if there was any knowledge that was not local and universal, simply meaning that any knowledge is about somewhere and that this knowledge is always everywhere knowledge, the universalisation of theorizing about national socials through the view of "spaces", advocated, to make any knowledge spatiologically constructed knowledge, that is to "provincialize" the European sciences as well as the sciences in the former colonies and, thus, completed a world of social thought consisting of a multiplicity of local relativisms—just as the epistemological dogma of the European social sciences is proclaiming as the nature of scientific thinking.

As a consequence, joining a world of a multiplicity of spatial relativism in the first place detects scientificy, the objectivity of knowledge, as its main obstacle, in the second place therefore opposes and abolishes scientificy for contributing social science thought to the world of a multiplicity of spatially constructed knowledges and, finally ends up where nationally constructed thinking about the world's social, consequently, ends up, in advocating global social thought as imperial thinking, theorizing as the creation of a multiplicity of "spatiologically". i.e. idealized nation state view on the world's social, nationally constructed social thought claiming to be social thought that rules theorizing across the world. .

The impact of introducing the "where" as an epistemological dimension of thoughts since then has flourished world wide and crafted the main stream opposition against what was from there on is called the "Western" sciences, social thought coined with the space they origin from, opposed under other spatiologically constructed notions, such as "Euro-centrism" and inspired the creation of patriotic theories under such notions as "local", "indigenous" or "southern" theories and the like.

It is obvious, that science in and about the spatiologically constructed knowledge islands is never about knowledge, but about a purposefully constructed politically "biased" patriotism and this is what the universalised social science world has learned from the science colonisers, both from the imperial nation states sciences as from the Historical Materialism, which both successfully universalised their dogma of thought both presented as an impact of the reality, the postcolonial thinkers, arguing in the name of the former colonised world, applied to their theory about the where as an epistemological dimension of social thought. Critiquing theories they oppose under the notion on "Eurocentrism" as one sided views they therefor propose to "provincialise" allowing them to create their own provincialise theories as a contribution to global social thought, consisting of spatiologial pre-occupied world views, critiquing any of the "Western" theory other than claiming to complement these downplayed as only one "provincial" view on the social by complementing them with their own provincial view, is the least option that would come to the minds of this opposition, since they know from the colonizers that theories must be a matter of any theory model one choses ex ante for theorizing and, thus, they argue, that since theories are anyway an impact of the location where they are created, the social science world must commit itself to all create locally pre-occupied social thought.

Re-discovering the obscurantism of religion as a way of scientific thinking

Hence, under the auspices of this postcolonial spatiological thinking, indigenous knowledge [14], once a discriminating notion from European sciences, excluding this knowledge from sciences via defining what scientific knowledge is beyond any argument about what indigenous knowledge said, is re-discovered and re-interpreted as a form of spatiological knowledge, that also not want to critique any theories it opposes, but aims at contributing another local unique knowledge with an exclusive local theory: For this very purpose, creating scientific patriotisms proving that the colonized world already owned spatiologically constructed theories long time before the "Western" sciences invaded the world of thinking with their "Eurocentric" theories, some social scientists, preferably from "the West", detect even pre-social science thinkers such as for example Khaldoun, a thinker, thinking about the 14th century, as the first spatiologically thinking sociologist, others admire poets like Rizal, who insisted that the Phillippinos are not lazy, as a local anti-hegemonic theorists, all re-detecting the colo-

---

[14] Indigenous knowledge is not a creature of indigenous people, but of the scientific colonisers. The critique indigenous knowledge was autochtonous is a revealing hypocrisy of thinkers who otherwise cultivate contextualized theorizing. The fact that all those indigenisation enterprises are the enterprises of the incriminated academics which serve the latest epistemological fashions of the apparently not only Western "post-structuralists" relativists freaks, does not bother the original holders of this indigenous knowledge: For the disappointment of the indigenous knowledge seekers they don't care about what indigenousness at all means.

nised world as a world that provides authentic local "southern" theories for todays global battle among all the locally pre-occupied theories, all representing the authenticity of a national social views in the battle about patriotic theories, which do no longer claim to understand the world, but to represent an exclusive national view, a scientifically ennobled local patriotism as their contributions to a world of provincialized theories...

It was and is this opposition against the theories called, in the logic of spatiological theorizing called "Western" theories, that paved the way for universalising the "where," presenting space, mostly politically defined, as a worldwide epistemological dimension of science, thus spreading the concept of social science thinking about and through nation state views across the world in a way, the social sciences from the imperial world never could, due to their own very political, i.e., nationalized "where" of theorizing, that basically did not care about what is going beyond their biotopish national socials.

Since then, thanks to a false opposition against the imposed "Eurocentric" theories and justified by the Gurus of post-structuralism social science thinking finally conquered the world of social thought as a multiplicity of relatively obscure spatialological social thought, only comprehensible for and through the obscureness of being part of a "space" in which it is created. Since then, the world of sciences consists of the global theoretical relative crux of anywhere valid and nowhere sharable theories and an intellectual scenario, in which the traditional obscurantism of religious thinking, once overcome by civic thinking, rises again from the dead as another spatiological view on the world.

Thus, it is the false opposition against the universalisation of the theories from the local knowledge island in Europe, which further develop global social though under the regime of social sciences and which finally opposes the scientificy of science for the sake of setting free the creation of all the local obscurantism and, thus help to abolish the only substantial achievement social science thinking has gained through its critique of the classical philosophies—with a consequent interpretation and application of the dogmas of social sciences to global social thought.

It returns to the obscurantism of thinking in which the mystification of some spatial particularism into a type of knowledge which can be only shared by those who share the mystic spatial "context", in which it is created. It is this scientifically reactionary opposition against social science thinking that gives birth to the emergence of a new wave of religious social sciences 200 years after the European sciences emerged from a critique of the obscurantism of religious thinking.

References

Adorno, T. W. (1971). *Erziehung zur Mündigkeit*. Frankfurt a.M.: Suhrkamp, 1. Auflage.

Chakrabarty, D. (2000). *Postcolonial Thought and Historical Difference*. Princeton University Press.

Rynko, M. (n.d.). *On the Measurement of Welfare, Happiness and Inequality*. European University Institut. Available online at: http://cadmus.eui.eu/handle/1814/20694

Bibliographical Notes

Michael Christie has worked with Yolngu Aboriginal people in Arnhem Land Northern Territory Australia as an educator and linguist since the early 1970s. He is currently Professor of Education at the Northern Institute at Charles Darwin University, undertaking collaborative transdisciplinary research generating intercultural practices of knowledge and agreement making, and designing governance structures for Aboriginal organisations which take seriously both ancestral and western imperatives of responsibility and accountability.
Email: Michael.Christie@cdu.edu.au

Christiane Hartnack (PhD, Free University of Berlin) is the director of the Intercultural Studies Programme at the Danube University Krems in Austria and adjunct lecturer at the Department of South Asian, Tibetan and Buddhist Studies at the University of Vienna.
Email: christiane.hartnack@donau-uni.ac.at

Michael Kuhn is President of the World Social Sciences and Humanities Network ad director of Knowwhy Global Research. His background is philosophy, political science and international economics. His current interests focus on theories of social sciences.
Email: michaelkuhn@knowwhy.net; mkuhn@worldsshnet.org

Claudia Magallanes-Blanco has a PhD from the University of Western Sydney, Australia. She is a professor and researcher at the Universidad Iberoamericana Puebla in Mexico where she currently chairs the masters' in communication for social change. She is member of Mexico's National Council for Science and Technology. Her research is focused on indigenous and community communication from a participatory approach.
E-mail: claudia.magallanes@iberopuebla.mx

Roger Magazine is Professor and Researcher in the Graduate Program in Social Anthropology at the Universidad Iberoamericana in Mexico City. His research interests include street children in Mexico City, football (soccer) fans, and local practices and understandings of personhood, action and sociality in rural Mexico.
E-mail: roger.magazine@ibero.mx

Ivan da Costa Marques is associate professor at the Federal University of Rio de Janeiro and the President of Brazilian Association for Social Studies of Science and Technology.
Email: imarques@nce.ufrj.br

Léon-Marie Nkolo Ndjodo is a philosopher at the department of philosophy of Higher Teachers' Traninig College of the University of Maroua in Cameoon. M. Nkolo Ndjodo general interests are on postmodernism, aesthetics of late capitalism, contemporary forms of global culture and African turn of postcolonial theory. He is also interested in the impact of civil society movements, the challenges of the reformation of social sciences in international context and its political implications for African societies.
Email: leonnkolo@yahoo.fr

Qodratullah Qorbani is Assistant Professor and Researcher of philosophy at Kharazmi University, in Tehran, Iran. His researcher interests are Comparative Philosophy, Philosophy of Religion, and Science and religion Issues.
E-Mail: qorbani48@gmail.com; qorbani@khu.ac.ir

Pablo Reyna Esteves is the director of Incidence Programs. Universidad Iberoamericana, Mexico.
Email: pablo.reyna@ibero.mx

Juan Pablo Vázquez Gutiérrez is professor of Social and Political Sciences Department. Universidad Iberoamericana, Mexico.
Email: juan.vazquez@ibero.mx

Kumaran Rajagopal is assistant professor at the Department of Sociology, Gandhigram Rural Institute – Deemed University, Gandhigram, Tamil Nadu India. His disciplinary background is sociology, his interests are alternative science practices and theories.
Email: rkumara@gmail.com

Leandro Rodriguez-Medina holds a PhD from University of Cambridge. He is associate professor at Universidad de las Américas Puebla, affiliated researcher at University of Cambridge, and member of the National System of Researchers, National Council for Science and Technology (Mexico). His research interests are international circulation of knowledge, materiality of socio-political processes and higher education in developing countries.
E-mail: leandro.rodriguez@udlap.mx

Hebe Vessuri is a social anthropologist, Emeritus researcher at the Center of Science Studies, Venezuelan Institute of Scientific Research (IVIC), Caracas, and a Collaborating Scholar at the Center for Environmental Geography (CIGA), National Autonomous University of Mexico (UNAM). Dr. Vessuri's general interests are on the sociology and contemporary history of science in Latin America, science policy, and sociology of technology. She is also interested in the challenges and dilemmas of expertise and democracy in developing country contexts.
Email: hvessuri@ivic.ve

ibidem-Verlag

Melchiorstr. 15

D-70439 Stuttgart

info@ibidem-verlag.de

www.ibidem-verlag.de
www.ibidem.eu
www.edition-noema.de
www.autorenbetreuung.de